ROALD DAHL AND PHILOSOPHY

ROALD DAHL AND PHILOSOPHY

A Little Nonsense Now and Then

Edited by Jacob M. Held

ROWMAN & LITTLEFIELD
Lanham • Boulder • New York • Toronto • Plymouth, UK

Published by Rowman & Littlefield
4501 Forbes Boulevard, Suite 200, Lanham, Maryland 20706
www.rowman.com

10 Thornbury Road, Plymouth PL6 7PP, United Kingdom

Distributed by National Book Network

British Library Cataloguing in Publication Information Available

Library of Congress Cataloging-in-Publication Data

Roald Dahl and philosophy : a little nonsense now and then / edited by Jacob M. Held.
pages cm
Includes index.
ISBN 978-1-4422-2252-6 (pbk. : alk. paper) — ISBN 978-1-4422-2253-3 (electronic)
1. Dahl, Roald—Criticism and interpretation. 2. Philosophy in literature. 3. Children's stories, English—History and criticism. I. Held, Jacob M., 1977– editor of compilation.
PR6054.A35Z857 2014
823'.914—dc23
2013048452

Printed in the United States of America

Dedicated to me, Jacob M. Held,
without whom none of this would have been possible.

CONTENTS

ACKNOWLEDGMENTS

I would like to acknowledge all of those who supported me during the completion of this project, from my loving family to all of my contributors. I would also like to thank Jon Sisk at Rowman & Littlefield for originally being receptive to *Dr. Seuss and Philosophy*. Thanks also to Marissa Parks, whose idea for another children's literature and philosophy book was the impetus for the one you currently hold.

Finally, early in the summer of 2013 I lost Vlad, my dog. The whole family loved him. But he was my dog. My wife convinced me to get him when I was in graduate school. He was my first child. With Vlad, everything changed. The impact he had on me was profound. I am a better person for having had him as a companion. I loved him dearly and miss him daily. Thank you, Mr. Puss, for everything.

> Hence we see the four-footed friendships of so many men of a better nature; for how could we recover from the endless dissimulation, duplicity, perfidy, and treachery of men if it were not for the dogs into whose open and honest eyes we can look without distrust?
> —Arthur Schopenhauer (1788–1860)

INTRODUCTION

Roald Dahl and Absurdity: Children's Literature and the Divorce between the Mind That Desires and the World That Disappoints[1]

Jacob M. Held

"There is but one truly serious philosophical problem, and that is suicide. Judging whether life is or is not worth living amounts to answering the fundamental question of philosophy. All the rest . . . comes afterwards."[2] So begins Camus, and so shall we also begin. It may seem odd, if not downright perverse, to open a book on Roald Dahl with a quote about suicide. Dahl is the author who brought us Matilda and Willy Wonka, James Henry Trotter, and the Big Friendly Giant. Dahl's works seem to speak to a love of life and a celebration of childhood that is antithetical to the depression and violence of taking one's own life. But nothing could be more fitting than to open this book with the question of what makes life worth living.

If we begin by revisiting Dahl's most well-known protagonists, Matilda Wormwood, Charlie Bucket, James Trotter, George Kranky, Danny, Sophie, and the boy from *The Witches*, we see that the question of suicide, or rather the question of finding value in a chaotic world, is not so out of place. Matilda's parents are abusive when not neglectful, and as a vulnerable child she seems to be helpless to escape her fate. Charlie is starving to death alongside his impoverished family; James's parents were killed by a rogue rhino, leaving him to the care of his physically and emotionally abusive aunts; and so on. Roald Dahl's stories don't begin joyfully. He never opens a book with the words "Everything was pleasant. . . ." Were he to do so, readers familiar with his other works would be waiting for the inevitable tragedy. Dahl would only start out uplifting to make the inevitable fall more poignant. *James and the Giant Peach* begins, "Here is James Henry Trotter when he was about four years old. Up until this time, he had a happy life."[3] Up until life struck. Dahl doesn't begin upbeat, so why should we?

Dahl begins where his protagonists, usually children, find themselves, where most human beings find themselves—in the thrall of existence, in the turmoil that is life, the divorce between our desires and a disappointing world. Dahl's children find themselves where humanity exists, somewhere between their ideals, their fantasies about what life should be, and the reality of their situation, disappointment, and suffering. James Trotter knew happiness, until his parents were eaten by a rhino. Now he lives in between his dreams of a happy life of family and friends and the reality of his Aunts Spiker and Sponge. Matilda finds herself caught between ideals she's formed, having read accounts of happy lives in books, and the reality of living among the Wormwoods, small-minded bullies who seem to revel in inhibiting Matilda's pursuit of happiness. And so we have the common theme among Dahl's stories: our lives speak to the absurdity of human existence, the fact that there is an unbridgeable gulf between what we demand of this world and what we know to be true. "The absurd is born of this confrontation between the human need and the unreasonable silence of the world."[4] We need meaning and purpose; we need hope, a reason to continue on. But the world is silent; it offers nothing. And so we find the connection between Roald Dahl's work and the question of suicide, the question of whether life is worth living.

The answer Albert Camus (1913–1960) offers is the answer Dahl shows us through each of his heroes and heroines: "Everything considered, a determined soul will always manage."[5] So even before she develops her powers of telekinesis, Matilda manages through her trips to the village library and by periodically exacting revenge on her parents. Even though he loses his magic crocodile tongues, James perseveres. He doesn't need magic; he is enough to overcome his situation. Magic may provide him opportunities, but it is through his ingenuity, through his actions, that the peach is saved from a shark attack, Cloud-Men, and every other tragedy that confronts him and his comrades on their journey. George takes matters into his own hands to deal with his wretched grandmother, making his marvelous medicine. It is Charlie, through a bit of luck but also through his own moral uprightness, who perseveres in the face of adversity and earns the right to be Willy Wonka's heir. Everything considered—being orphaned, poor, abused, young, weak, vulnerable, a mouse—the determined souls, like James, Charlie, Matilda, and the boy from *The Witches*, will manage. And they don't simply manage—they succeed; they revel in their rebellion against a chaotic world.

In the work of Roald Dahl, there is no shortage of pain and suffering. His protagonists never come from happy homes. And that is probably a good thing. Who wants to read about a spoiled child or one who has always had things easy? Such a story wouldn't resonate because we'd see it for what it was: an irrelevant fantasy, a simple distraction. But no child's life will be pain-free or easy; we all have to struggle and suffer, and we have to learn how to deal with that fact, how to cope with what life is: hard. So we see James, whose parents are killed by a rogue rhino and who is forced to live with emotionally and physically abusive aunts. Or we see Charlie Bucket, a poor child on the verge of starvation struggling to make it in a world of gluttonous, spoiled brats. Sophie, before she meets the Big Friendly Giant, lives in an orphanage. Matilda is neglected and emotionally abused at home and sent to a school where education looks strikingly like punishment. Even Dahl's autobiography, *Boy*, includes a tale of child abuse at the hands of school administrators.

Dahl begins from the fact that life is chaotic and often painful. Life isn't what it should be; it simply is, a random series of events that we suffer through. In this regard, he begins from the position of Camus—the world is absurd. As humans, we seek meaning in the face of absurdity, in the face of seemingly senseless suffering. Why is the world a place where children starve, are abused, lose parents, suffer at the hands of tyrannical teachers, and so on? Surely, some of these problems could be solved. But even though Dahl offers us the occasional happy ending, the lessons we learn from watching Matilda, Charlie, or James resonate. We can't ignore the fact that life is chaotic and often painful. To delude ourselves with the hope for magic or miraculous salvation is to simply deny the problem and refuse to admit what is right in front of our faces. Although Matilda exercises magic (telekinesis), that doesn't remove her problems—it merely affords her an additional tool with which to face them. Matilda still has to face down the Trunchbull; she still has to deal with the Wormwoods. James's magic crocodile tongues don't solve his problems; they merely offer him an alternative. But James must still choose what he does with that opportunity—how he will use it to craft a life for himself. And his journey is wrought with troubles. There is no easy solution. We can't ignore the problem, and to accept a magical solution would be to, "like the donkey, feed on the roses of illusion."[6]

Somehow, we must continue onward. Somehow we must find the strength to press forward in a chaotic world that offers no promise of salvation, no semblance of order. At some point the world just is a place where you suffer; as parents are prone to remind children, it doesn't revolve around you. In fact, the world doesn't care two licks about you. This is an important fact that children need to learn and that many adults need to be reminded of. And simply recognizing as much doesn't mean we despair of our condition and lament how horrible life is. It is merely about recognizing the nature of our condition so we can begin to craft a response. For Camus, as for Dahl's protagonists, "the only coherent philosophical position is . . . revolt."[7]

If we're going to talk about what it means to revolt in the face of the absurd, we need to talk about *The Witches*. *The Witches* is a good story. It's entertaining. But what is profound about it is the way in which the characters respond to their hardships. Near the end, the boy is turned into a mouse. It's not what he'd prefer, and surely his grandmother is less than pleased. The reader may even be a bit taken aback. But these things happen in adventure stories, so we roll with the character. It'll be all right in the end. And by "all right," I mean that we assume things will turn out well for the boy and his grandmother. But what is really great about the story, what is important, is that the boy doesn't get changed back into a child—things are not "righted." He is forever stuck being a mouse. He is totally altered and his life is significantly shortened, and that's just how it is. He wonders about how long he'll live. His grandmother tells him he's only got a few years; that's just how long mice live. He's special, so maybe he'll get a few more, but he's fated to die soon. What's his response? Does he cry, lament his condition, bemoan the injustice of it all, and scream that "it's not fair"? No. He accepts his irrevocable situation and notes that it's not how long you live but how well. He may only live a few more years, but his grandmother is old as well. They'll live their last years out together doing something meaningful, tracking down and ridding the world of as many witches as possible. "It will be a triumph, my darling!"[8] In the face of a chaotic world, they will revolt; they will respond in a manner of their choosing, without hope but with purpose. "But what fun and excitement it's going to be!"[9]

Matilda, and most of Dahl's corpus, recapitulates this theme. We always begin in grim circumstances; the kinds of circumstances that, were an adult forced into them, would surely encourage suicidal thoughts. Who could live in the abject poverty in which the Buckets find themselves and not wonder if it is worth carrying on? Who could tolerate James Trotter's life for more than a month before the thought of ending it all entered their mind? These children are given the worst the world can offer, and they are vulnerable and weak, often unable to do anything about it. The stories change when an opportunity appears: a golden ticket, telekinesis, a magician offering salvation in the form of a bag full of tongues. But the children still must seize the opportunity. They still must find the strength and the determination to do something about it all. The world doesn't cease to put up obstacles, become easier, or cooperate; rather, they find the strength, even if they are granted a leg up, to finally take control and revolt against the world, against the chaos and the pain. They are defiant. That is their strength. They are stronger than their enemies, they are tougher than their circumstances, and so—in the face of the absurdity that is life, chaos without meaning, pain without hope—they revolt. What else could they do?

This idea of rebellion in the face of an absurd world is what children (and adults) need to hear, learn, and continually be reminded of. For the most part, you don't choose your life or circumstances. Life is the result of a whole lot of luck, and usually bad luck. But in the midst of it all, you control one thing—your choices, your responses to it—and this means you control your happiness. Whoever you are and wherever you find yourself, you can always be the best right there at that moment. And so Dahl presents children with the real world and offers them valuable coping skills for dealing with it. Challenge injustice always, rebel, forge a life of your choosing, and live well. When you can't change the world, don't let it corrupt you and don't relent; continue onward—a determined soul will always manage. In this way Dahl doesn't lie to children, like so many fantasy tales. So much of children's literature ends cheerfully. What a letdown life must be for children who buy into this lie. How incapable these children must be of becoming adults who can handle the real world of failure and misery.

Dahl's stories communicate a perspective on life and a disposition toward it. He advocates for certain values, like integrity and justice, and demonstrates their value through the lives of his protagonists as they struggle through an unjust and chaotic world. These narratives are powerful in that they give children scripts through which they see the value of living virtuously. If Dahl's worlds were all sunshine and roses, these narratives, these scripts, would be worthless; they wouldn't translate to the lived lives of his readers. But his worlds, as painful and unjust as they are, offer scripts that can be transposed into our lives and offer models that children can mimic in theirs. The boy turned mouse continues on, and so can you. And how silly and trivial your problems look in light of what could be, and what for so many children actually is. Matilda managed to live with the Wormwoods and successfully navigate Crunchem Hall and the Trunchbull. You, too, can understand and deal with your bullies, your parents, those who insult you for being different or smart or for questioning their authority. Stories show children how things can be, how *they* can be. Dahl provides a workable and laudable model for his readers, and he does this by bringing philosophical wisdom to bear on the real world through fantasy.

Dahl's work is profoundly philosophical and promotes a philosophical disposition in the reader. Through work on Dr. Seuss and now this volume, I have come to appreciate the brilliance of good children's authors[10] as well as to truly dislike bad children's literature, even to despise it as harmful insofar as it promotes flawed ideals and false hope and creates a generation of delusional, spoiled children incapable of coping with life as they will experience it. Dahl presents a fantasy world strikingly similar to our own, a chaotic world of meaningless suffering. Through his protagonists he provides models for responding to the world as it is, not as it should be. And so the reader is provided a vision of how to respond to the world they find themselves in; as such, Dahl's works facilitate a reflective, philosophical approach to life. But don't just take my word for it. Keep reading.

I

EPICURUS AND THE CHOCOLATE FACTORY

Benjamin A. Rider

Charlie Bucket is not like other children. His singular perspective on life, which we see even in the opening chapters of *Charlie and the Chocolate Factory*, becomes particularly evident when he visits the chocolate factory with the other children holding Golden Tickets. As each of the other children falls prey to his or her immoderate desires and spoiled impulses, Charlie is able to calmly relish the wonders that he is experiencing in the amazing and fanciful factory. So how is Charlie different? The philosophy of Epicurus offers an insightful perspective for understanding why Charlie is special and why, in the end, he deserves to share in the joys of Willy Wonka's creation.

"WELCOME TO THE FACTORY!" THE EPICUREAN LIFE

Living amid the rich variety of philosophical ideas that proliferated in the ancient Greek and Roman world, Epicurus (341–270 BCE) took a distinctive approach. Earlier philosophers, such as Aristotle and Plato, believed that only a select group of people were blessed with the natural talent or external resources necessary to achieve a truly worthy and happy life. In contrast, Epicurus sought to create a philosophy of life accessible to *anyone*—noble born or working class, rich or poor, young or old, man or woman. He claimed that *pleasure* is the goal of life: "We say that pleasure is the starting point and goal of living blessedly. For we recognized this as our first innate good, and this is the starting point of every choice and avoidance and we come to this by judging every good by the criterion of feeling."[1]

From the moment we're born, he explained, we pursue pleasure and avoid its opposite, pain. A newborn infant, who knows nothing else, seeks pleasure in the warmth of a parent's caress, cries when hungry or cold or afraid, and rests peacefully when her needs are satisfied and fears soothed.[2] Now, as we grow up and internalize the (often arbitrary) social norms and expectations of our culture, we may begin to convince ourselves and each other that we pursue higher or nobler goals, but, still, what we really seek and want, deep down, is pleasure and freedom from pain.

According to Epicureanism, therefore, attaining a good and happy life is much simpler than people often think it is. Nevertheless, many people fail to live good lives. Why? Because, Epicurus explained, it's easy to become confused about what a good life is and what it requires and as a result to get involved in pursuits that cause more harm than good. According to Epicurus, the pleasure that matters and creates a true and lasting happiness comes not from the pleasures of excess or indulgence— from extravagant feasts, death-defying thrills, or expensive purchases. Instead, the highest pleasure arises from the healthy, natural state of body and mind: "When we say that pleasure is the goal we do not mean the pleasures of the profligate or the pleasures of consumption, as some believe . . . but rather the lack of pain in the body and disturbance in the soul."[3]

This idea has struck many as strange—what is *pleasant* about mere freedom from pain? Think about it, though: When do you most *enjoy* your experiences? It is when you are fully absorbed in what you are doing, in the activity of *living*, without physical or mental distractions. Imagine laughing with friends, reading a good book, or playing your favorite sport. You aren't experiencing thrills of sensual pleasure, but at that moment you enjoy being alive. You lose track of time, engrossed in the moment. On the other hand, a persistent physical pain, such as a toothache, makes enjoying any activity or experience difficult. And when your *mind* is buffeted by anxiety, stress, and fear, the simple enjoyment of living becomes impossible.

Charlie and his family have a hard life. But even in poverty and discomfort, they share moments of happiness when, because of the joy of each other's company, they forget their cares and lose themselves in the stories told by Charlie's four ancient grandparents:

> As soon as they heard Charlie's voice saying, "Good evening, Grandpa Joe and Grandma Josephine, and Grandpa George and Grandma Georgina," then all four of them would suddenly sit up, and their old wrinkled faces would light up with smiles of pleasure—and the talking would begin. For they loved this little boy. . . . Often, Charlie's mother and father would come in as well, and stand by the door, listening to the stories that the old people told; and thus, for perhaps half an hour every night, this room would become a happy place, and the whole family would forget that it was poor.[4]

Epicurus writes, "Poverty, if measured by the goal of nature, is great wealth; and wealth, if limits are not set for it, is great poverty."[5] Money, as Epicurus would acknowledge, has uses—the Buckets certainly could use more of it. But money isn't the most important thing, since it's possible to be wealthy and miserable, or, conversely, to have much happiness in life without a lot in the way of material possessions. The most important thing is the *attitude* you take and the joy you are able to find in what life gives you.

Moreover, as Epicurus explains, a person who gets used to little can better appreciate those times when life provides the opportunity for special enjoyments. Epicurus writes, "We believe that self-sufficiency is a great good, not in order that we might make do with few things under all circumstances, but so that if we do not have a lot we can make do with few, being genuinely convinced that those who least need extravagance enjoy it most."[6]

The circumstances of his life have forced Charlie to do without most luxuries, but he does have one indulgence: chocolate. Once a year, on his birthday, Charlie receives a Wonka chocolate bar. Other children, blessed with the resources for casual extravagance, take their chocolate bars for granted, munching bar after bar without much thought or gratitude for what they have. Charlie does not. As a result, he treasures every moment of enjoyment from his chocolate:

> Each time he received [his birthday chocolate], he would place it carefully in a small wooden box that he owned, and treasure it as though it were a bar of solid gold; and for the next few days, he would allow

himself only to look at it, but never to touch it. Then, at last, when he could stand it no longer, he would peel back a *tiny* bit of the paper wrapping at one corner to expose a *tiny* bit of chocolate, and then he would take a *tiny* nibble—just enough to allow the lovely sweet taste to spread out slowly over his tongue. . . . In this way, he would make his ten-cent bar of birthday chocolate last for more than a month.[7]

This story tells us two things about Charlie: First, he has an incredible amount of self-control! But, more important, he's learned how to extract more pleasure from one small piece of chocolate than most children would have from mounds of candy. Because he does not get to enjoy this experience very often, he knows to be grateful for it when it comes.

THE CURIOUS WISDOM OF SMALL CHILDREN IN TIMES OF HARDSHIP: NEEDS AND WANTS

As I've explained, the goal of Epicurus's philosophy was not bursts of wild, sensuous excitement, to be followed by headaches and regret, but rather a steady, healthy state of body and mind in which one could maintain pleasurable experience over the long term. But what does a person need for a healthy life? In his usual way, Epicurus sought to reduce this problem to a simple idea that anyone could understand. There are, he explained, three types of desire: natural and necessary; natural, but not necessary; and unnatural, unnecessary desires, which, as Epicurus put it, "are produced by a groundless opinion."[8] Understanding this distinction provides a clear standard for managing our lives and knowing how to respond to the chance events that life throws at us.

Natural and necessary desires are, as the name suggests, the desires that you *must* satisfy to keep your body and mind in a healthy state.[9] To stay healthy and free from mental disturbance, you must eat; you must drink; you must have shelter from cold and wet. If any of these desires were left unsatisfied, pain would inevitably result, of the sort that disturbs your tranquility and enjoyment.[10] It is hard to engage in the activities of life with enjoyment when your stomach aches with hunger, when your head throbs because of dehydration, or when you're shivering with cold or illness. Epicurus insisted that, with prudent life management, the basics of life should be "easy to acquire."[11] Not everyone can afford gourmet meals and a lush mansion, but Epicurus was confident that a prudent person would always find enough to keep her stomach filled and the pains of need at bay. [12]

The plight of Charlie and his family, however, reveals a harsher reality—sometimes, through no fault of their own, people just do not have enough of what they need to keep themselves pain-free and satisfied. The first chapter explains the Buckets' situation:

> In the summertime, [sleeping on the floor] wasn't too bad, but in the winter, freezing drafts blew across the floor all night long, and it was awful. There wasn't any question of them being able to buy a better house—or even one more bed to sleep in. They were far too poor for that. . . .
>
> There wasn't even enough money to buy proper food for them all. The only meals they could afford were bread and margarine for breakfast, boiled potatoes and cabbage for lunch, and cabbage soup for supper. . . . The Buckets, of course, didn't starve, but every one of them . . . went about from morning till night with a horrible empty feeling in their tummies. [13]

Later, the situation becomes even worse. The weather grows colder; the factory where Mr. Bucket makes his minimal salary, screwing caps onto toothpaste tubes, closes down; and an already lean life turns desperate: "Every day, Charlie Bucket grew thinner and thinner. His face became frighteningly white and pinched. His skin was drawn so tightly over the cheeks that you could see the shapes of the bones underneath. It seemed doubtful whether he could go on much longer like this without becoming dangerously ill."[14]

Any person in extreme poverty *knows* they must satisfy natural and necessary desires—it is their daily reality—but they also realize that circumstances do not always cooperate.

Despite having every reason for despair, however, Charlie and his family cope as well as one might expect by following the advice Epicurus might have offered. Epicurus wrote, "Of the things which wisdom provides for the blessedness of one's whole life, by far the greatest is the possession of friendship."[15] He had in mind a group of like-minded friends, creating a bulwark against life's vagaries through their love, support, and advice to each other. Epicurus himself established this kind of community, called the Garden, on an estate outside Athens where he lived together with his friends, growing their own food and enjoying each other's company. In such a community, Epicurus reasoned, a person need fear nothing that life could throw at him, because his friends would always be there to encourage him, cheer him up, and lend a hand in trouble. Similarly, Charlie's family—his careworn father and mother and four bedridden grandparents—has created this kind of community. They are not doing well. It's clear that their situation is not sustainable in the long run, with so many mouths depending on Mr. Bucket's meager earnings. Still, they love each other and sustain each other through the cold and privation of their existence.

BEASTLY GIRLS AND BOYS: EXCEEDING THE LIMITS OF DESIRE

Once your basic human needs are satisfied—once your body and mind are healthy and undisturbed, and you have like-minded friends to love and take care of you and create confidence about the future—then, according to Epicurus, you don't need anything else to be happy. Minimal material resources are enough to keep the pain of need at bay: "As soon as we achieve this state, every storm in the soul is dispelled, since the animal is not in a position to go after some need nor to seek something else to complete the good of the body and the soul."[16]

Epicurus admits, however, that it is natural to want some "variation" in your experiences. Bread and margarine and cabbage and potato soup keep a body alive, but they are not very interesting. This is where natural but not necessary desires come in: desires for varied foods, more stylish clothing, a soft bed, or a more spacious, luxurious house. If you have the chance to enjoy these things, Epicurus held, there is no harm in indulging.[17] Charlie's love of chocolate is an example—he takes great enjoyment in chocolate, because it varies the usual blandness of his diet and daily routine. It's natural that he should want it and look forward to his limited opportunities to enjoy it. But he also knows he does not *need* chocolate to live.

The unnatural, unnecessary desires, however, are one of the greatest scourges of human life. Epicurus calls these desires "empty" or "occurring as a result of a groundless opinion." In his view, these desires are a chief source of human misery—we become convinced that we *need* things that, in fact, aren't necessary. We yearn for them, valuing them all out of proportion with their actual benefit. And the more we get, the more we want, until these insatiable appetites consume our lives and relationships and tear our minds apart with anxiety and craving. In *Charlie and the Chocolate Factory*, Augustus Gloop, Veruca Salt, Violet Beauregarde, and Mike Teavee provide object lessons in the consequences of empty, unnatural desires gone amok.

The cycle of psychological degradation Epicurus describes is not uncommon. It starts with an occasional luxury, a novel variation to break the boredom. It could be a beer or two at dinner, a candy bar after school, a salty snack in the afternoon, a few hours playing a video game. At this level, these pleasures are innocent. They satisfy natural—though unnecessary—desires, adding variety and spice to life.[18] The danger, however, is that what begins as harmless fun does not remain that way. The occasional treat soon becomes a habit, then a craving, and finally—at least in one's own mind—a necessity.[19] In the end, what once served you and your happiness now becomes your master.

So how did Veruca Salt, Mike Teavee, and the other children become the despicable creatures we see in the book? They weren't *born* that way—Epicurus calls these desires "unnatural" precisely because a healthy and properly developed body and mind would not experience them. On the contrary, their degradation was gradual, rooted in natural and apparently harmless desires.

Consider the first child to find a Golden Ticket, Augustus Gloop:

> Mr. Bucket's newspaper carried a large picture of him on the front page. The picture showed a nine-year-old boy who was so enormously fat he looked as though he had been blown up with a powerful pump. . . .
>
> "I just *knew* Augustus would find a Golden Ticket," his mother had told the newspaperman. "He eats so *many* candy bars a day that it is almost *impossible* for him *not* to find one. Eating is his hobby, you know. That's *all* he's interested in."[20]

Eating starts off as a "hobby"—a way to stave off boredom and vary experience—but it's clear that, for Augustus, it's now become much more than that, a fact that his mother fails to recognize.

The second child to find a Golden Ticket is Veruca Salt, a girl whose rich parents dare deny her nothing:

"You see, fellers," [Mr. Salt] had said, "as soon as my little girl told me that she simply *had* to have one of those Golden Tickets, I went out into the town and started buying up all the Wonka candy bars I could lay my hands on. *Thousands* of them, I must have bought. *Hundreds* of thousands! . . . Oh, it was terrible! My little Veruca got more and more upset each day, and every time I went home she would scream at me, '*Where's my Golden Ticket! I want my Golden Ticket!*' And she would lie for hours on the floor, kicking and yelling in the most disturbing way."[21]

The others have similar stories—because their parents can't tell them no and they were never compelled to learn their limits or develop self-control, their "hobbies" became obsessions, indulgences became entitlements, and before long, their empty and unnatural desires took over their lives.

The only way for a person in this state to regain equilibrium and mental health, according to Epicurus, is to learn the true limits of human happiness and desire. That makes it sound easy, as if all you need to do is to read Epicurus's "Letter to Menoeceus" and *Principle Doctrines* and you'll be cured. But Epicurus (like other Greek philosophers) realized that beliefs—especially the deep beliefs that make up one's identity and way of life—are not changed so easily. It's not a matter merely of reading a book or hearing an argument. A long-term smoker does not quit because he reads statistics on lung cancer or sees a warning on a pack of cigarettes. Someone hooked on chocolate, gum, or TV does not give up their obsession because some adult tells them to stop. Sometimes one must confront an experience that vividly brings a truth home for change to begin. And even then, habits of thought are stubborn. Relapses are likely.

When Augustus Gloop sees the river of melted chocolate in Willy Wonka's factory, he cannot resist. While the others are marveling at the amazing room, he sneaks down to the edge of the river and begins "scooping hot melted chocolate into his mouth as fast as he could." Willy Wonka and his parents yell for him to stop, "but Augustus was deaf to everything except the call of his enormous stomach," and soon he plunges into the river, to be sucked up the pipe to the Fudge Room.[22] As Epicurus would put it, "nothing is enough to someone for whom enough is little."[23]

This pattern repeats for each of the other spoiled children: First, Violet, puffed up by pride in her world-record gum-chewing prowess, snatches Wonka's experimental chewing-gum meal, only to be literally

EPICURUS AND THE CHOCOLATE FACTORY

puffed up by the gum's (known) side effects.[24] Then Veruca is tossed down the garbage shoot, rejected as a bad nut, after insisting on having her own pet squirrel in the Nut Room.[25] Finally, Mike is shrunk down small enough to fit into the palm of his mother's hand, after he runs recklessly into Wonka's television-chocolate machine.[26] In each case, the children's obsessive desires take over, and they ignore all warnings as they plunge headlong into trouble.

While the other children spend their time in the chocolate factory alternately complaining and getting into trouble, however, Charlie simply takes in the experience with delight and wonder:

> Charlie was holding tightly onto his grandfather's bony old hand. He was in a whirl of excitement. Everything that he had seen so far—the great chocolate river, the waterfall, the huge sucking pipes, the candy meadows, the Oompa-Loompas, the beautiful pink boat, and most of all, Mr. Willy Wonka himself—had been so astonishing that he began to wonder whether there could possibly be any more astonishments left.[27]

Even the astonishing delights of the factory are not enough for the other children—they want more. But for Charlie, everything is wonderful and amazing.

As we learn near the end of the book, all of the bad children go home from the factory eventually, transformed but otherwise unharmed.[28] Are Augustus, Violet, Veruca, and Mike reformed and redeemed by their experiences in the chocolate factory? Have they and their parents learned to appreciate life's simple pleasures? We don't know, but we might hope so.

AN EXTRAORDINARY LITTLE MAN: WILLY WONKA

Ultimately, the most memorable character in *Charlie and the Chocolate Factory* is not Charlie or the corrupted children, but Willy Wonka. (There is a reason, I think, that the 1971 movie adaptation was called *Willy Wonka and the Chocolate Factory* and that Johnny Depp was brought in to play the role in the 2005 remake.) He is reclusive and mysterious. He locked himself away inside his factory for ten years after firing all his workers and replacing them with Oompa-Loompas when rival spies stole his recipes. [29] He bursts with manic energy when he greets the children:

> And his eyes—his eyes were the most marvelously bright. They seemed to be sparkling and twinkling at you all the time. The whole face, in fact, was alight with fun and laughter. And oh, how clever he looked! How quick and sharp and full of life! He kept making quick jerky little movements with his head, cocking it this way and that, and taking everything in with those bright twinkling eyes. He was like a squirrel in the quickness of his movements, like a quick clever old squirrel from the park. [30]

In each version, he's a strange, almost inhuman figure, more force of nature than person. One might be tempted to read Wonka as a sort of whimsical god, who—through the world he created—metes out justice to the humans in his realm, punishing the wicked (the four bad children) and rewarding the good (Charlie). [31] Indeed, the fates suffered by the four bad children recall the divine justice in Dante's *Inferno*—their misfortunes seem particularly matched to their sins.

I would argue, however, that Willy Wonka is closer to Epicurus's way of thinking about the gods than to either the ancient Greek or Judeo-Christian conceptions. [32] Contrary to the prevailing beliefs of his time, Epicurus argued that the gods don't actually care about humans, nor are they responsible for anything good or bad that happens to us. They exist apart from our world, in state of perfect happiness and tranquility, and, as Epicurus argues, neither anger nor gratitude would be appropriate for such beings. [33] Among other things, that means that they do not mete out punishments or rewards, either in this life or in an afterlife. On the contrary, as the Epicurean poet Lucretius so vividly explains, the "punishments" we imagine the gods inflicting on us actually represent the misery we bring on *ourselves* through our own foolishness:

> And Sisyphus exists in life, right here before our eyes:
> The man consumed with seeking the accoutrements of office
> From the people, who always come back sad and beaten. To be driven
> To seek power—an illusion after all—which is never given,
> And undergo endless hard toil in striving for it still,
> This is the act of struggling to shove a stone uphill,
> Which, at the very peak, only goes bounding down again. [34]

Sisyphus is not real. Instead, his story represents one kind of self-inflicted misery we encounter in this life. In this way, Lucretius concludes, "at last, the life of fools becomes a Hell on Earth."[35] The same is true of the children in Willy Wonka's factory—he did not set up his factory *intentionally* to trap and punish bad children. When Violet hastily pops the experimental gum into her mouth, or when Veruca races into the Nut Room to snatch a pet squirrel, he's as surprised as anyone. Like Epicurus's gods, he inhabits a special region of space, separate for the most part from the normal human realm, where he remains absorbed in the pure joy of his own activities. (He's odd largely because he seems so oblivious to anything outside of his factory and his experiments.) The misery the children suffer is brought on themselves because of their own unnatural desires.

At the climax of the story, after the other children are gone, Willy Wonka invites Charlie to be the heir to his factory. Wonka recognizes a kindred spirit in the boy, someone who can truly appreciate and care for his factory and its wonders:

> "How I love my chocolate factory," said Mr. Wonka, gazing down. Then he paused, and he turned to Charlie with a most serious expression on his face. "Do *you* love it, too, Charlie?" he asked.
> "Oh, yes," cried Charlie, "I think it's the most wonderful place in the whole world!"
> "I am very pleased to hear you say that," said Mr. Wonka, looking more serious than ever. . . . Mr. Wonka cocked his head to one side and all at once the tiny twinkling wrinkles of a smile appeared around the corners of his eyes, and he said, "You see, my dear boy, I have decided to make you a present of the whole place."[36]

But Epicurus promises the same for anyone who understands and internalizes the truths of his philosophy: "Practice these and the related precepts day and night, by yourself and with a like-minded friend, and you will never be disturbed either when awake or in sleep, and you will live as a god among men. For a man who lives among immortal goods is in no respect like a mere mortal animal."[37]

We don't become immortal, but by living an Epicurean life, we do enjoy the same *quality* of experience as the gods. The immortal goods of happiness are available to all of us, if only we are willing to take them. Charlie had the good fortune to find the Golden Ticket, and that lucky chance may have saved him and his family from starvation. But the keys to happiness were already within him.

2

ON GETTING OUR JUST DESSERTS[1]

Willy Wonka, Immanuel Kant, and the *Summum Bonum*

Jacob M. Held

At first blush, *Charlie and the Chocolate Factory* is a classic underdog story.[2] Charlie and his family struggle from day to day. The extended family lives in a small shack while Mr. Bucket works at a toothpaste factory screwing caps on tubes of toothpaste for a wage barely large enough to sustain the basic biological functions for his wife, son, elderly parents, and in-laws. Charlie has nothing, and for him, as for so many born into debilitating poverty, his future will likely resemble that of his father. As an underdog, as a child born into destitute poverty, we root for him; we want better for him. We see him doing everything right and accepting the meager reward he ekes out of a frugal world: his one bar of birthday chocolate that he savors over the course of weeks.

Yet, even given their hardships, his family provides a loving home. And we find some measure of satisfaction in the fact that at least Charlie has a happy home life. He'll be loved as he starves to death. So we hope alongside Charlie for something better. We want it to work out for the Buckets. They deserve better. But we know in the real world this scenario rarely turns out well. In the real world what you deserve has very little to do with what you get. We can wish for things to be better, but if wishes were horses, beggars would ride.[3] However, in Roald Dahl's world, where children are victorious and justice wins the day, we will root for Charlie because we want him to succeed—he deserves to, and we know our efforts won't be in vain. Beneath the simple underdog tale lies our desire for something more. We desire justice—and a particular kind of justice. We long to see the good rewarded for being good and decent, because they deserve to reap the benefits of having lived virtuously, of having done everything right. If the world were fair, if the world were just, the good would prosper and Charlie would live happily ever after.

But *Charlie and the Chocolate Factory* isn't simply a story about a decent, honest, child who overcomes hardship and, through the beneficence of his benefactor, Willy Wonka, lives happily ever after. *Charlie and the Chocolate Factory* is also about punishment. A great deal of the book focuses on the punishment of the bad children. A significant amount of the text is committed to developing Veruca, Augustus, Mike, and Violet and to providing the context for their eventual punishments. This is a major part of the book, and it is the flip side of us wanting to see Charlie succeed: we also want to see these rotten children fail. In fact, we delight in their punishments, perhaps too much. We are, after all, enjoying the thought of children being brutalized in an eccentric's factory because they are gluttonous, spoiled, obnoxious, or otherwise misbehaving.

Thinking about Willy Wonka, we might then ask: On what basis do we demand our just deserts? Every child has screamed at the top of their lungs, "That's not fair!" Often they do so when they don't get their way. Children often find it unfair that they don't get what they want when they want it. Too many children are Veruca Salt. But sometimes this lamentation is focused at the right object: actual injustice. Why do some people's children get all the breaks just because they are lucky enough to have been born to privileged parents? Why do these children get to go to the best schools and have every possible opportunity afforded to them, for no other reason than that their parents have accumulated wealth in some fashion?

Now some parents respond to the charge that "It's not fair" with "Life's not fair." This response is troubling for several reasons. First, it accepts that the world is inherently unfair, and so it implies that one's response to injustice ought to be acquiescence—suck it up. This attitude conveys to the child that they need to accept injustice as a fact of life and simply cross their fingers and hope that they will be on the winning side sometimes. Second, some scenarios in which a child yells about something being unfair are scenarios that allow a parent to fix the injustice. To simply respond that the world is unfair is for a parent to be lazy, either by failing to explain how the contested situation is in fact fair, by failing to explain how certain unfair situations are beyond the parent's current control but still regrettable, or by refusing to do what is within their power to rectify the injustice. Regardless, from a very early age children recognize that the world isn't fair and demand that it be made more so. As adults, we, hopefully, have a more cultivated sense of what is and is not unjust as well as a better sense of how to fix the world to make a bit more so. This insight is the heart of *Charlie and the Chocolate Factory*: the recognition that the world isn't fair paired with the desire to make it so and the hope that someday it will be. The hope that the good will prosper, and the wicked will be punished.

IMMANUEL KANT'S WORLD OF PURE IMAGINATION

We know that the world isn't fair, and we know, deep down, that no matter how hard we hope and work for it to be so, the world will never be perfectly just. We know that the world is not the kind of place where the good are rewarded for their virtue and the wicked punished. We know that on the rare occasions when this does happen it's probably luck or mere coincidence. But we still harbor that belief, that faith. And we lie to children and ourselves through stories like *Charlie and the Chocolate Factory*. We lie that good will win in the end. Why do we do so? Why is that lie so appealing?

In his *Critique of Pure Reason*, Immanuel Kant (1724–1804) famously claimed that the interests of reason combine in three questions, one of which is "What may I hope?"[4] Kant recognized that a fundamental aspect of the human condition is to hope for something greater, for meaning in an otherwise meaningless universe. His third question expresses the idea that "If I do what I ought to do, what may I hope?"[5] Can I hope for happiness? Without hope—hope for justice, hope for happiness, hope that it will all work out in the end—we would quickly be driven to despair. And so Kant sought to answer this question, to offer us hope. His solution: We may hope for the ultimate good, the *summum bonum*—happiness in proportion to virtue. But in order to understand his answer, we need to begin at the beginning of Kant's practical philosophy; we need begin with the good will.

Kant claims that the only thing in this world valuable in itself is a good will.[6] By this he means simply that everything in this world aside from a rational, free will is only instrumentally valuable. Tables, desks, pens, chocolate bars, everlasting gobstoppers, and other things are only valuable because we value them. Their monetary value stems from vague economic forces and their use value stems from our interest in doing things with them. But were there no one around to use the table, desk, or chair, or to taste a Wonka's Whipple-Scrumptious Fudgemallow Delight, they would be worthless. This is obviously an anthropocentric world view, a vision of the world with humans at the center, but Kant supports it for the following reasons.

A good will is good in itself because it is autonomous. This means that a will is able to choose for itself, it can give the law to itself, or, more simply put, it can choose on what principle to act. This type of will is not determined by instinct or programming; it's able to decide for itself how it will relate to the world around it, including how it will relate to other wills. Now, for humans, this will is embodied; it's placed in a human meat sack and so driven by (and often seemingly determined by) biological processes. Yet even though our wills seem to be governed by natural forces, such as neurological processes and biochemical reactions, we're still justified in our belief that we are in fact free. Even though it appears as if our body is determined by natural processes, and even though our best science aims to give a complete account of how everything is caused by various material processes, there will always be doubt. Our minds are wired to understand the world in a certain way—according to the laws of cause and effect and beholden to linear time. But that is just how our minds interpret reality; how things really are might be quite different. There might be some things, like wills, that are spontaneous, that aren't governed by law like other physical phenomena. The doubt that results from the fact that we can only know so much, and in a very specific way, allows us to believe, to have a rational faith in things like free wills. So we are permitted to believe that our will is free. And this is good, because the idea of a free will does a lot of heavy lifting for value theory, specifically ethics.

Since our wills are free, we can choose to act rationally—that is, according to reason, and not simply according to desires, which are given to us from our bodies. We don't decide to enjoy chocolate or sweets; we simply do. And our tastes, although they can be cultivated to an extent, are very much out of our control. So if we simply listened to our body and, when it demanded chocolate, proceeded to shovel it down our gullet as quickly as possible, we wouldn't be free, but rather a slave to our compulsions and whims, much like the gluttonous Augustus Gloop, a one-dimensional walking appetite. But we are rational and therefore free, autonomous wills. In this regard, we are unlike anything else on the planet. But with the ability to choose comes the responsibility to choose well. How do we choose well? We choose rationally.

Kant's ethics revolves around the categorical imperative, one formulation of which is "So act that you use humanity, whether in your own person or in the person of any other, always at the same time as an end, never merely as a means."[7] This imperative, or command, demands from us and compels us via reason to act in a way that respects others by treating them as dignified in themselves. It also commands that we respect our own freedom and so our own dignity. And this is the main point, the big idea. As autonomous beings, humans possess dignity—that is, a value beyond price. We are valuable simply by existing because of the kind of thing we are: free, rational agents. Likewise, when we find other beings that appear free and rational we are compelled to respect them. This is our duty. This is the crux of Kantian ethics, respect for free, rational beings, for dignified beings. This respect vindicates the inherent worth that all people have and is the only protection for this value. Whereas everything else in the world is only instrumentally valuable, people are valuable in themselves. But this value only truly exists, it only means something, so long as we behave as if it does. When we respect the dignity of others, that dignity becomes real and their value is affirmed. When we behave morally, according to the categorical imperative, we treat ourselves as dignified and this dignity then has meaning. We are stewards of value, the source of the only inherent, priceless value in the universe. It's a big deal, a big responsibility.

So consider why we like Charlie so much, why we root for him. His life is dreary. He lives in destitute poverty. Yet, despite all of this, he lives honorably, and he is a moral boy. He respects his parents and grandparents. He doesn't get into trouble. We see here a boy who values morality above all else. He could steal. He could sell the gobstopper to Slugworth (if one is considering the 1971 film version of the story). But instead he perseveres, morally speaking. The other characters don't. They live for bodily pleasures—they live for stuff, always wanting more and wanting it "NOW!" They use and abuse other people. But Charlie is a steward of human dignity, exhibiting it in how he behaves, how he treats himself, and how he treats others.

Yet, as stewards of value, we have to tend not only to our dignity but also to that of others. We have to make sure proper respect is being shown; that those who deserve respect are being given it, and that those who fall short are being reprimanded. Praise and blame are essential elements to this idea. We praise ethical human beings. But most important, at least for our discussion of *Charlie and the Chocolate Factory*, we blame those who fall short. When someone comes up short, when their behavior is lacking in some way, we hold them accountable. If the only value that exists in its own right is the value we create and maintain through our respectful, good actions, then we praise those who help us build a world worth living in and condemn those who make things harder, uglier, and wicked. And so we come to punishment.

Kant is a retributivist. He believes punishment is about retribution, or payback. In this way, punishment blames people for having acted poorly and vindicates the dignity of the victim and even the criminal while affirming a moral world order. When someone commits a wrong, they do harm to the victim, whether it be monetarily, physically, or emotionally. But most important, their action harms the victim and the community morally—that is, it speaks to a lack of respect for the other and for our shared values. The criminal shirks morality and dishonors himself and humanity in the process. Punishment is meant to rectify this. By punishing the criminal we reassert the values they rejected. We don't punish to prevent future crimes or to teach lessons. Doing so would be disrespectful to the criminal. We don't have to hurt you to teach you; you're not an animal to be trained. Likewise, we don't punish criminals merely to send a message. Doing so would be using them, not respecting them. If we punish a criminal simply to send a message to other criminals, we're exploiting him. We punish in order to make dignity real, in order to establish, reinforce, and reproduce a moral order in the universe. For Kant, "The moral law . . . also defines for us a final end . . . and makes it obligatory upon us to strive towards its attainment. This end is the *summum bonum*, as the highest good in the world possible through freedom."[8] Punishment speaks to a natural need or desire that we all have for the *summum bonum*, the greatest good.

We all want to be happy, and we want to be happy most when we deserve to be. "Virtue and happiness together constitute possession of the highest good in a person, and happiness distributed in exact proportion to morality (as the worth of a person and his worthiness to be happy) constitutes the *highest good* of a possible world."[9] Likewise, "Virtue is the greatest worth of the person, but our state must also be worth wishing for. The greatest worth of one's state is happiness. So virtue combined with happiness is the highest good."[10] So we want happiness in proportion to our virtue. In this world that isn't going to happen. This world is not driven by forces that guarantee that we'll get what's coming to us. But Kant tells us we can hope. One answer to the question "what may I hope?" is that when I die, I'll get what's coming to me, and so will you. I can hope for an afterlife in which I'm as happy as I deserve to be, and you suffer as much as you ought. Kant claimed, "Only if religion is added . . . does there also enter the hope of some day participating in happiness to the degree that we have been intent upon not being unworthy of it."[11] This hope is for Kant a rational faith, one that, although it can't be known, is not contradictory. "Morality and the expectation of a happiness proportionate to it as its result can at least be thought as possible . . . since no one can want to maintain that a worthiness of rational beings in the world to be happy in conformity with the moral law combined with a possession of this happiness proportioned to it is impossible in itself."[12] This requires a leap of faith, a practical faith or pure rational belief. But even this is cold comfort. Faith won't fill Charlie's empty belly, find a job for his recently unemployed father, or keep his bedridden grandparents from succumbing to hunger or illness. We all still suffer so long as we live. And the afterlife is a bit of a gamble. So isn't there something more we can do?

Well, there is more we can do; we can try to construct this world to mimic the ideal. We can set up institutions that reward goodness and punish the wicked, at least as much as is possible. We can live as morally as possible, demand the same from others, and enforce this demand through the law, through punishment. Then this world would begin to look like a manifestation of an ideal moral order. It's this demand that we all have for our just deserts—that we get what we are owed, morally speaking—that causes us to revel in Charlie's success and enjoy the suffering and punishment of the other children. Willy Wonka has created a world of pure imagination, a world where we are given a glimpse into the *summum bonum*, where people are given happiness in proportion to goodness and are punished in proportion to their wickedness.

IT ALWAYS GOES RIGHT, WHEN WONKA COMES TO THE DESSERT [13]

There is an odd satisfaction we get from seeing bad people punished. Now, some might simply classify this as sadism, or schadenfreude, or an expression of our own resentment. [14] But, arguably, there is much more to the pleasure we take in seeing people punished than a simple desire for control, power, or sadism. We call it justice, and we justify it with a claim to just deserts. Let's consider the children in *Charlie and the Chocolate Factory*.

The children in *Charlie and the Chocolate Factory* are fitting examples to illustrate retribution because their infractions are moral shortcomings. They are punished for failing to live up to a moral ideal. Willy Wonka's factory is not law driven. Things run according to his whims. Yet each of the children, even Charlie at the end of the 1971 film, is punished for some perceived immorality.

Augustus Gloop is a glutton. He is described as a fat child, with "great flabby folds of fat" bulging all around his body and a "face like a monstrous ball of dough." [15] But, more important, as a glutton Augustus lacks self-control. "Eating is his hobby. . . . That's *all* he's interested in." [16] Augustus has thus developed into a one-dimensional human being, a walking appetite unable to control himself. In fact, it is this failure to curb his own desire for sweets, his succumbing to his irrational cravings, that leads to his downfall. His gluttony leads to him falling into the chocolate river, as he exclaims, "I need a bucket to drink it properly." [17] But nobody "properly" drinks chocolate by the bucketful. Augustus is subsequently sucked up a pipe and sent to the strawberry-flavored chocolate-coated fudge room, where he may very well be dumped into a fudge boiler. One can only begin to imagine the processes through which Augustus will be converted into "uneatable" fudge.

Why does Augustus deserve such a punishment? Why do we enjoy his plight? We enjoy watching Augustus punished simply because he lacks self-respect, or else he wouldn't have let himself devolve into such a state in which, like a ravenous animal, he is driven by appetite alone. He has turned the enjoyment of an occasional sweet into a perverse hobby; more animal than human, he is driven by his stomach, not his mind, not reason. His whims, his desires determine his actions, not his free will. In behaving like an animal, Augustus fails to respect himself; he fails to respect his own dignity. He is an affront to human dignity itself, not because he is overweight but because he lacks self-control. "Augustus Gloop! Augustus Gloop! The great big greedy nincompoop! How long could you allow this beast / To gorge and guzzle, feed and feast?"[18] This glutton who brought not even "the smallest bit of fun" to anyone, due to his greed, will bring joy as delicious fudge. "For who could hate or bear a grudge / Against a luscious bit of fudge."[19] The punishment for gorging on treats is to be turned into one, and by one's own hand. Augustus fell into the river of his own accord; his unwieldy appetite was his own undoing.

Then there is Violet Beauregarde. Violet lacks manners. She is disgusting, as evidenced by her incessant gum chewing. The Oompa-Loompas claim, "There's almost nothing worse to see / Than some repulsive little bum / Who's always chewing chewing gum."[20] They even suggest it's as bad as somebody picking their nose. Violet gnaws and pops, chews and slops her gum nonstop, making a mockery of eating itself. Her gum chewing borders on the obscene; it's a perverse distortion of a natural life function. It is also obnoxious, as anyone who has been subjected to an incessant gum chewer can attest. The constant visual and aural assault of a gum chewer is poor etiquette; it fails to account for the comfort of those who are subjected it. And, like all the children, her behavior is punished through her own misdeed. She stuffs an experimental piece of gum in her craw before Wonka can stop her, although he doesn't seem terribly interested in doing so. He yells for her to stop, but his attitude seems dismissive. Wonka has no intention of stopping these children from being their own undoing. His factory merely provides the perfect environment for them to get their own comeuppance, to get what they deserve. Wonka's response to Violet's fate is telling: "It always happens like that,"[21] he sighs. Violet's lack of self-control, like Augustus, leads to her predicament. But unlike that of Augustus, her behavior is also disrespectful of others. Her disgusting habit smacks of a total lack of respect for others in public situations. She doesn't simply lack self-control; she is also self-centered to the point that she disregards others.

Mike Teavee meets his end also due to a lack of self-control, specifically with regard to a questionable pastime. Mike watches too much television and doesn't read. The Oompa-Loompas iterate, "[TV] ROTS THE SENSES IN THE HEAD! IT KILLS IMAGINATION DEAD! IT CLOGS AND CLUTTERS UP THE MIND! IT MAKES A CHILD SO DULL AND BLIND / HE CAN NO LONGER UNDERSTAND. A

FANTASY, A FAIRYLAND! HIS BRAIN BECOMES AS SOFT AS CHEESE! HIS POWERS OF THINKING RUST AND FREEZE! HE *CANNOT* THINK—HE ONLY *SEES*!"[22] Mike's behavior betrays disrespect for himself. He is not interested in developing his own potential; he treats himself as an object, a pleasure machine, a being that only "sees," passively receiving his entertainment, not actively "thinking" and crafting his existence. Like Augustus, Mike is a one-dimensional person, driven by appetite alone.

Finally, there is Veruca Salt. Her greed, the fact that she is spoiled rotten, a bad nut, leads to her and her parents' potential incineration. Veruca's moral failing seems to be that she uses others as a means to her own pleasure. Veruca doesn't respect others, but sees in them only a means to get more of what she wants. Her lack of respect for others is obvious. Yet, in Veruca's case, both she and her parents get punished, since all of them bear some responsibility. Mr. and Mrs. Salt did spoil her. All of the parents bear some responsibility. Augustus wouldn't be a glutton with an insatiable appetite for junk food if his parents hadn't fed him poorly and not looked after him properly. Mike's parents obviously don't encourage reading or monitor his television watching. And Violet's parents do nothing to curb her bad habit. But in the end, all of these children get punished for having run afoul of a moral code that demands self-control, respect, proper habits, and manners. A moral law that demands that people be decent and respectful, of themselves and others. We can see why we enjoy reading about these children's punishments if we take seriously the idea that a moral order, a civil order, needs to be maintained because it demonstrates respect for dignity, the value of all human life.

But beyond being what they deserve, the children's punishments may also function to rectify the cause of their moral failings. Augustus has been squeezed thin (although his weight wasn't his problem—his appetite was). Mike is tall and can look forward to a basketball career. Violet leaves the factory purple, and now she'll see her moral failing as much as others saw and heard it as she chomped her gum; perhaps this constant reminder will motivate her to behave more appropriately. And Veruca and her parents leave the factory covered in garbage; perhaps this humiliation will bring them down a notch or two, so they can see that they are not so special and should treat all people with the same respect they demand for themselves. Shame and humiliation have an odd way of bringing those who think a bit too highly of themselves back down to everyone's level, a level of equal respect. So these four children deserve their punishments, and those who want a civil society built on mutual respect will enjoy, or at least appreciate, their being punished for their moral transgressions; if the punishment helps them learn a lesson, then so much the better.

That leaves Charlie Bucket, our hero. Charlie seems to be a good kid. From all indications, he doesn't get into trouble at home or at school. He is well behaved towards his parents and grandparents, and the family as a whole is loving and supportive. When Charlie gets home, the grandparents light up, and "for perhaps half an hour every night, this room would become a happy place, and the whole family would forget that it was hungry and poor."[23] It's good that Charlie has a loving home, and although we know happiness is the most important thing in life, his poverty isn't something that can be ignored; if not remedied, Charlie and his family will starve to death. Although poverty itself is lamentable, especially when it is not one's fault, it seems even worse in Charlie's case. His father works hard at the toothpaste factory until the factory closes and leaves him unemployed. His grandparents are indigent and his mother labors hard to care for them all. They seem to be doing everything right, but the world isn't cooperating. So they are gravely poor, to the point that "It seemed doubtful whether [Charlie] could go on much longer like this without becoming dangerously ill."[24] It's a matter of when, not if, they succumb to poverty.

It's especially hard to see Charlie go through this. As Grandpa Joe says, "It doesn't matter about us. We're too old to bother with. But a *growing boy*! He can't go on like this!! He's beginning to look like a skeleton!"[25] Surely some of what bothers us most about Charlie's plight is that he is a child, and it's always harder to see children suffer than adults. But mostly the reader is frustrated because Charlie deserves better. Not that anyone deserves to die of starvation, but Charlie is a child, a good, sweet, gentle child. Our sympathies are only deepened when we are regaled with tales of how he savors his birthday chocolate, placing it in a small wooden box, looking at it first, "until he could stand it no longer." Then he would only take tiny nibbles so that he "could make his ten-cent bar of birthday chocolate last him for more than a month."[26] This sensitive boy does everything right and appreciates the meager offerings this world affords him. He remains hopeful and good in a world that seems hell-bent on seeing him and his family fail. Meanwhile, we hear of these other children, these rotten, spoiled, gluttonous, ungrateful children who are afforded every luxury, and have every whim satisfied for no other reason than that they were lucky enough to be born into wealth and privilege. As his mother states when he's hoping for a Golden Ticket, "You mustn't be too disappointed, my darling, if you don't find what you're looking for underneath the wrapper. You really can't expect to be as lucky as all that."[27] But what can you expect in this world? There's only so much luck, so much privilege to go around. And as Grandma Georgina says, "The thing to remember . . . is that whatever happens, you'll still have the bar of candy."[28] Charlie can't expect much, but these little things may make his miserable life tolerable, even if just for a little bit.

Charlie doesn't deserve to suffer, and the wretched brats don't deserve to have so much when he has so little. And so we don't simply want to see them fall, we don't just want them to be punished for their moral failings; we want to see Charlie rewarded for his virtue, his goodness. The Golden Ticket offers him this reward. Charlie has a chance to receive happiness in proportion to his virtue, to achieve the *summum bonum* through Willy Wonka, an eccentric with the power to establish justice on earth, even if it is only within the walls of his factory.

When Charlie finds his Golden Ticket it's more than just a free tour of a chocolate factory. The Golden Ticket is a way to redeem his life, to redeem the world. Perhaps, he can get what he deserves. After the bad children are all punished, Charlie is rewarded for being good, for being a "good sensible loving child, one to whom [Wonka] can tell all [his] most precious candy-making secrets."[29]

The book and the 1971 movie differ significantly at the end. The book has Wonka simply hand the factory over to Charlie when he realizes that all the other children are gone. He is given it because he loves it; he earned it by being morally disposed to not get into trouble, to do things the right way. And so he is honored with the gift of the factory and is as happy as he deserves to be. But the film is different.

SO SHINES A GOOD DEED

At the end of the 1971 film, Charlie is originally dismissed without getting the factory or any chocolate. He is kicked out by Wonka for having stolen Fizzy Lifting drinks. Grandpa Joe figures they can square things by selling the everlasting gobstopper to Slugworth, a competitor of Wonka's who would love his candy-making secrets. But Charlie is too good for that. He's been through tough times, he's handled the worst the world can throw at him, and it hasn't made him bitter or spiteful. So this setback won't either. He'll still do what's right even if the world seems once again to have turned its back on him. He returns the gobstopper by wordlessly placing it on Wonka's desk as his back is turned and he seems to be working furiously.

Charlie does not do so for a reward or because he wants to avoid punishment. In fact, at that moment taking and selling the gobstopper to Slugworth is probably the only hope Charlie has of providing for his family. He returns the gobstopper simply because it seems the right thing to do. As he turns to walk away Wonka places his hand on the gobstopper and utters, almost inaudibly, "So shines a good deed, in a weary world." These nine words may be the most impactful of the film, of nearly any film, because of their poignancy. This simple sentence communicates this entire chapter, and in fact inspired it. This weary world, this world of poverty, starvation, greed, pain—simply put, this world of vice and suffering—is enough to wear down even the strongest among us. Yet, in spite of it all, in spite of having suffered the worst life can throw at him, Charlie shines like a beacon; Charlie is good. The world can be loathsome and dark, sinister and rotten, but Charlie will not be so. He will not let the darkness of this world dim his light, and so he shines through his good deed in this weary world. Charlie's goodness reaffirms Wonka's faith in humankind; there are still decent people among us. Charlie reaffirms the value of the world, its beauty. Charlie is a proper steward of value. Here Wonka sees it, and Charlie proves he deserves everything.

This world can't justify itself; it isn't good in itself. It is just stuff and events, most of which are painful. But human beings, moral beings, can redeem this world by making it a place worth living in, a place of morality and order, a place of justice and worth. Through his simple act, Charlie redeems this weary world and proves to Wonka that it is worth it; the world is valuable and good because people like Charlie are in it. To hell with the rotten kids, the spoiled children. The world will always be full of such profligate, wretched beings, but compared with Charlie, compared with the good and the just, they are nothing.

Charlie incites in us our demand that the good be rewarded and given what they deserve and the wicked punished. Charlie makes us want to demand justice. Wonka provides it, and so the story provides a glimpse into that world where we may hope for justice, where we're allowed to believe the lie that it will be all right in the end. Because without that lie, with what are we left? Charlie offers us a glimpse of human dignity, of a value beyond price, a value that reaffirms the worth of the world and gives us hope for something better. This hope invigorates us and gives us the strength to persevere as moral beings among the slag and refuse of humanity that surrounds us. And perhaps if enough of us persevere, this world will someday be worthy of us. We can always hope. To quote another British author, "You need to believe in things that aren't true. How else can they become?"[30]

3

MATILDA, EXISTENTIALIST SUPERHERO

Elizabeth Butterfield

Once upon a time, there was a young girl named Matilda. She was polite and good-hearted and kind, but there was also something different about her—she possessed remarkable mental abilities. It would not be a stretch to say that Matilda was a genius. Now, you might think that any parent would be overjoyed to have a daughter like that. Most parents would swoon over a child with such abilities and would thank their lucky stars to have such a pleasant and helpful child in the family to boot. And you might suspect that most teachers and principals would treasure the chance to nurture a young intellect like Matilda's. With her abilities and eagerness to learn, Matilda was the kind of student that any teacher would be lucky to come across once in a lifetime.

Yes, in so many ways, Matilda was the child most adults would dream of having. But what is surprising, as Roald Dahl tells us, is that at home Matilda's gifts were not met with praise, or support, or even love. It was not just that her genius was unnoticed, or unappreciated, or even taken for granted, which would be a crime in itself. Oh, no—unfortunately, the reprehensible reaction Matilda received from the most important adults in her life was one of resentment.

How can we make sense of the strange and heartbreaking scenario in which Matilda found herself? Well, regrettably, Matilda was not the first person of genius to encounter resistance as she rose above the mediocrity of her surroundings. In fact, two nineteenth-century European philosophers, Søren Kierkegaard (1813–1855) and Friedrich Nietzsche (1844–1900), wrote strikingly similar descriptions of exactly such experiences in their own societies. Both philosophers were concerned with what they saw as the growing mediocrity of average society and the increasing difficulty of living as a true individual who stands out from the crowd. They both noticed that when the strengths of a particularly talented individual begin to show, in general the crowd reacts by trying to cut down this extraordinary individual however possible, in order to restore the group to the safety of mediocrity—all in the name of "equality."

Though there are many differences between the philosophies of Kierkegaard and Nietzsche, they obviously witnessed and described very similar forces at work in the Europe of the nineteenth century. Today, both are generally categorized as "existentialist" philosophers. Existentialism can be understood as "a philosophy about the concrete individual,"[1] which understands individuality to be not a given, but rather an accomplishment. As Thomas Flynn writes, "Because of the almost irresistible pull toward conformity in modern society, what we shall call 'existential individuality' is an achievement, and not a permanent one at that. We are born biological beings but we must become existential individuals."[2]

Roald Dahl's character Matilda can be understood as an existentialist hero or even, considering her remarkable abilities, an existentialist *superhero*. We will see that as Matilda with her genius rises above the mediocrity of her surroundings, she encounters resentment from most of the adults in her life. But as the existentialist superhero, she finds ways to counter the obstacles they put in her path. Instead of becoming bogged down in feelings of victimhood or resentment, she uses her strength of character as well as her genius and superpowers to take the initiative to do something about the situation, first executing revenge and ultimately creating a better life for herself and others she cares about. She also inspires others to do the same. And she does all of this without arrogance or a sense of self-importance, but rather with goodness, cheerfulness, and an affirmation of life.

MATILDA AT HOME

Keep your nasty mouth shut so we can all watch this programme in peace.

—Mrs. Wormwood[3]

When Roald Dahl introduces us to Matilda, we learn that while she might have been small and not very physically strong, she was "sensitive and brilliant," with a mind that was "nimble" and "so quick to learn." She was also "gutsy and adventurous" and "interested in everything." All in all, he writes, she was "something to make your eyes pop."[4] However, we are also told right from the beginning that she is modest and friendly and not at all a show-off. She seems to have an innate sense of moral decency and often feels righteous indignation when she witnesses the wrongful cheating or abuse of others.

But Matilda couldn't have been more different from her parents. Dahl describes Mr. and Mrs. Wormwood as "gormless" and unintelligent, and they spend every evening completely absorbed in watching television. Interestingly, Dahl also describes Matilda's mother and father as especially *tacky*. He makes frequent references to the tackiness of their clothes, hair color, and style, as well as to the mother's makeup and the father's mustache and hat.[5]

Matilda's parents have no interest in learning, and the only book in the house is one titled *Easy Cooking*. Mr. Wormwood explains, "We don't hold with book-reading. . . . You can't make a living from sitting on your fanny and reading story-books. We don't keep them in the house." And Mrs. Wormwood adds, "Looks is more important than books." However, in contrast to Matilda's natural modesty, Mr. Wormwood seems to be naturally boastful. He *thinks* that he has "a fine brain," comparing himself to geniuses and inventors, and he finds proof of his brilliance in his ability as a secondhand car salesman to cheat his customers and bring home a fortune.[6]

Dahl tells us that Mr. and Mrs. Wormwood are not at all interested in parenting their children. They are "so wrapped up in their own silly little lives" that they take no interest in their children and can't wait for the day to come when they could be rid of them.[7] So when her parents don't parent her, Matilda takes responsibility for doing so herself. As a young child left alone in the house all day, she learns to care for herself not only in practical matters but also in feeding her desire to learn. Matilda teaches herself to read, and when her parents refuse her request for a book, she discovers that she can walk to the library by herself. In this way, she finds things to stimulate her intellect, and she begins reading everything she can find.

If we could simply say that Matilda's parents took no interest in her at all, and simply left her alone to explore the world on her own, that might have been better. But what Matilda experienced at home was actually much worse. It didn't help that Mr. Wormwood was by nature a bully, and when he came home irritated by something, he would take it out on others. Matilda was a convenient target. But worse than that, whenever Matilda gave a sign of how very special she was—how intelligent and precocious, or how interesting, or curious, or morally decent—her parents would shut her down. It was as if Matilda's specialness was somehow a bother, or worse, a challenge. For example, Dahl tells us that at age one and a half, when Matilda could speak perfectly, her parents responded by calling her a "noisy chatterbox." As she grew, her father regularly referred to her as "an ignorant little twit" and "stupid." And one day, when Matilda effortlessly completed a difficult calculation in her head, instead of appreciating her amazing mathematical abilities, her father angrily accused her of cheating, saying that no one could have done that, "especially a girl."[8]

At the root of her parents' reactions seems to be more than just annoyance with children or the loss of patience. Dahl tells us that Mr. Wormwood actually *resents* Matilda for her brilliance. We see this one evening in particular, early in the story, when Mr. Wormwood returns home from work and turns on the television as usual. While the rest of the family watches TV, Matilda blocks out the noise from the program and continues to read her book. On this particular night, the fact that Matilda goes on reading seems to drive her father crazy. As Dahl writes, "She kept right on reading, and for some reason this infuriated the father. Perhaps his anger was intensified because he saw her getting pleasure from something that was beyond his reach."[9]

Here we have the boastful and arrogant Mr. Wormwood, who must at some level actually be aware of his lack of intelligence or his inferior state, resentful of the fact that his daughter is able to comprehend and enjoy something he cannot. Instead of wanting to learn about it too, so that he can enjoy it with her, he resents the idea that something could be beyond his reach—he rejects the idea of "high culture" altogether, in favor of middle-class tackiness and television—and reacts hatefully toward his daughter. Matilda's enjoyment of reading in some way suggests a high-culture criticism of who and what he is, and he reacts violently. As Mr. Wormwood in a rage rips her library book to shreds, Dahl writes,

"There seemed little doubt that the man felt some kind of jealousy. How dare she, he seemed to be saying with each rip of a page, how dare she enjoy reading books when he couldn't? How dare she?"[10]

It is this theme of resentment that leads us to nineteenth-century existentialist philosophy. Friedrich Nietzsche, a German philosopher, argued that the mediocre masses tend to want to huddle together, as if in a herd, in order to protect themselves and to keep everyone safe. Nietzsche writes that "morality is the herd-instinct in the individual," because, as he sees it, the goal of conventional morality is to protect the safety of the herd. In this context, whenever an individual of outstanding qualities begins to rise above the group, the masses not only feel resentment toward this individual but also experience him or her as a dangerous threat to their safety. For this reason, they also attempt to restrain the individual and force him or her into repressing these strengths. Nietzsche writes, "One herd! Everybody wants the same, everybody is the same: whoever feels different goes voluntarily into a madhouse."[11]

Søren Kierkegaard, a Danish philosopher, described a dynamic similar to Nietzsche's. In his work *The Present Age*, Kierkegaard describes the majority of people in his society as lazy, passionless, running from their own freedom, refusing to take responsibility for making their own choices, and losing themselves in the media. For these people who live without depth, boredom is the greatest danger, and so there is a constant call for entertainment and distraction. Even in the nineteenth century, without televisions and radios, Kierkegaard was particularly troubled by the development of mass media, which for his time meant newspapers and periodicals. He writes, "Ours is the age of advertisement and publicity. Nothing ever happens but there is instantaneous publicity everywhere."[12] He argued that the distraction and entertainment of the mass media shaped society into a "gallery public," a group of anonymous bystanders who observe from a distance, as if observing artwork in a gallery. The gallery public craves entertainment, and the papers oblige by criticizing and mocking others. However, this was often done under the use of pseudonyms, so that no one ever had to take responsibility for the vicious attacks. Kierkegaard himself was subject to this sort of attack from unnamed voices in the papers, and he became well known on the streets of Copenhagen as a character to be mocked.

Another reason that Kierkegaard was critical of the public was that he saw in society a tendency to run away from the responsibility of making one's own choices and to look outside oneself for direction. And the newspapers were right there, ready to tell anyone what opinions to hold, how to vote, what to buy, what is fashionable, what to believe, how to live, and so on. Many people flee the responsibility of making their own choices, into busyness, distraction, and inauthenticity, trying to conform to what "they" say one should do. In many ways, Kierkegaard's description of "the present age" resembles what we find in Matilda's parents, who seek constant distraction in the television. They take no responsibility for parenting their children, no responsibility as members of their community, and no moral responsibility either, as their livelihood is based on criminal activities at the car dealership.

Kierkegaard was especially concerned with what he saw as the increasing resentment of the masses toward anyone of special talent or individuality, and he wrote, "The *ressentiment* which is establishing itself is the process of leveling." It is called leveling because the goal is to cut down those that rise above the crowd "in order that everything may be reduced to the same level."[13] He describes a desire among the masses to preserve the value of equality above all else, which in his eyes meant being equally mediocre and the same as everyone else. He writes that in the present age, there is "contempt for the individual" and "no one wants to be an individual human being."[14]

We can understand Mr. Wormwood's resentment of Matilda in terms of Kierkegaard's notion of leveling. As he tears up her library book, tells her she is stupid, and refuses to allow her teacher, Miss Honey, to offer Matilda private lessons, Mr. Wormwood is experiencing the world from a position of mediocrity, and he resents her genius. His attacks can be seen as an attempt at leveling, trying to bring Matilda back down to his level. Since he is an arrogant and boastful man, the child prodigy who challenges his authority must be cut down so that he can feel superior.

MATILDA TAKES ACTION

Being very small and very young, the only power Matilda had over anyone in her family was brain-power. For sheer cleverness she could run rings around them all. But the fact remained that any five-year-old girl in any family was always obliged to do as she was told, however asinine the orders might be.[15]

Matilda was in a tough position. It was not simply that her genius was unappreciated; she was also in the difficult situation of having to suffer abuse from an authority who was thoroughly incompetent. Dahl writes, "She knew it was wrong to hate her parents like this, but she was finding it very hard not to do so. All the reading she had done had given her a view of life that they had never seen. If only they would read a little Dickens or Kipling they would soon discover there was more to life than cheating people and watching television."[16]

While other people in a situation like this might begin to feel sorry for themselves or become bogged down in feelings of victimhood, stewing in resentment toward their oppressors, Matilda takes a different route—she takes the initiative and decides to do something about it! She takes revenge! As Dahl tells us, "She resented being told constantly that she was ignorant or stupid when she knew she wasn't. The anger inside her went on boiling and boiling, and as she lay in bed that night she made a decision. She decided that every time her father or her mother was beastly to her, she would get her own back in some way or another. A small victory or two would help her to tolerate their idiocies and would stop her from going crazy."[17] Matilda adopts the principle of "when attacked, counterattack," and she finds that punishing her parents makes her life a little more bearable. Instead of letting the situation weigh her down, she takes matters into her own hands.

Now, up until this point, we have emphasized that Matilda seemed to have been born with an innate moral goodness and sense of right and wrong, which rendered her superior to her corrupt parents. But the situation is actually a little more complex than that, for when Matilda decides to take revenge on her parents, she chooses to do many things that would actually appear to be *immoral* according to the principles of conventional morality. Matilda acts in ways that are dishonest, harmful, and disrespectful. For example, to punish her father for cheating people at the car dealership, she puts superglue into the rim of his hat. When it can't be removed, the hat is destroyed, her father's skin is injured, and he looks like a fool. Later, to punish her father for ripping up her library book, Matilda tricks her parents into believing there is a ghost in the house, lying to them and frightening them. And after her father claims that Matilda could not possibly have completed a difficult math problem and calls her a cheater, she punishes him by switching his hair oil with her mother's hair dye, making him look ridiculously blonde and eventually leading to all of his hair falling out. Are these the actions of a child who is morally good?

To answer this question, we can return to the philosophy of Søren Kierkegaard. Kierkegaard developed an untraditional approach to ethics that can be called "three stages on life's way."[18] I say that his approach is untraditional because, while we usually tend to think of ethics in terms of simply following or breaking the rules, Kierkegaard suggests that sometimes conventional rules don't apply.

Kierkegaard describes three stages of moral development. At the first stage, called the "aesthetic stage," we find someone who is amoral, or even pre-moral. This person lives for pleasure in the present and is focused on entertainment and selfish desires. At this level, the person does not feel any pull of moral responsibility because the very concepts of right and wrong have not yet taken on meaning. At this stage we might find Mr. and Mrs. Wormwood, who pay no attention to moral rules of right and wrong or to the duty to care for their children and who spend their lives watching television.

Kierkegaard calls the second stage of moral development the "ethical stage." At this level, the person has developed a conscience and a sense of the meaningfulness of right and wrong. The ethical person recognizes that the moral law exists and strives to fulfill his or her duty to this law. Here we find someone with a strong respect for the rules and for authority, and this is also where we might find Matilda's teacher, Miss Honey. While Miss Honey is one of the few adults who value and care for Matilda, she herself is restrained by her own respect for authority. Again and again, Miss Honey tries to do things in the conventional way, following the typical protocol that would normally be respected. For example, when she first realizes that Matilda is special, her first instinct is to rush to the principal to share the news. That seems like a very normal response, until you realize that the principal is a monster (and Miss Honey should have known better). Later, Miss Honey again follows normal protocol, wanting to speak to Matilda's parents about giving her special lessons. And in her own personal life, in which she has been abused and cheated, instead of going to the authorities or asking for help, Miss Honey dutifully works through her own problems according to conventional values. Although she would make more money by quitting work and taking unemployment payments, she chooses to live according to the values of hard work and thrift, hoping that maybe in ten years or so she might find some relief from the duress. It is as if Miss Honey has such a respect for traditional power and the institutions of authority that she has a hard time remembering that not all people are good.

While most people tend to think that the ethical stage is all there is to ethics, Kierkegaard's innovative approach was to suggest that there are some individuals who are capable of maturing past this point. Sometimes, some special individuals realize that the right thing to do is to break the rules. He called this a "teleological suspension of the ethical"—a situation in which the individual can temporarily suspend the normal rules of morality for the sake of achieving a higher goal, or *telos*. Taking this action may appear immoral to everyone else, and there may be no way to explain to others that it was the right thing to do. But the existential individual, who is the hero of Kierkegaard's narrative, is able to transcend conventional morality and find the path of "right" action for herself. Instead of looking outside herself for direction, the existential individual makes her own way.[19]

In this way, while Matilda behaves in ways that may appear immoral to others, using Kierkegaard's framework we can understand her actions as teleological suspensions of the ethical. Instead of accepting her lot as Miss Honey does, Matilda challenges authorities when she sees that they are unjust and doing a terrible job. She is a trickster and a rule-breaker, but always for a higher purpose. She shows that in extraordinary circumstances, the rules of conventional morality like "respect your elders" do not always apply. The higher *telos* of her actions is at first to help herself survive, then to teach her parents a lesson, and later, at school, to help other abused children and Miss Honey. When Matilda transcends conventional morality to find her own way, she again appears as the existentialist hero.

MATILDA CONFRONTS A VILLAIN

If we think of Matilda as a superhero, when she is finally able to attend school and arrives at Crunchem Hall Primary School, she finds the character we might consider to be her arch-nemesis, Principal Trunchbull. The Trunchbull, as she is called, has several traits in common with Matilda's father. For example, she insists that she is always right and won't accept any criticism whatsoever, and she demands respect for her authority even when she is obviously wrong. But in the Trunchbull, we also encounter a very different sort of villain. She does not express the weakness we might find in a fearful herd mentality or in the demand for equality in mediocrity. No, here instead we find a crude, explicitly animalistic expression of power. We are told that she is "a gigantic holy terror, a fierce tyrannical monster," a "storm trooper," and "a tank" who snorts like an animal.[20]

Friedrich Nietzsche's own existentialist approach to moral philosophy can help us to understand the character of this villain. Like Kierkegaard, Nietzsche also presents us with an account of morality in three stages. But instead of addressing personal moral development, Nietzsche's approach is to examine the development of moral values throughout history.[21] Nietzsche's work is founded on the idea that there is a primal life force, called the will to power, that motivates all that we do. It is like a will to live and drives us to want to survive and to flourish. Nietzsche presents the development of morality throughout history as varying expressions of this will to power.

At the first stage of morality, we find the "masters," who express the will to power in a very direct, crude, and animalistic way. The masters are the strongest members of society. They simply assert, "I am strong, I am powerful, and thus I am good and beautiful. Whatever is different from me, and weak, is bad." We can locate the Trunchbull at this stage, as she expresses her power in a crude and animalistic way. Like the masters, in her power she possesses the privilege of naming and judging, so she asserts her strength, demands respect for her authority, and reserves the right to declare what is true and what is false (even when it clearly contradicts the facts). This can also help us to understand the Trunchbull's hatred for children. She claims that she herself was never a child and that she hates all children who are small and weak. Like the masters Nietzsche describes, she asserts that all children, as her opposites, are innately bad. For example, to a boy named Eric who misspells a word, she says, "You were *wrong*! . . . In fact you strike me as the sort of poisonous little pockmark that will *always* be wrong! You sit wrong! You look wrong! You speak wrong! You are wrong all round!"[22]

According to Nietzsche, everyone experiences the driving force of the will to power, but while the masters can express it openly and directly, those who are the oppressed have to turn the will to power inward. This leads, he claims, to the development of a conscience and great intellectual power, and he also claims that this is the moment when humanity becomes interesting. Eventually, historically speaking, the pendulum of power swings in the other direction, and the values of master morality give way to what Nietzsche calls "slave morality." This morality of the oppressed directly contradicts the values of the masters. Where they praised strength, the slave morality cares for the weak. Where the masters appreciated shows of power, slaves praise virtues of meekness, gentleness, and compassion. Here we find the imagery of the lion that lies down peacefully next to the lamb (instead of ripping the lamb to shreds and having it for dinner). Again, we might say that Miss Honey is a good example of slave morality. In her own life, she has been dominated and oppressed by her aunt, the Trunchbull. After having the courage knocked out of her when she was young, she eventually finds a way to get on her own two feet and make her way. But still, in what she values most, she embodies the values of slave morality. We see this most strongly in the fact that she makes it her mission at Crunchem Hall to protect the weak children however she can.

Finally, Nietzsche comes to the third stage of the historical development of morality. This, he believes, calls for a return to a sort of master morality. But at this stage, instead of a crude and animalistic expression of the will to power, the new masters will have acquired the depth of soul and intellect of slave morality, and this means that their strengths will not be physical but spiritual, and that their expressions of the will to power will be artistic creations. Similar to Kierkegaard's hero, who can suspend the ethical, the new hero for Nietzsche is someone who has the courage and creativity to find his or her own path. Nietzsche refers to this person as the *Übermensch*, or super-human, or the beyond-the-human. The *Übermensch* comes to realize that moral rules were never more than human creations and that no one else can really give you the right answer to the question of how you should live. The *Übermensch* sees that we are the creators of meaning for ourselves and we must find our own way.

We can understand Matilda as an *Übermensch*. With her incredible "brain power," as Dahl calls it, she is practically buzzing and overflowing with the will to power. In school, when she is falsely accused by the Trunchbull, her anger grows and grows until it becomes so intense that the first "miracle" occurs—Matilda uses telekinesis to overturn a glass of water. Dahl writes that after the first miracle, which we could interpret as an expression of this surplus of will to power, Matilda was "sensing her own possibility" and had an "exalted" look on her face.[23] While Miss Honey cautions Matilda to take it slowly and be careful, Matilda ignores this advice and acts independently to practice using her superpower and find what she is capable of:

> It seemed as though a valve had burst inside her and a great gush of energy was being released. She trotted beside Miss Honey with wild little hops and her fingers flew as if she would scatter them to the four winds and her words went off like fireworks, with terrific speed. It was Miss Honey this and Miss Honey that and Miss Honey I do honestly feel I could move almost anything in the world.[24]

As an existentialist *super*-hero, Matilda then uses her power to confront and conquer the Trunchbull, something that no one else had ever been able to do.

When we come to the end of Dahl's tale, thanks to Matilda, she and Miss Honey are freed from both the Wormwoods and the Trunchbull. Finally, Matilda is able to give and receive the love that she so deserved, and she is able to move up to a higher grade in school and to be challenged by more difficult studies. At this point she finds that she is no longer capable of telekinesis. Miss Honey surmises that this is because her superpower arose from an excess of frustrated brain power (or will to power). Now that her brain is genuinely challenged in the way it had craved, her brain power can be actively expressed, and telekinesis is no longer necessary. Matilda replies, "I'm glad it's happened. . . . I wouldn't want to go through life as a miracle-worker."[25]

MATILDA AS EXISTENTIALIST SUPERHERO

Critics of the philosophies of Kierkegaard and Nietzsche often point out that these thinkers seem to embody a sort of bitterness and resentment of their own toward their historical periods, and many critics have questioned how the heroes they present, at the most advanced stages of moral development—these "authentic individuals" who create their own paths in life—might live well together with others. One worry has been that their conceptions of the existentialist hero might take individualism too far.

But what is most remarkable about Matilda is the way that she does all of these things while still remaining gentle, kind, and almost unaware of her brilliance. Dahl tells us again that she is able to express her unique strengths and show that she is smart without showing off and that this makes it possible for her to make friends. Even under duress, repressed and abused, even when she has her own feelings of anger and resentment, we find that she is able to creatively put them to use in positive ways, and she is able to maintain loving relationships. I would argue that this is partly due to her total lack of arrogance (in contrast to the boastful Mr. Wormwood and Principal Trunchbull).

In Matilda's story, we see that when facing a situation with multiple obstacles, she took the initiative to make something out of it for herself. In this way, Matilda emerges as a great example of an existentialist superhero. She rises above the mediocrity of her situation to take the reins to her future, creating a life for herself—a life that *she* wants and that is of her *own* design. Taking responsibility for teaching herself, she comes to create a life that is full of the learning and the loving relationships she craves. Finally, she throws off the limitations of conventional morality to follow her own path and to do what she knows is right, even when that means challenging authority and taking risks. In the end it pays off, and she has helped both herself and others, while also inspiring Miss Honey and the other children around her. Matilda's story brings to life the slogan of another great existentialist philosopher, Jean-Paul Sartre (1905–1980): "You can always make something out of what you've been made into."[26]

4

THE EXISTENTIAL JOURNEY OF JAMES HENRY TROTTER

Kierkegaard, Freedom, and Despair in *James and the Giant Peach*

Matthew Bokma and Adam Barkman

As the stories of Roald Dahl echo down the halls of elementary schools, his creation of fanciful worlds and whimsical characters continue to captivate the imaginations of both children and adults alike. One might be inclined to ask, however, how often do stories like *Charlie and the Chocolate Factory* or *Fantastic Mr. Fox* amuse the ears of academics? Don't assume that academics imprison themselves in their dark and dusty study-rooms, neglecting humor, irony, playfulness, and youthful reminiscences. In fact, it is possible for *James and the Giant Peach* to be associated with the father of existentialism, Søren Kierkegaard (1813–1855).

In Dahl's *James and the Giant Peach*, the protagonist is faced with the same existential struggles that characterize the lives of every human being: How can one loosen the grip of despair, given the chaotic reality of existence, and find genuine joy? Where can one find meaning in a world full of absurdities and ethical conundrums? What does it mean to exist as a human individual in the midst of everyone else? These questions are linked to a characteristically Dahlian and Kierkegaardian theme: self-actualization (or becoming a fully developed human), the fundamental task of every individual. One's journey toward self-actualization not only involves the aesthetic and ethical dimensions of life but also invokes a higher, mysterious reality—the fantastic—in order to qualify the former dimensions as stages geared toward developing a more mature, self-actu-alized individual.[1] On his journey, the fantastic provides James with the passion required for him to embrace his freedom, seize his opportunities, and participate in both the aesthetic and the ethical stages of existence, thereby transforming him into a more self-actualized being.

PRAEFATUS TO THE PEACH

Isolating a purely Kierkegaardian position concerning ethical theory is a daunting task due to his frequent use of often dissenting pseudonyms.[2] However, our intention is not to convey Kierkegaard's actual beliefs, but rather to apply his insights from a variety of his works in order to defend our own position. Second, instead of paralleling the structure of our chap-ter with Dahl's narrative chronologically, we've chosen a thematic ap-proach, arguing that each stage of existence—the aesthetic, the ethical, and the religious—manifests itself in James's choices. And third, the crux of Kierkegaard's authorship deals explicitly with Christian themes; there-fore, in order to justly adopt a Kierkegaardian approach we can't divorce his scholarship from his own mission statement: to "reintroduce Chris-tianity to Christendom."[3] Perhaps we will take James's mother's advice from the movie rendition of Dahl's work and "try looking at it [the narrative] another way":[4] we will broaden the notion of religion, and speak not of God explicitly, but rather God implicitly, God as a higher, incomprehensible, mystical power—the fantastic.

THE WHOLE PEACH

In order to fully appreciate the scope of Kierkegaard's existentialism, a distinction needs to be made: while most North American philosophers are typically analytic philosophers, Kierkegaard is a continental or exis-tential one. Although there is much debate concerning the distinction between these two philosophical movements, existentialism thinks, right-ly or wrongly, that it provides a richer appreciation of the whole human condition. The totality of what it means to be an existing human—includ-ing rationality, the imagination, and the passions—is considered. On the other hand, analytical philosophy is characterized by abstraction—that is, it takes a fragment of reality and cuts it off from the whole in order to subject it to theoretical analysis. Furthermore, the vehicle or medium through which abstraction is conducted is language and propositions. In other words, analytical philosophers appear to reduce reality to symbols and logic. And what often occurs is that once a fragment is removed from the whole, it loses its dynamic character—the organic movement of existing things. To use an illustration: Upon discovering that they are about to be eaten by sharks, James's fellow travelers fix their gaze on him in hopes that he will rescue them. If James operated solely on analytical principles and an elementary understanding of physics, given the approximate density of the air and the weight of the peach, it follows that harnessing the negligible lift of the seagulls as a rescue procedure would be utterly absurd. In fact, his fellow passengers claim he's mad and decry his plan as "Ridiculous . . . Absurd . . . Poppycock . . . Balderdash . . . [and] Madness."[5] Surprisingly, however, it is James's imagination, passion, and—despite a brief period of hesitation—his unfaltering leap into the fantastic that rescue him and his crew. Therefore, existentialists are not satisfied with pure abstraction; rather, they wish to develop a philosophy that appreciates not just the narrowly demarcated rational dimensions of life that often characterize the supposedly mature minds of adults (ironically, in his narratives Dahl depicts adults as immature fools, whereas children are existentially established individuals) but also the grandeur of what it means to *be* in the broadest sense—in the sense that allows the individual to participate in the fantastical, mysterious, and imaginative aspects of our experience. In other words, the human task is more than just isolating substances in tests tubes or speaking or writing in a strictly formal demeanor; rather, our creativity works upon the malleable inexhaustible data of our experience. We are artists, musicians, mystics, and, as another of Dahl's creations states, "We are the music makers, and we are the dreamers of dreams."[6] And perhaps James will show us how to embrace the breadth and depth of human existence.

AUTHENTICITY AND AWFUL AUNTS

A close look at Kierkegaard's psychological work *The Sickness Unto Death* will be our point of departure for James's existential journey. Under the pseudonym Anti-Climacus, Kierkegaard describes self-actualization—although with dense syntax and cryptic vocabulary—as a subjective dialectical process that includes the synthesis of diametrically opposed extremes: "the infinite and the finite, of the temporal and the eternal, of freedom and necessity."[7] In other words, human beings are more than just finite, temporal biological entities that operate according to physical laws; the soul and spirit are inextricably linked to the body. The body is limited by finitude, for it belongs to the concrete life that people find themselves in. This includes one's professional occupation, marital status, nationality, favorite children's book—everything that belongs to spatial-temporal reality. The soul is infinite—that is, it is immortal and carries with it the locus of every intellectual capacity. The soul possesses the capacity to abstract, rationalize, and imagine. It is the seat of possibility, whereas the finite is synonymous with actuality. Most important, however, humans are to be understood as unfolding *spirits*. Spirit can be understood as the dynamic unifying mechanism that exists between the body and soul, or the finite and the infinite. It is that which transforms possibility into actuality. And, generally speaking, it is the force that drives the process of self-actualization.

In the first chapter of *James and the Giant Peach*, Dahl establishes the tension that exists between the infinite and the finite in the life of young James Henry Trotter. This tension between the two poles manifests itself as anxiety that, according to Kierkegaard, becomes an unavoidable reality given the fact of human freedom in the face of a multitude of possibilities.[8] James exists not in a vacuum but in a concrete life: he is only four years old, beloved by his parents, living in a cozy house on the beach with plenty of opportunities to play with other children. It seems that the finite is in harmony with the infinite and the tension that exists between the two is reduced to a minimum. In other words, James embodies the ideal, and therefore the anxiety that is associated with a discrepancy between the actual and the ideal is minimized. However, James's parents "suddenly got eaten up (in full daylight, mind you, and on a crowded street) by an enormous angry rhinoceros which had escaped from the London Zoo . . . and they were dead and gone in thirty-five seconds flat."[9] The manner in which James's parents die illustrates the sheer power of the finite. It seems, along the thought of Jean-Paul Sartre (1905–1980), that humans are thrown into the finite and that in a jiffy the rather absurd movements of fate can extinguish one's existence. Once his evil aunts Spiker and Sponge adopt James, a radical discontinuity between the infinite and the finite emerges. He is no longer James Henry Trotter, but "the filthy nuisance"; rather than living on the beach, he lives on the peak of a hill that is barricaded by a dense garden and a fence. Moreover, the only social interaction he has is with his awful aunts, who not only prevent James from eating a hearty meal or playing with other children down at the beach but also abuse him both verbally and physically. However, although James remains obedient to his abusive aunts, he refuses to be manipulated by their demeaning remarks. Nevertheless, James continues to suffer. Under the abusive authority of his aunts, is there any hope left? How can he still manage to achieve self-actualization in this stultifying situation?

A glimmer of hope is found in the seat of James's own soul. Life and existence provide possibilities, but the will to embrace opportunities lies in the individual himself. Every moment the individual—James—is in a state of reconciliation, for there is a constant tension between the infinite quality of freedom and the finite quality of physical necessity, and the spirit continues to unite these two extremes into a concrete choice or action.[10] James is fundamentally free, but in order for reconciliation to occur, he needs enough willpower to make a choice. The moment of choice, the pinnacle of spiritual activity, is what releases the tension that exists between the infinite and the finite, thereby affording James a measure of spiritual peace.

Throughout the narrative, James is confronted with many possibilities, many windows of opportunity through which a choice must be made—such as whether he should drink the magic concoction of "one thousand long slimy crocodile tongues boiled up in the skull of a dead witch for twenty days and nights with the eyeballs of a lizard."[11] Only by embracing these choices will reconciliation be possible. However, although some opportunities aid one's journey toward self-actualization, many lead to despair.

DESPAIR; OR, LETTING YOUR AUNTS KEEP YOU DOWN

According to Kierkegaard, despair is a sickness of the spirit—a failure to become self-actualized. Paradoxically, despair indicates both human worth and human demise.[12] The capacity to despair is valuable because it is how humans differ from animals—animals cannot despair because they do not have spirit—they lack the transformative capabilities that are present in the human condition. Nevertheless, to be in despair is a human's greatest misfortune. In a sense, despair is a fate worse than death; it's no less than an unwillingness to become one's self. Most, if not all, people participate in some form of despair, for most of life's struggles can be understood primarily as the result of an imbalance between the infinite and the finite. As in the case of James, living with his aunts does nothing but oppress his spirit. The finite—his desperate state of affairs—overwhelms the infinite, reducing his intellectual and creative abilities that are required to conjure up possibilities. Kierkegaard identifies three forms of despair: (1) a failure to realize that you are a despairing, eternal self; (2) a realization that you are despairing, yet an unwillingness to become self-actualized; and (3) despairing in order that you might become self-actualized. [13] If one wishes to restore a proper balance between the infinite and the finite, thereby avoiding despair and reducing anxiety, individuals need to make choices in accordance with all three stages of existence: the aesthetic, the ethical, and the religious.

AESTHETE AUNTS

"Such loveliness as I possess can only truly shine in Hollywood!" Aunt Sponge declared. "Oh wouldn't that be fine! I'd capture all the nations' hearts! They'd give me all the leading parts! The stars would all resign!" [14]

According to the aesthete, freedom is about the individual choosing in accordance with their selfish desires. Every ambition of the aesthetes is a selfish ambition. On their view, happiness can only be attained with a hedonistic—pleasure first—outlook on life. Within the aesthetic sphere there are two classes of people: the immediate aesthete and the reflective aesthete. The former is characterized by reckless hedonism and concurs with Solomon's words: "Let us eat and drink, for tomorrow we die." [15] On the other hand, the reflective aesthete is characterized by a more sophisticated hedonism, in which moderation is employed in order to avoid the pitfalls of the former. For example, a glutton whose only source of pleasure stems from eating peaches all day is an immediate aesthete. For the immediate aesthete, their pleasure is also their demise. Pleasure merely provides the illusion of well-being, for immediate aesthetes don't realize how their vice is slowly killing them, whether it is through extreme sugar intake or what-have-you. Immediate aesthetes participate in the most primitive form of despair: they fail to realize that they are despairing, eternal selves who, in their ignorance, pass up every possibility to become actualized. They fail to realize the transformative power of the ethical as a tool for moral guidance, and the fantastic when approached with a proper measure of humility and awe.

James's Aunt Spiker deems herself "as lovely as a rose," someone whose loveliness "can only truly shine in Hollywood" despite being, as Aunt Sponge interjects, "only bones and skin." The fat, short Aunt Sponge is also fraught with self-grandiosity as she beholds her supposedly "gorgeous curvy shape" and "charming grin." Indeed, they even believe that they will become famous in Hollywood, so much so that the remaining "stars would all resign!" [16] Furthermore, the aunts' greed drives them to charge spectators who wish to see the giant peach. Eventually, however, the very thing that tempts their insatiable need for money or pleasure crushes them to death, and their bodies remain "ironed on the grass as flat and thin and lifeless" [17]—as lifeless as their pathetic, actual lives fixed in the aesthetic stage of existence.

In order to avoid the suffering induced by crass hedonism, the reflective aesthete embraces a more sophisticated notion of pleasure, similar to what is spoken of in Kierkegaard's *Seducer's Diary*: "One must limit oneself—that is the primary condition for all enjoyment." [18] A food connoisseur like the Centipede, who knows how to appreciate fine dishes such as "Scrambled dregs and stinkbugs' eggs and hornets stewed in tar, / And pails of snails and lizards' tails, / And beetles by the jar," [19] can be classified as a reflective aesthete. The food connoisseur does not gorge himself with delicious food. He savors every aspect of it and is educated in its taste, smell, and presentation. However, pleasure is fleeting. Thus another characteristic of reflective aesthetes is that they participate in the second form of despair: a realization that they are despairing. Their spirits are stifled by the shear meaninglessness of fleeting pleasure. In *Either/ Or*, Kierkegaard remorsefully expresses the inevitable consequences of this meaningless existence:

> To a knowledge of truth, I have come; to salvation, surely not. What shall I do? Be active in the world people say. Should I then communicate my sorrow to the world, make one more contribution to prove how pitiable and wretched everything is, perhaps discovering a new,

hitherto undetected stain in human life? I could then reap the rare reward of becoming famous, just like the man who discovered the spots on Jupiter. I still prefer to remain silent. [20]

Whereas immediate aesthetes suffer from despairing ignorance, the reflective aesthetic is fully aware of his state, yet unwilling to promote self-actualization. Thus, the reflective aesthete ends up in a lazy stupor, unable to find enjoyment in life's pleasures. However, it is important to remember that the existentialist wants to appreciate the entire scope of human life—including aesthetic pleasures.

A fundamental similarity between James, his aunts, and the Centipede is that they all participate in the aesthetic dimension in life. James himself yearns for the youthful pleasures of life, such as going down to the beach to play. In contrast with the others, however, James is not fixated on the aesthetic sphere. On his journey he performs acts that establish him as an *ethical hero*.

JAMES: THE ETHICAL HERO?

The second volume of Kierkegaard's *Either/Or* is a response by a character, Judge Williams, to the aesthete. Judge Williams uses the institution of marriage as an example that demonstrates the superiority of the ethical way of life over that of the aesthetic: So long as he remains docile toward his wife, a man rises above his primitive sexual passions and takes control of his life. Men are disposed to boredom, for habit and repetition often characterizes the married life. However, the wife transforms the trivialities of existence and provides them with "a meaning, a value, a beauty that enchants."[21] Consequently, the married man more fully appreciates the scope of concrete living. He manages to find the modest beauty in everything, not just in the wanton pleasure of aesthetic living. Through his willingness to provide for his family and remain faithful to his wife, he actualizes himself. According to Judge Williams, "it takes a great soul to save his soul from minutiae, but he can if he will, because to will makes the great soul, and the person who loves, wills."[22] The measure of restraint practiced by married couples represents an ethical way of living. The freedom of choice is no longer subject merely to the whims of one's own desires, but it also takes into account the well-being of others. The ethical sphere doesn't abolish the aesthetic, but it validates it in a more noble way of living—there needs to be equilibrium between the two spheres.

Throughout his journey, James experiences the tension between the aesthetic and the ethical, and this tension is only released through decisive action. The centipede, spider, earthworm, ladybug, grasshopper, and glow-worm, as insects, are typically unappreciated and are often the target of insecticide. James, however, learns to appreciate their existence, particularly the beautiful music created by the Old-Green-Grasshopper: "And to think that up until now I had never even *wondered* how a grasshopper made his sounds."[23] He even chooses to risk his own life to save the obnoxious Centipede—the insect who takes pride in only being a nuisance to others. James's ethical actions contribute to his own self-actualization: he is no longer an isolated unit, divorced from the rest of society on the top of a hill; his fellow travelers—despite being the lowliest of the low—become the family he lost.

However, despite many ethical accomplishments, the ethical hero fails to appreciate the entire scope of existence and therefore participates in the third form of despair: a despairing desire to become a self. Regardless of how ethically one chooses to live one's life, the individual is continually bombarded with aesthetic temptations, and ethical perfectibility becomes physically impossible. It follows, in accordance with Saint Paul's teaching, that self-actualization is attained "not because of works, lest any man should boast."[24] Something more is needed. According to Kierkegaard, in order to eradicate despair, one must have a docile relationship with the mysterious power that established one's selfhood.

JAMES AND THE FANTASTIC: THE HERO OF FAITH

> For now, there came a morning when something rather peculiar happened to him. And this thing, which as I say was only *rather* peculiar, soon caused a second thing to happen which was *very* peculiar. And then the *very* peculiar thing, in its own turn, caused a really *fantastically* peculiar thing to occur.[25]

A popular theme among existential philosophers (and often ridiculed, and sometimes rightly so, by those in the analytical camp) is the notion of the absurd, or, in our case, the fantastic. As mentioned above, Kierkegaard is a Christian, and his mission was to "reintroduce Christianity to Christendom."[26] By doing so he explored the notion of *faith* in light of the human experience—faith is not, as many scholastics believed, merely an intellectual achievement; rather, faith is the highest passion that encompasses not only rationality but also its corresponding emotions and experiences. Faith is the capacity to persevere in one's beliefs—to endure—despite momentary intellectual challenges. Faith is fantastical in the sense that it suspends common sense as well as scientific principles in order for one to yield before the miraculous. Furthermore, passion is what ultimately drives one to do *something* with his life, whether it is the intellectual and formal demeanor of the ethicist or the primitive drives of the aesthete. According to Kierkegaard, a person can dwell on the question of whether to perform a particular action for his entire life, reducing the possibility of the act itself to mere propositions; yet so long as an individual continues to do so, that person will remain spiritless and will inevitably spiral into despair. Thus, faith is a holy passion; it was the courage that enabled Abraham[27] to approach the fantastic with fear, trembling, and a childlike confidence. Can James be compared to Abraham—the Father of Faith?

In James's journey, faith in the fantastic plays a crucial role. The fantastical events begin with James's encounter with the crazy old magician wearing a dark green suit. As the magician approaches, James shudders with anxiety as opportunity himself draws near, beckoning "Come closer to me, little boy."[28] His experience can be characterized as what Kierkegaard calls "antipathetic sympathy."[29] Although James freezes with fright, the tension is too great, and his curiosity anticipates James's leap of faith whereby his finite and infinite qualities morph into a concrete decision—a movement of spirit.[30] The magician pushes the paper bag full of crocodile tongues into James's hand and teaches him the necessary procedure. And James—without entertaining the possibility that he might be deceived by mystery's seduction—embraces his opportunity and leaps into the fantastic. James does not conceptualize the circumstance; he lives it. James possesses faith—a childlike confidence in the fantastic. And by doing so he has the courage to embark on a journey to an unknown place, come face to face with giant bugs, soar with the seagulls on the top of a giant peach, evade the Cloud-Men, and land safely on the peak of the Empire State Building. When the travelers begin their journey, they do not know where they are headed. What they do know, however, is that they are journeying to a land far better than the desolate hilltop. Just as Abraham's descendants anticipated a land flowing with milk and honey, James's fellow travelers shout, "Here we go, boys! The Promised Land! I can't wait to see it!"[31]

The fantastic not only accompanies James on his journey as an external force but also operates as a living reality inside James's soul. As mentioned above, the qualities of the infinite and finite enter into a dynamic relationship with the spirit. The soul posits an ideal future self and the spirit tries to bring such ideality into a finite actuality. Regarding the fantastical power, the future self is of particular importance. Near the beginning of the novel, the magician reveals to James a fundamental truth of his condition: After drinking the magical concoction, the magician maintains, "*marvelous* things will start happening to you, *fabulous*, *unbelievable* things—and you will never be miserable again in your life. Because you are miserable, aren't you?"[32] The magician is implying that James's existential journey has a fixed destiny that excludes despair. A Kierkegaardian approach invokes a higher power in order to establish James's future self, James *who he should be.* And by the end of the book, living in the pit of the peach is the famous "JAMES HENRY TROTTER himself."[33]

But each passing moment also confronts James with an opportunity to doubt the marvelous things that are happening to him. If he doubts, where would his journey take him? If he called it all a dream, would he continue to be a guiding star for the rest of the travelers? It follows that the fantastic is the power that develops and ultimately establishes James's selfhood. To remain with his aunts is to remain static, spiritless, and fundamentally unwilling to stimulate his imagination and develop future possibilities. He will eventually learn to suppress the aesthetic idea of going down to the beach to play with other children. Furthermore, if James remains merely an ethical hero, his duties will become overwhelming, for no one can tame the storming passions through their own strength. Without embracing the whole of life—the aesthetic, ethical, and faith in the fantastic—he would remain in a state of internal contradiction. His existence entails freedom, but a failure to embrace freedom's possibilities will result in despair. Therefore, if we as individuals hope to escape despair—whether it be in the form of ignorance, the anxiety that is associated with a mid-life crisis, or the eternal desperation that is associated with the redundant cultivation of ethical perfection—we must follow in James's footsteps, acknowledge our freedom, seize our opportunities, and perhaps come to terms with the incomprehensible, the mysteri-ous, the fantastic. And who knows? You might find it nice to sit down one day and write the story of your adventures.

5

OF MICE AND (POSTHU)MAN

Roald Dahl's *The Witches* and Ethics beyond Humanism

Taine Duncan

Roald Dahl's books for children ignite the imaginations of young and old alike, creating spectacular and wondrous worlds filled with simultaneous delight and terror, dread and excitement, as only the most profound tales and fables can. In the fabulous imaginary worlds Dahl creates, children and fantastical creatures often interact, as in *The BFG*. Sometimes children *become* the fantastical creatures. Such is the case in Roald Dahl's *The Witches*. In this book, Dahl offers up a tragicomic and suspenseful tale of heroics, familial love, and vulnerability, all couched within familiar fantasy tropes of witches and spells. It is in his subversive take on the familiar that Dahl's stories often become the most philosophical.

Perhaps one of the most controversial children's books in Roald Dahl's oeuvre, *The Witches* has often irked feminists, censors, and Wiccans for its portrayal of an all-female band of demonic witches hell-bent on killing the children of the world. This adventure tale of an unnamed boy and his unnamed grandmother saving the world's children, however, can also serve to provide examples for exploring posthumanism, a transformative ethical theory. In this chapter, I explore this legacy of transformative ethics through the lens of continental feminist philosophy. Using examples of transformation from *The Witches*, such as the boy's final transfiguration into a sentient mouse-boy, I explore the theories of Donna Harraway, Rosi Braidotti, Karen Barad, and Drucilla Cornell and the implications for contemporary posthumanist philosophy.

A WITCH IS ALWAYS A WOMAN

> A witch is always a woman. I do not wish to speak badly about wom-
> en. Most women are lovely. But the fact remains that all witches *are*
> women. There is no such thing as a male witch.[1]

Dahl writes the lines above in the first few pages of *The Witches*, and it is
this passage that makes many feminists, Wiccans, and literary theorists
squeamish about the book. It is not simply that these sentences seem so
overtly sexist on their own; instead, these words encapsulate hundreds of
years of fear and hatred of powerful women. The persecution of women
in the Inquisition, the Salem witch trials, and even the marginalization of
Caribbean women practicing *vodou* are just a few of the tragic chronicles
of women who were killed using the excuse of fear of witchcraft. Making
the central antagonists of *The Witches* a group of evil, magical, maniacal
women (who do meet often violent ends) plays into a long and storied
history of justifying or providing apologia for the historical violence per-
petrated against marginalized women. So how can I make the claim here
that Dahl's *The Witches* can be interpreted *not* as a misogynist treatise in
the guise of a kid's fairytale but as representing an imaginative literary
representation of many contemporary feminist ethical ideals?[2]

Particularly in England, where the novel was first released, there were
several feminist critiques of *The Witches* produced shortly after its initial
publication. Catherine Itzin is most often cited for her criticism that the
novel "reinforces culturally conditioned misogyny."[3] Itzin and other critics emphasize that the novel relies on the sex-specific identification of
witches and women, and that the boy is recognized only as an anonymous
male child. They explain that the novel's plotline doesn't simply replay
the fantasy of patriarchal violence against powerful women, but actively
teaches that lesson through the model of a young boy learning to hate and
fear women. Although this concern is valid, and the critiques are well
researched, I would like to offer an alternative reading that might salvage
the story's other elements of transformation and interrelation for feminist
ethics.

Grandmamma—Dahl's own oft-cited evidence against sexism in *The
Witches*—chastises the boy for equivocating human women and witches.
She says, "You don't seem to understand that witches are not actually
women at all. They *look* like women. They talk like women. And they are

able to act like women. But in actual fact, *they are totally different animals*. They are demons in human shape."[4]

Grandmamma is clearly the expert on witches; she has had a long life, which she describes autobiographically as devoted to identifying, and steering clear of, witches. So when she says that witches are not real women but "totally different animals," she, as the primary human female character in the book, is the authority on both women and witches. And she carefully instructs her grandson not to collapse the two categories.

It may be the case that witches are always women, but women are not always witches. In Dahl's grotesque and fantastic world, good and evil are always waiting just around the bend. Women in this world, like all adults in Dahl's children's books, can be good or bad. This recognition of potentiality is actually a feature of a complex understanding of adult female characters; rather than being relegated to exchangeable archetypes of angels and vixens, Dahl's women in *The Witches* are complex. The titular witches themselves are evil, but instead of simply playing with conventional tropes of witchcraft as the means for disempowering men in patriarchal culture, their evil is exclusively understood and felt by children and those sympathetic to children. Most adults do not notice or care about the witches, and it is their everyday banality that makes them so terrifyingly good at eliminating the world's children.

Grandmamma, on the other hand, is also no demure and angelic paragon of femininity. She smokes cigars, she tells frightening stories to the boy, and she scoffs at following laws and rules in the hotel. In fact, it is precisely this rebellious streak that enlivens the grandmother to assist the boy in hunting witches. Additionally, the boy's transformation into a mouse-boy eliminates the possibility of his participation in adult human gender norms. The macabre reality that he will not live long after the timeline of the book means that the boy will never reach adolescence as a human. The usual tropes of witches as bewitching for love or related to psychoanalytic fears of castration cannot apply to the prepubescent boy. In fact, these witches seem to have no interest in harming adult men, simply in ridding the world of all children—boys and girls alike.[5]

METAMORPHOSIS

> As far as children are concerned, a REAL WITCH is easily the most
> dangerous of all the living creatures on earth. What makes her doubly
> dangerous is the fact that she doesn't *look* dangerous. Even when you
> know all the secrets (you will hear about those in a minute), you can
> still never be quite sure whether it is a witch you are gazing at or just a
> kind lady. If a tiger were able to make himself look like a large dog
> with a waggy tail, you would probably go up and pat him on the head.
> And that would be the end of you. It is the same with witches. They all
> look like nice ladies. [6]

The Witches is a dark fable. Death and dying are never far from the
narrator, but the novel escapes despairing in the boy's tragic circumstances. The boy's parents die in an accident before the events in the book
take place. His elderly grandmother becomes his caretaker, and the two
are forced by the terms of his late father's will to live in England rather
than the grandmother's native Norway. Tragedy strikes once more, when
a summer vacation to Norway is impeded by a debilitating bout of pneu-
monia, and the grandmother's age and physical frailty become very real.
Instead, the boy and his grandmother decide to take a British seaside
vacation, and it is in their vacation hotel, the Hotel Magnificent, where
the dramatic confrontation with the witches takes place. And this confrontation serves as a fulcrum for the story to turn the tragic into an
opportunity for growth, change, and hopefulness. This process mirrors
that by which the goals of humanism are subverted and expanded in
posthumanism.

Traditionally, all the values by which we ground philosophical and
practical ethics center on what we perceive to be exclusively human
attributes: autonomy, freedom, and even norms of "selfhood." Generally,
when philosophers use the word "autonomy," they mean something like
the concept that it is good to be able to make your own rational choices;
therefore, it gives a value to the ideas of reason, choice, and individuality.
In the philosophical context, "freedom" is often used to describe the
possibility for the individual to act on such rational choices without coercion. The idealized person who can accomplish the feat of attaining
autonomy, and therefore freedom, is the goal of the humanist projects of
subjectivity and emancipation. We are supposed to create ourselves and

our identities in the image of Immanuel Kant's rational man, and by so doing we can help to cultivate a moral and ethical world of free people. [7]

However, as many critics have noted, the image of the universal human in humanism is not a generic and inclusive figure; it is both explicitly and implicitly identified with a set of European and masculine norms. As Rosi Braidotti describes in her book *The Posthuman*, "Universal 'Man', in fact, is implicitly assumed to be masculine, white, urbanized, speaking a standard language, heterosexually inscribed in a reproductive unit and a full citizen of a recognized polity."[8] This set of characteristics, far from promoting freedom and equality, tends to exclude through a universalization of a narrowly applicable identity. How are women, racial minorities, homosexuals, immigrants, and the rural poor to gain recognition, respect, and freedom if they can never fit the model of emancipated rational man in the first place?

Further, Braidotti in particular argues that these norms function to eliminate differences that allow for innovation—the real goal of practical freedom. She also explains that the ever-looming specter of "universal man" has been removed from its historical content. Immanuel Kant (1724–1804) created the figure that continues to guide much of Western philosophical thought and explicitly grounds most contemporary humanistic ethics in his 1788 *The Critique of Practical Reason*. It only makes sense that his conception would have been guided by the philosophy, science, and morality of his time, and eighteenth-century European norms were openly racist, sexist, and classist.[9] Braidotti explains,

> The human of Humanism is neither an ideal nor an objective statistical average or middle ground. It rather spells out a systematized standard of recognizability—of Sameness—by which all others can be assessed, regulated and allotted to a designated social location. The human is a normative convention, which does not make it inherently negative, just highly regulatory and hence instrumental to practices of exclusion and discrimination. The human norm stands for normality, normalcy and normativity. It functions by transposing a specific mode of being human into a generalized standard, which acquires transcendent values as the human: from male to masculine and onto human as the universalized format of humanity. This standard is posited as categorically and qualitatively distinct from the sexualized, racialized, naturalized others and also in opposition to the technological artefact. The human is a

historical construct that became a social convention about "human nature."[10]

This historical construct no longer matches the lived realities of the contemporary world, where our philosophy, science, and morality are increasingly globalized, technological, and diverse.

In thinking of alternatives to the limits of "universal man," a new branch of philosophy labeled *posthumanism* has emerged. Posthumanism can be defined as a branch of philosophical thinking that includes the recognition of ethics beyond humanism and of existence beyond the human. It challenges the limitations of humanism by articulating a new ethical and ontological theory. Ethical theories focus on evaluating the rules and values we should live by, while ontological theories attempt to explain the meanings and manifestations of existence. As a cipher for the ideal ethical existence, humanist theories of the "universal man" make claims on both how we should live and how to define our very existence. Posthumanism offers alternatives to both of these perspectives.

By contesting humanism's standards, posthumanist feminism proposes that the discrete and particularized interests of women, children, and other marginalized groups are not simply lacking the means for attaining autonomy and reason; it asserts that the values of autonomy and reason are themselves masculinized ideals. Posthumanist feminists argue that as an aspirational figure, "universal man" reinforces social norms and practices that privilege the already dominant figures in society. In contrast, posthumanist models reinforce ideals of innovation, differentiation, and transformation. The ground for liberation is not based on rational autonomous choice but on material relations. Our minds, bodies, and interactions with the world are ripe with possibilities and fraught with new ethical challenges. Posthumanism focuses on liberation and transformation for a future, but a future that imagines a world in which humans will not be the center.

Posthumanism engages the idea that a globalized world is a planetary model. Our environment and social relationships are no longer exclusively dependent on our interactions with other *people* but on our interactions with animals, technology, and even the environment itself. Pets, computers, and global climate change have forever altered the way that we interact with the world and have tended towards greater interdependence and interaction between humans and nonhumans. Rather than seeing posthumanism as a legacy of Kant, Braidotti argues that posthumanism is part of a tradition that builds on the seventeenth-century philosopher Baruch Spinoza (1632–1677). Spinoza argued that the universe is made of a single substance, a theory known as monism. For Spinoza, this theory contrasted with dualism, the theory that mind and body are separate. For contemporary posthumanists, a modified monism describes the way in which human minds and bodies participate in a much larger world. It also helps to describe the ways in which circumstances can change, intellectually, materially, and in our interactions. Braidotti writes,

> The conceptual frame of reference I have adopted for the method of de-familiarization is monism. It implies the open-ended, interrelational, multi-sexed and trans-species flows of becoming through interaction with multiple others. A posthuman subject thus constituted exceeds the boundaries of both anthropocentrism and of compensatory humanism, to acquire a planetary dimension. [11]

Braidotti's monism, then, emphasizes both goals of posthumanism. It allows for a relational ethics, in which the world, other species, and other humans are taken into consideration. Additionally, this theory explains that existence itself is fluid and interrelational; rather than focusing on what it means to already *be* something or someone, it focuses on the activity of *becoming.*

The emphasis on interdependence and transformation at the root of posthumanist theory is expressed in the plot of Dahl's *The Witches.* The boy learns that the world is a place that is quite difficult to navigate, with the possibilities of tragedy on every horizon. His parents' deaths, his grandmother's illness, and the threat of the witches themselves could reasonably cause despair. In fact, since he will never be a fully realized rational man, it is reasonable that he would want to die. However, the boy imaginatively learns to renegotiate the world. He develops a deep and meaningful relationship of trust and mutuality with his grandmother, he adapts to his bodily transformation into a mouse, and he aspires to a future (albeit short-lived) in which he can make the world a better place for others. This fluidity of becoming corresponds to the new ideal of posthuman being. In replacing "universal man," posthumanist feminists suggest the model of a cyborg. In one of the earliest posthumanist texts, Donna Harraway described the cyborg as "a kind of disassembled and reassembled, postmodern collective and personal self. This is the self feminists must code."[12] Despite the boy's disassemblement from being a son, a human boy, and even a child who would have grown into "universal man," the boy is able, with help, to reassemble as "a talking thinking intelligent mouse-person."[13]

A TALKING, THINKING, INTELLIGENT MOUSE-PERSON

> A REAL WITCH spends all her time plotting to get rid of the children in her particular territory. Her passion is to do away with them, one by one. It is all she thinks about the whole day long. Even if she is working as a cashier in a supermarket or typing letters for a businessman or driving around in a fancy car (and she could be doing any of these things), her mind will always be plotting and scheming and churning and burning and whizzing and phizzing with murderous bloodthirsty thoughts.[14]

Harraway explains that the figure of the cyborg in posthumanism emerges "precisely where the boundary between human and animal is transgressed."[15] In *The Witches*, this boundary is transgressed several times, from the account of the boy and his grandmother violating the human laws of the hotel to accommodate pet mice, to the boy's transformation into a mouse, to the mouse-boy's unique ability to creatively fight against the evil witches.

Before the boy *becomes* a mouse, he has two pet mice, William and Mary, whom he trains to do tricks and keeps as constant companions.[16] His grandmother, who gives him these mice as pets, also protects his ability to keep his companions at the hotel. She slyly challenges the hotelier, saying that she will report his hotel as rat-infested if he does not allow the mice to stay.[17] This affection between the boy, the rodents, and the grandmother foreshadows the boy's happiness as a mouse and the grandmother's ease with the boy in his transformed state. However, I also see this scene as illustrative of some of the major tenets of posthuman feminist ethics. In the theories of Harraway, Braidotti, and Karen Barad, posthuman ethics maintains a special sensitivity to nonhuman animals. Calling into question the legitimacy of an anthropocentric grounding for ethics (and metaphysics and epistemology, although those are beyond the bounds of our discussion here), posthumanist feminists use the importance of companionate relationships with animals to test the limits of humanist ethics. [18]

In contemporary American society, our relationship to animals is clearly a mixed bag. The industrialization of meat production, environmental pollution, and scientific experimentation causes unimaginable suffering for the animals who share the world. At the same time, we understand more and more of the complexity of animals, pets live in most American homes, and social organizations protecting the rights of animals are growing. So, how do we understand this antagonism and interdependence? The most inclusive humanist model would say that we, as rational beings, hold superiority over other species. Our responsibility to nonhuman animals would then be predicated on an anthropocentric hierarchy; where man is at the center of the environment, our duties and obligations rely on the fact that mistreating animals may lead to mistreating other people. This estimation of our ethical duties does not simply devalue animals, but it also devalues our species, by expecting us to be violent and hegemonic: "As if this line of criticism is not enough, this 'Man' is also called to task and brought back to its species specificity as *anthropos*, that is to say as the representative of a hierarchical, hegemonic and generally violent species whose centrality is now challenged by a combination of scientific advances and global economic concerns." [19]

This humanist approach to animal ethics appears to guide most of the adults in *The Witches*. When witches turned one of Grandmamma's childhood friends into a porpoise, the adults played with it as long as it was usefully giving rides, and then they watched it swim away. [20] They did not harm the porpoise, as it was no threat, but they also only saw the porpoise as useful and amusing to humans. However, when the witches turn children into mice, the adults see the mice as pests to be killed, since humans see mice as a threat to hygiene. In fact, except for Grandmamma, the other adult humans in Dahl's world see mice as disposable, whereas human children are not. This hierarchy of relationship to humans is a decidedly anthropocentric model for humanistic ethics.

In contrast, posthumanist ethics sees the boundaries between human and nonhuman worlds as flexible and even the boundaries between human and nonhuman *beings* as fluid. When the boy is caught by the witches in the chapter "Metamorphosis," the boy describes his transformation from boy to mouse-boy. At first the change is painful, and he describes burning and itching and pinching. Then the change is disorienting, and the boy narrates his first awareness of his mouse paws. But, finally, the transformation is enjoyable; he sees potential and possibilities to escape as a mouse, when he couldn't escape as a boy: "What I especially liked was the fact that I made no sound at all as I ran. I was a swift and silent mover. And quite amazingly, the pain had all gone now. I was feeling quite remarkably well. *It is not a bad thing after all*, I thought to myself, *to be tiny as well as speedy when there are a bunch of dangerous females after your blood.*"[21]

Witches turn the boy into a mouse as a way of punishing him, and they even attempt to kill him, but he is able to appropriate his new posthuman identity and respond in kind to the witches. Karen Barad explains in her article, "Posthumanist Performativity: Toward an Understanding of How Matter Comes to Matter," that our very natures and sense of the natural world are in fact historically grounded constructs, subject to change. Just as the boy can become a mouse, "A posthumanist account calls into question the givenness of the differential categories of 'human' and 'non-human', examining the practices through which these differential boundaries are stabilized and destabilized."[22] The boy echoes the posthumanist ideal of fluid becoming by explaining that he is not only a mouse but also a hybrid or cyborg mouse-person, and a thoughtful one at that: "I became a talking thinking intelligent mouse-person who wouldn't go *near* a mousetrap."[23]

HOWEVER PECULIAR I MAY LOOK

> Very carefully a victim is chosen. Then the witch stalks the wretched child like a hunter stalking a little bird in the forest. She treads softly. She moves quietly. She gets closer and closer. Then at last, when everything is ready . . . *phwisst!* . . . and she swoops! Sparks fly. Flames leap. Oil boils. Rats howl. Skin shrivels. And the child disappears.[24]

Posthumanism emphasizes collectivity and the importance of working with and relying on others. Whereas humanism explicitly values autonomy and independence as the source of freedom, posthumanism argues that interdependence and alliances are required for navigating our collectively uncertain futures. In fact, posthumanism identifies very unlikely alliances as some of the most fruitful and liberating. Donna Harraway highlights our relationships with machines, Karen Barad points out the relationship between our sense of self and changing biologies, and Rosi Braidotti argues that humans and nonhumans must interact for our planetary future. These unlikely alliances offer spaces of innovation and hope, but, even further, they respect the importance and uniqueness of difference. The radical difference of becoming a mouse-person might seem insurmountable even for a sense of self-identity, but in a humanist model the even more difficult transition would be in relating to others. Put differently, how can a mouse have a Grandmamma? The (now) mouse-boy narrator claims, "The fact that I am still here and able to speak to you (however peculiar I may look) is due entirely to my wonderful grandmother."[25] His grandmother does not simply accept that the boy has transformed but also actively supports his continued existence; they continue to rely on one another, although in a way very different from when they were both human.

The concept of "natality" is used in political and existential philosophies, including Drucilla Cornell's, as a challenge to Kantian notions of autonomy. As opposed to autonomy, natality emphasizes the importance of growth and rebirth. The "natal" in natality is from the Latin word *natalis*, which means "birth" or "origin." By relying on a metaphor of birth, natality emphasizes both a relationship to others and an opportunity for the "I" to self-innovate rather than to absolutely self-determine. Cornell explains that the Kantian autonomous subject of reason is defined as a subject of control and regulation as opposed to innovation.[26] In contrast, the posthumanist subjects of relation are defined by their intersections with one another and their ability to grow and find potential.[27] Cornell is not alone in seeing innovation in collaboration; Braidotti also argues that her work "rests on the firm belief that we, early third millennium posthuman subjects in our multiple and differential locations, are perfectly capable of rising to the challenge of our times, provided we make it into a collective endeavor and joint project."[28] This promise for a better future together is echoed in Dahl's simultaneously sweet and moribund tale. The boy's final moral lesson about his posthuman life is this: "'I don't mind at all,' I said. 'It doesn't matter who you are or what you look like as long as somebody loves you.'"[29]

YOU'RE A MAGICIAN!

> I am not, of course, telling you for one second that your teacher actual-
> ly is a witch. All I am saying is that she *might* be one. It is most
> unlikely. But—and here comes the big "but"—*it is not impossible.*[30]

Posthuman critical philosophy works to address environmental, ethical,
and ontological concerns together via the "creative imaginary." This theory uses a future and future-present, rather than an idealized past, to place
emphasis on possibility and the virtual. Writing about Dolly the cloned
sheep and the genetically altered, cancer-susceptible oncomouse, Braidotti argues that these material and biological creatures transcend their physical presence and become images for contemplating the near future: "Fig-
urations like Dolly and oncomouse are no metaphors, but rather vehicles
to imaginatively ground our powers of understanding within the shifting
landscapes of the present."[31] This future is sometimes imagined as magical, mythical, or mystical, although the posthumanist feminists are also
hyperaware of material realities.

This balance between material limitations and illimitable potential is
also reflected in Dahl's book. As the mouse-boy brainstorms possible
ways to defeat the threat of the witches, his grandmother is increasingly
awed by his creativity. At one point, she even exclaims, *"You're a Magician!"*[32] What makes the boy so magical is precisely his ability to creatively imagine possibilities for the future, even as he faces despair, drama,
and death. His new reality has changed his possible future, in ways that
he is still struggling to understand, but also in ways that seem to keep
opening and expanding. This changing horizon seems to match our own
current planetary experience:

> Human embodiment and subjectivity are currently undergoing a pro-
> found mutation. Like all people living in an age of transition, we are
> not always lucid or clear about where we are going, or even capable of
> explaining what exactly is happening to and around us. Some of these
> events strike us in awe and fear, while others startle us with delight. It
> is as if our current context kept on throwing open the doors of our
> collective perception, forcing us to hear the roar of cosmic energy that
> lies on the other side of silence and to stretch the measure of what has
> become possible.[33]

The mouse-boy and his grandmother clearly see their world changing, and they are enthusiastic about what they can do in this new world. As a mouse-boy with nothing to lose and a grandmother filled with love and experience, they imagine traveling their new world and eliminating the dangerous witches. The changing horizons of their experience not only alter their choices and means of interacting with both each other and the world but also cause them (and us as readers) to reconsider their obligations in light of their new potential. Barad explains that posthumanist ethics is transforming and open-ended, but it is also an ethical theory that requires sensitivity and responsibility: "Particular possibilities for acting exist at every moment, and these changing possibilities entail a responsibility to intervene in the world's becoming, to contest and rework what matters and what is excluded from mattering."[34] What matters to the boy and his grandmother is each other, and the short time they have left to make the world safer.

Formula 86 Delayed Action Mouse-Maker turns the boy into a talking, thinking, and intelligent mouse-person. But, even more than that, it opens the possibilities for his interaction with the world. When one person might see the shortened life span and physical transfiguration as limitations, the boy and his grandmother see possibility. As a transfigured subject—a cyborg in the language of the posthumanists—the boy's relation to the world is forever changed, and in that changed relation, he can also see the potentials of a new world for others. He sees the potential for the best possible world he can imagine—a world free of witches.

Braidotti claims that this is the position we should all find ourselves in, as people living in a time and place in which humanism is no longer relevant. She challenges and encourages us by writing, "This is a new situation we find ourselves in: the immanent here and now of a posthuman planet. It is one of the possible worlds we have made for ourselves, and insofar as it is the result of our joint efforts and collective imaginings, it is quite simply the best of all possible posthuman worlds."[35] As though hearing this challenge from posthumanists, Dahl's mouse-boy is ready to save the world's children from the witches; he has a new perspective and the possibility for sneaking into witches' homes when a regular human boy would be caught. And Grandmamma has always wanted to fight the witches anyway: "'You can say that again!' my grandmother cried, giving me another kiss. 'I can't wait to get started!'"[36] And neither can I!

6

"WHO IS THIS CRAZY MAN?"

Willy Wonka's Uneasy Predicament

Cam Cobb[1]

Willy Wonka gets called a great many things in *Charlie and the Choco-late Factory*. Strangers and acquaintances seem keen to comment on his state of mind throughout the novel. The parents who tour his factory proclaim that he is "balmy," "nutty," "screwy," "batty," "wacky," "loony," and "crazy." One father tells him he's "off his rocker."[2] Even Charlie's dear old Grandma Josephine declares that Wonka is "dotty" near the beginning of the story and refers to him as "crazy" near the end.[3] While the novel was initially published nearly half a century ago, these eight words and one idiomatic expression are still commonly used to describe a person's behavior. And they locate that behavior somewhere beyond the realm of normalcy, on a continuum that ranges from eccentric to insane. Throughout the story many characters use a wide variety of derogatory labels to question the sanity of—and ascribe madness to— Willy Wonka. The man they are critiquing is a creative, energetic, and tremendously successful inventor, but he is also unconventional, which links to the idea of normalization.

According to normalization theory, social perceptions of the normal and the abnormal act as a way of monitoring and manipulating the behav-ior of people in a society.[4] In other words, social views of normalcy, at least in part, control the behaviors of those in a society. It is important to reflect on normalization because it can help us to better understand the tension between freedom and constraint in a society. Drawing from normalization theory, the core question I address in this chapter is: How does Willy Wonka come to be seen as a "crazy man" throughout *Charlie and the Chocolate Factory*? To explore this question, I delve into different aspects of how Wonka is perceived by those around him. Two key dimensions of his supposed madness will be examined, including his hubris and his appearance/behavior. Along the way, I will draw from the work of French philosopher Michel Foucault (1926–1984) as well as Plato's *Phaedrus*.

OUTSIDE THE FACTORY GATES

What is normal? What is abnormal? And what exactly leads some actions to be perceived as normal and others to be seen as abnormal? Everything an individual does, from the way she talks to the way she walks, from the way she laughs at jokes to the way she eats her meals, could be placed on a continuum of normalcy. And this continuum is a product of social construction. According to Foucault, within a society, people become "bound by a system of natural obligations."[5] A set of "essential virtues of society"[6] is not only *acknowledged* by people but also *imposed* upon those who do not follow its parameters.[7] Foucault described this constraining dynamic as the "homogenous rule of morality," which rigorously extends "to all those who try to escape from it."[8]

In a variety of ways and contexts individuals live under constant social observation, and their words and actions are viewed, assessed, and judged by those around them. It occurs in neighborhoods and it also occurs in workplaces and schoolyards. Try doing a pirouette as you wait in front of the photocopier at work and see what happens. Or perhaps try doing a cartwheel as you approach the local bus stop on your way home from work and see how people respond. You might note that I have used the less provocative word *observation* to describe what Foucault called *surveillance*. And this sociological theory—which links social surveillance to the idea of normalcy and social control—is known as normalization. It is useful to keep normalization theory in mind while reflecting on different spheres of Willy Wonka's supposed madness because his actions so often fall outside what his guests view as *normal* behavior. Yet, although the inventor is under the constant gaze of society, he never allows himself to be constrained by his guests' views of normalcy.

"NOTHING IS IMPOSSIBLE!"

On one level, Willy Wonka's ascribed madness is linked to his hubris. A popular theme in ancient Greek mythology, hubris could be defined as excessive self-confidence or overinflated pride. To illustrate the depth of Wonka's great confidence and pride, I will begin with his startling Chocolate Room. When Charlie, Grandpa Joe, and the other families begin their tour of Wonka's factory, the inventor initially leads them into a vast underground lair known as the Chocolate Room. In this enormous room, "There was a tremendous waterfall halfway along the river—a steep cliff over which the water curled and rolled in a solid sheet, and then went crashing down into a boiling churning whirlpool of froth and spray."[9] Describing the underground waterfall, Wonka excitedly informs his guests, "It's *all* chocolate! Every drop of that river is hot melted chocolate of the finest quality. The very finest quality. There's enough chocolate in there to fill *every* bathtub in the entire country!"[10] Explaining the rationale behind this elaborate architectural design, Wonka adds, "The waterfall is most important! . . . It mixes the chocolate! It churns it up! It makes it light and frothy! No other factory in the world mixes its chocolate by waterfall! But it's the *only* way to do it properly! The *only* way!"[11] Rather than using machines to churn and mix chocolate, Willy Wonka dreamed up something far more elaborate. For him, anything less than an immense waterfall is unacceptable. And his readiness to reach for things that are seemingly impossible stems from his immense self-confidence as an inventor and entrepreneur.

But creating a waterfall chocolate mixer is only one of many examples of Willy Wonka's hubris. Later in the story, the candy magnate leads his visitors into his Inventing Room, where he shows them the Great Gum Machine. As they stand around the machine, Wonka excitedly announces, "THIS GUM . . . is my latest, my greatest, my most fascinating invention! It's a chewing-gum meal! . . . that tiny little strip of gum lying there is a whole three-course dinner all by itself!" Exciting as this concept sounds, it is only a part of Wonka's grand scheme, and he elaborates, "When I start selling this gum in the shops it will change everything! It will be the end of all kitchens and cooking! There will be no more marketing to do! No more buying of meat and groceries!" Summing up his revolutionary plan, Wonka states, "No plates! No washing up! No garbage! No mess! Just a little strip of Wonka's magic chewing gum—and that's all you'll ever need at breakfast, lunch, and supper!"[12] For Willy Wonka, developing and selling regular chewing gum is not enough. And he imagines himself producing and selling a kind of gum that will alter the way people eat and ultimately change the entire planet.

Wonka's hubris is, in part at least, linked to his immense love for his factory. Near the end of the novel, Wonka confides to Charlie, "How I love my chocolate factory."[13] According to Plato (427–347 BCE), passionate love leads people to a certain type of madness in which "a lover admits that he is sick rather than in his right mind; he knows he is deranged, but is incapable of self-control."[14] Plato outlined this idea of madness in the *Phaedrus*, and he sums it up as follows: "After all, we did say that love was a kind of madness. . . . But there are two kinds of madness, one caused by human illnesses, the other by a divine release from the norms of conventional behavior."[15] Foucault described a similar connection between love and madness, in which "unreason transformed into delirium of the heart, madness of desire, the insane dialogue of love and death in the limitless presumption of appetite."[16]

Ultimately, the chocolate waterfall and chewing-gum meal are but two examples of Willy Wonka's hubris. He has great dreams indeed, and some might even say they are too great. After perusing Wonka's elaborate contest announcement in the newspaper—and the notion of finding a suitable heir to his empire through a chocolate bar contest is another example of Wonka's hubris—Charlie's Grandma Josephine mutters, "The man's dotty!"[17] While Wonka's great dreams do not conform to commonplace views of *reasonable objectives*, the great inventor might repeat what he exclaimed as he stepped into his glass elevator: "Nothing is impossible! You watch!"[18]

Yet, like the Greek hero Icarus, who dared to fly too close to the sun with his waxen wings, Willy Wonka has great hubris. And if Wonka could be seen as a sort of Icarus of modern times, it would be important to ask: Does he hope to achieve too much? Does he want the impossible? No matter how these questions are answered, it is clear that Willy Wonka refuses to be constrained by perceptions of what is possible and what is impossible.

"HE WAS LIKE A SQUIRREL"

Another aspect of Willy Wonka's ascribed madness is rooted in his appearance and behavior. Simply put, he does not look, move, or talk in a way that his guests expect. And this divergence occurs time and time again as he interacts with the families who tour his chocolate factory.

When Wonka first appears at the gates of his factory to welcome the five children and nine grownup guests, Dahl states that he is "clearly just as excited as everybody else." And regarding his physical appearance Dahl states that "his eyes were most marvelously bright. They seemed to be sparkling and twinkling at you all the time. The whole face, in fact, was alight with fun and laughter." As he stood at his factory gates, "He kept making quick jerky little movements with his head, cocking it this way and that, and taking everything in with those bright twinkling eyes." Summing up Wonka's entrance, Dahl notes, "He was like a squirrel in the quickness of his movements, like a quick clever old squirrel from the park."[19] Partly in awe, and perhaps a bit in fear, Grandpa Joe whispers to his grandson, "Don't you let go of my hand, Charlie."[20]

But there are also Willy Wonka's physical actions to consider. When first approaching the winners of his Golden Ticket contest, "he did a funny little skipping dance in the snow."[21] And as he showed the chocolate waterfall to the visitors, Wonka was "dancing up and down and pointing his gold-topped cane at the great brown river."[22] While riding in his boat (a giant pink hollowed-out piece of boiled candy), "Mr. Wonka was jumping up and down in the back of the boat and calling to the rowers to row faster and faster still." As Dahl explains, "He seemed to love the sensation of whizzing through a white tunnel in a pink boat on a chocolate river, and he clapped his hands and laughed and kept glancing at his passengers to see if they were enjoying it as much as he." While riding in Wonka's boat one of the fathers on the tour shouts out, "He's gone off his rocker!" And the entire group of parents chimes in, shouting, "He's crazy!"[23] Clearly, Wonka's physical behavior is seen as unacceptable to his guests. It is a key reason the candy bar magnate is perceived as a mad, albeit successful, inventor-entrepreneur.

Another important aspect of Willy Wonka's appearance/behavior is his speech. Willy Wonka is often surprisingly casual in the face of potentially dire situations. When Augustus Gloop falls into the chocolate river and gets sucked up by a giant pipe, his mother immediately worries that her son will be made into chocolate fudge. "I won't allow it!" Wonka cries out. "And why not?" asks Mrs. Gloop. "Because the taste would be terrible," Wonka explains.[24] And when Violet Beauregarde is transformed into a gigantic blueberry after trying a stick of gum she was told not to touch, Wonka casually sighs, "It always happens like that."[25] Later, when Veruca Salt is thrown down a garbage chute by Wonka's trained squirrels (heading down a pipe toward the furnace), Wonka comforts her parents by saying, "Don't worry . . . there's always a chance they've decided not to light it today."[26] And when there is the possibility of Mike Teavee completely disappearing after he teleports himself in the Television-Chocolate Room, Wonka says to the child's parents, "I do hope that no part of him gets left behind!"[27] Four emergencies, four possible tragedies, and Willy Wonka remains surprisingly casual. It is as though he completely disregards the feelings of the worried parents. But how much of this thoughtlessness is an act?

After Augustus vanishes up a vacuum pipe, Willy Wonka asks an Oompa-Loompa to assist the boy's frantic parents. Approaching the parents, "The Oompa-Loompa took one look at Mrs. Gloop and exploded into peals of laughter." Aware of the parents' worried state, Wonka chides the Oompa-Loompa with gusto, "Oh, do be quiet! . . . Control yourself! Pull yourself together! Mrs. Gloop doesn't think it's at all funny!"[28] For a man who often appears to be thoughtlessly casual, Willy Wonka clearly grasps the concerns of the visiting parents as their children disappear one by one on his factory tour. And his often casual behavior could be interpreted as a form of deception, perhaps even a wily example of dissimulation. According to Francis Bacon (1561–1626), dissimulation "is but a faint kind of policy or wisdom" through which one "can discern what things are to be laid open, and what to be secreted, and what to be showed at half lights, and to whom and when."[29] Because Willy Wonka presents a combination of half-truths and false information he can be seen as a savvy purveyor of underhanded messages.

Perhaps, by exhibiting an outwardly casual attitude to the disappearance of rule-breaking children, Wonka is implying that these children are not really worth worrying about. One cannot be certain that Wonka is practicing dissimulation here, but it certainly is a possibility. And it is not the only possible instance of Wonka's dissimulation in the novel. Another is rooted in his verbal exchanges with Mike Teavee, a precocious boy who challenges Wonka regularly. When Mike Teavee disagrees with

Wonka on the usefulness of finding a cure for child hair loss and helping children to fulfill their desire to grow beards, Wonka chides, "Don't argue, my dear child, please don't argue!"[30] Here, rather than countering Mike Teavee's arguments, Wonka asks him to stop questioning what he has to say. But the candy magnate soon learns that this strategy doesn't work.

After a short while, Mike challenges Wonka in a different way. After hearing the candy baron criticize gum chewing—and gum itself—the boy astutely asks, "If you think gum is so disgusting . . . then why do you make it in your factory?" Wonka discards this question by stating, "I do wish you wouldn't mumble . . . I can't hear a word you're saying."[31] Here Willy Wonka uses a different tactic to counter Mike Teavee's sharp criticisms. He neither asks Mike to stop arguing nor offers a counterargument. By claiming not to hear Mike Teavee, Willy Wonka avoids the boy's difficult questions altogether. Shortly thereafter, when Mike Teavee asks another difficult question—"But what *does* a snozzberry taste like?"—Wonka responds, "You're mumbling again. . . . Speak louder next time."[32] Clearly, Wonka is satisfied with this tactic of avoidance, and it becomes a strategy he continues to use in his verbal sparring with Mike Teavee. Later in the tour, after Wonka explains how the science behind television operates, Mike Teavee rebuts, "That isn't exactly how it works."[33] Escalating his strategy of avoidance, Wonka remarks, "I'm a little deaf in my left ear. . . . You must forgive me if I don't hear everything you say."[34]

But is Willy Wonka truly deaf in his left ear? And was Mike Teavee *really* mumbling all those times? Perhaps in those instances Wonka was overcome by his imagination. Perhaps he was hallucinating. Describing one idea of madness, Foucault wrote, "The ultimate language of madness is that of reason, but the language of reason enveloped in the prestige of the image, limited to the locus of appearance which the image defines."[35] According to this perspective, madness isn't the absence of reason, but rather the overpowering of the imagination. And while Wonka certainly may have been imagining things, there is also the possibility that he wasn't.

Instead of asking whether Wonka is deaf in his left ear, and whether he truly believed that Mike Teavee was mumbling, perhaps it would be better to ask: Just what exactly does Willy Wonka gain from claiming to have hearing loss? And what does he gain from claiming that Mike is mumbling? And these questions link back to dissimulation. When verbally sparring with Mike Teavee, perhaps Wonka *acts* hard of hearing to avoid having to answer the boy's difficult questions. And by pretending not to hear the precocious boy, perhaps Wonka is actually implying that the boy just doesn't have anything to say that is worth hearing.

CONCLUSION

Candy baron Willy Wonka breaks multiple rules of normativity throughout *Charlie and the Chocolate Factory*. We might even say that he rebels against the normalizing forces of his society, and of his gaggle of guests in particular. Appraising the entrepreneur's animated physical behavior, Grandpa Joe urges Charlie to hold on to his hand as they step into the factory. When Wonka ecstatically jumps up and down in his candy boat he is called a variety of derogatory labels, all of which critique his state of mind. Perhaps Wonka's ascribed madness stems from his liberty. In isolation the inventor has complete freedom to pursue his numerous physics-defying projects.[36] According to some, as Foucault observed, madness comes from having *too much* liberty.[37] And Willy Wonka is certainly someone who refuses to be constrained by his guests' perceptions of what is *acceptable* or *normal*. But his perceived madness might also be a matter of lifestyle and dreams.

Willy Wonka lives in a vast factory that is shut off from the outside world, a place where he is free to pursue his candy-making dreams—which range from hot ice cubes and fizzy lifting drinks to everlasting gobstoppers—and prove that nothing is impossible. Perhaps Wonka's dreams and methods are just too complicated for his guests. As Foucault noted, people once believed that "the more abstract or complex knowledge becomes, the greater the risk of madness."[38] Wonka's perceived madness also might be linked to his tremendous hubris and extraordinary appearance/behavior. He is, after all, constantly being judged on his unconventional aims and extraordinary actions.[39] While the space between being *seen* as a genius and being *called* a madman appears to be a difficult one for Wonka to traverse, it is one that he navigates with zest throughout Dahl's classic novel. And by countering social expectations with such zest, perhaps Willy Wonka is meant to subvert—and prompt readers to question—the constraints of normalization.

7

"HE WILL BE ALTERED QUITE A BIT"

Discipline and Punishment in Willy Wonka's Factory

Marc Napolitano

Charlie and the Chocolate Factory is a book about punishment. For all of its creative confectionary sweetness, the most dominant reoccurring theme in the text is chastisement. The episodic structure of the story supports this theme, as each visit to a room in Willy Wonka's factory is punctuated by the punishment of a disobedient child; the initial spectacle of Willy Wonka's wonders thus shifts to the equally spectacular punishment of the bratty youngster. On the surface, Dahl's emphasis on reprimanding naughty youths hints at the rudimentary moralism of traditional children's literature: if a child disobeys, he or she will be punished. Nevertheless, Dahl's concept of punishment is somewhat more complicated: Are the naughty children punished for their general disobedience or for their specific behavioral problems? Is Charlie Bucket rewarded for his active adherence to the rules of Wonka's factory or for his passive adoption of societal standards of good behavior? The complex dimensions of punishment in *Charlie and the Chocolate Factory* provide a unique lens through which to study an even more complicated philosophy of punishment.

In his analysis of the evolution of punishment in Western society, Michel Foucault (1926–1984) traces the shift from the physical, public punishments of the past to the penal, private punishments of the present. While the punishments in Wonka's factory seem old-fashioned (perhaps even medieval), the contexts and consequences of the children's penalties actually align with Foucault's assertions regarding the contemporary function of punishment. Ultimately, the chastisement of the naughty children is not meant to promote fear of physical punishment from a sovereign power, but rather to promote self-discipline and social conformity, traits epitomized by the novel's hero: Charlie Bucket.

CHURLISH CHILDREN, BRUTALIZED BODIES

In chapter 28 of *Charlie and the Chocolate Factory*—a chapter somewhat ominously titled "Only Charlie Left"—Willy Wonka feigns disbelief upon discovering that, of the five children who entered his factory, only Charlie remains. Though Wonka is "pretending to be surprised,"[1] his astonishment is not unfounded. In spite of the fact that the text bears his name, it is actually quite easy to lose track of Charlie. He is an endearing and enduring underdog: small, vulnerable, yet highly moral. However, he never seems as visible as the gluttonous Augustus Gloop, the spoiled Veruca Salt, the vulgar Violet Beauregarde, or the obnoxious Mike Teavee. A cynical reader might attribute Charlie's success in navigating the perils of Wonka's factory to his ability to fade into the background and watch as his peers tie the nooses by which they will ultimately hang themselves—a morbid metaphor, to be sure, but a fitting one given Dahl's pronouncedly public approach to punishing bad behavior. Throughout *Charlie and the Chocolate Factory*, Charlie's small, undernourished body allows him to disappear against the spectacular backdrop of Wonka's plant; his body thus remains unchanged, for by escaping punishment, Charlie likewise escapes the physical disfigurements suffered by his peers.

Dahl's emphasis on the bodies of the disobedient children as the primary sites of punishment is somewhat surprising, especially in light of his negative depiction of physical punishment in his other children's books. In *Danny, the Champion of the World* and his autobiographical work, *Boy*, the practice of caning is presented as inherently unjust, due not only to its physical severity but also to the emotional trauma produced by the spectacle. Dahl uses nearly identical language in describing these two scenes of corporal punishment, highlighting both the grotesque exhibition and the physical pain:

I could hardly believe what I was seeing. It was like some awful pantomime. The violence was bad enough, and being made to watch it was even worse. . . . At first I heard only the *crack* and felt absolutely nothing at all, but a fraction of a second later the burning sting that flooded across my buttocks was so terrific that all I could do was gasp. . . . It felt, I promise you, as though someone had laid a red-hot poker against my flesh and was pressing down on it hard.[2]

As I stepped out from my desk and began walking up toward the front of the class, I knew exactly what was going to happen. I had seen it happen to others many times, both to boys and girls. But up until now, it had never happened to me. Each time I had seen it, it had made me feel quite sick inside. . . . I heard the crack first and about two seconds later I felt the pain. . . . It was as though someone were pressing a red-hot poker against my palm and holding it there.[3]

Despite these unwaveringly negative descriptions, Dahl's own attitude toward corporal punishment was ambiguous; biographer Donald Sturrock reflects that Dahl "did not see any particular harm in boys having their bottoms 'tickled' from time to time, if only the human dimension of the beater could be removed."[4] To rectify this problem, Dahl once jokingly proposed that a machine should be developed to administer such punishments.[5] It is not surprising that all of the physical punishments enacted upon the children in Wonka's factory are carried out by mechanical devices: tubes, pipes, pullers, and juicers. Though Willy Wonka carries a cane, he seems fundamentally incapable of applying it. Nevertheless, the sting of the cane fades in time; the physical scars of Wonka's factory are not so easily mended. Of the four children who disobey Wonka, three see their bodies permanently altered: Augustus Gloop's fat frame is compressed, Violet's skin is permanently colored purple, and Mike Teavee is distorted into a wiry giant. The medieval emphasis on punishing the body is fully realized in the case of Mike, who is placed on the chewing-gum puller, the chocolate factory's counterpart to the rack!

Though the comparison may be something of a stretch (pun intended), Dahl's focus on public punishment of the body is evocative of Foucault's initial assessment of "the great spectacle of physical punishment" in *Discipline and Punish*.[6] In this landmark text, Foucault chronicles "the disappearance of the . . . body as the major target of penal repression."[7] In the context of Foucault's analysis, the forms of punishment that exist in

Wonka's factory are old-fashioned: not only is the body the target of punitive action, but the spectacle surrounding the punishment is also essential. Under the watchful eye of Willy Wonka, punishment becomes what Foucault calls a "great theatrical ritual,"[8] as the Oompa-Loompas transform public punishments into moralistic musical performances.

However brutal these punishments may be, Foucault would likely argue that they are no more sinister than the "gentle" punishments of the nineteenth and twentieth centuries, for Foucault's central assertion in *Discipline and Punish* is that the transition from public torture to private imprisonment has resulted in the creation of a pervasive system of strict societal control. Traditionally, physical torture was associated with the terrifying power of the sovereign, and the punishment was thus framed as a conflict between individuals: the transgressor, in violating the law of the land, had defied the sovereign. Conversely, imprisonment is the result of a conflict between the transgressor and society as a whole, as in order for this "gentle way in punishment" to function effectively, "punishment must be regarded as a retribution that the guilty man makes to each of his fellow citizens, for the crime has wronged them all."[9] The entire society thus takes part in the foundation, administration, and perpetuation of a system of punishment resulting in the creation of the modern prison. Notably, Foucault sees this omnipresent and oppressive emphasis on widespread societal discipline as vital to the very fabric of contemporary civilization; as such, he traces significant connections between the prison and other contemporary institutions including the factory and the modern schoolroom. It is not surprising that the title setting of *Charlie and the Chocolate Factory* takes on characteristics of all three institutions; obviously, Wonka's plant is a factory, but it is likewise a "schoolroom" inasmuch as the children, all of school age, are taught important lessons about proper conduct. It is a prison inasmuch as their failure to embrace these lessons transforms the space into a place of punishment. And though Wonka's invasive punishments seem contradictory to the passive punitive philosophy of the modern prison, the philosophy behind those punishments is inherently modern.

WILLY WONKA: PUNITIVE SOVEREIGN OR DISCIPLINARY SOCIETAL REP?

To justify my claim that the tenets of punishment in Wonka's factory are modern as opposed to classical, it is useful to compare and contrast the conflict between the four disobedient children and Willy Wonka with the traditional conflict between the criminal and the sovereign. Although Wonka lacks the oppressive and tyrannical power of the Wormwoods from *Matilda*, Aunts Sponge and Spiker from *James and the Giant Peach*, and the other horrid adults who populate Dahl's novels, this does not change the fact that the children are punished under his authority. Furthermore, though the children's transgressions vary, the underlying factor that connects the perpetrators is that they disobey Wonka, the sovereign. In this context, the spectacular nature of the children's physical punishments seems reminiscent of the public executions carried out in previous centuries, which were intended to underscore the sovereign's power. The emphasis on the body reinforces the connection between Willy Wonka and the sovereign in that the physical torture of bodies at the command of the ruler "made it possible to reproduce the crime on the visible body of the criminal. . . . It also made the body of the condemned man the place where the vengeance of the sovereign was applied."[10] The disfigured bodies of Augustus Gloop, Violet Beauregarde, and Mike Teavee (and, to a lesser extent, the soiled body of Veruca Salt) stand as warnings to those who would violate Wonka's will.

From this perspective, Wonka's factory seems to embody all of the traits that Foucault associates with the old order. What complicates this reading, however, is the fact that although the only system of law in Wonka's factory is the word of Willy Wonka himself, the administration of punishment is *not* arbitrarily carried out at the whim of the sovereign. The children are punished while under Wonka's power, but their behavior has already been deemed socially unacceptable before they ever set foot in the factory. Thus, instead of the power to punish being conferred entirely on the sovereign (which would result in Wonka's transforming into a tyrannical figure like Miss Trunchbull or Captain Lancaster), the system of punishment that will be employed against the children has more to do with a general societal understanding of behavioral norms.

The portrait Dahl paints when introducing the naughty children is quite negative: Augustus Gloop is a glutton, Veruca Salt is a spoiled brat,

Violet Beauregarde is ill-mannered and mischievous, and Mike Teavee is a violent TV addict. The Bucket family immediately predicts that these unpleasant children will come to no good: Grandma Georgina prophesies that Violet will "come to a sticky end one day,"[11] and Grandpa Joe warns that "no good can come from spoiling [Veruca] like that . . . you mark my words."[12] This foreshadowing by Charlie's grandparents creates a sense of inevitability regarding the downfalls of these characters, and the predictability of their chastisements further underscores the contemporary philosophy of punishment in Wonka's factory. While the public spectacle that defines Wonka's approach to punishment seems antithetical to Foucault's analysis of a contemporary society in which punishment is carried out clandestinely, Foucault likewise notes that the efficacy of contemporary punishment is based on the notion of inevitability as opposed to physicality: "it is the certainty of being punished and not the horrifying spectacle of public punishment that must discourage crime."[13] From the perspective of the child reader, the certainty of the nasty children's punishments is of far greater instructional value than the physicality of the punishments. Most children need not fear being sent up a chocolate pipe or down a garbage chute, nor being turned into a blueberry or stretched out on a gum-pulling machine. However, a child should indeed fear becoming gluttonous, disrespectful, spoiled, or temperamental due to the fact that such behavior will invariably lead to punishment.

While the Buckets, as the downtrodden yet loving family, serve as the moral center of the book, it is important to note that they are not alone in their condemnation of Augustus, Veruca, Violet, and Mike. The widespread perception of the naughty children by the larger society within the text is also uniformly negative, and the minor supporting characters in the "crowd scenes" clearly disapprove of these children. While congregating outside Wonka's factory, the various spectators murmur that Mr. Salt's spoiling of Veruca is "dreadful."[14] They likewise view Mike's fondness for guns and violent TV programs as "crazy."[15] Similarly negative comments are leveled against Violet and Augustus,[16] and, like the Buckets, the crowd seems convinced that these children will receive some comeuppance for their naughty behavior.[17] Though the actual punishment takes place within the factory, the threat of punishment hangs over the children from the beginning and is framed as a defense of the societal norms that the children have flouted. This is in keeping with Foucault's assertion that in the contemporary world, the power to punish is conferred upon the general society, which results in the outlining of strict and specific behavioral codes.

THE RULES OF WONKA'S FACTORY VS. FOUCAULT'S "FIVE OR SIX MAJOR RULES"

Foucault lays out "five or six major rules"[18] regarding his contemporary philosophy of punishment. Here again, Dahl's text initially seems to illustrate a medieval view, rejecting "rules" and conferring the power to punish solely upon the sovereign. The first rule, "the rule of minimum quantity,"[19] does not apply in the chocolate factory, where the penalties are harsh and retaliatory. More significantly, Foucault's fourth rule, "the rule of perfect certainty,"[20] which demands that the legal and penal code be laid out in explicit detail, is nonexistent. There is no published code of crime and punishment in the Wonka factory.[21] Though Wonka repeatedly puts forth a set of verbal instructions, he does not specifically define the consequences of failing to adhere to these commands: "But now, listen to me! I want no messing about when you go in! No touching, no meddling, and no tasting!"[22] In the absence of a specific code of law, it seems that the one overarching rule of Willy Wonka's factory is an old-fashioned and autocratic one: you must obey Willy Wonka and, to a lesser extent, your parents (whatever their failures in the upbringing of their children, the Gloops, the Salts, and the Teavees all echo Wonka's warnings to their offspring—only the Beauregardes actively encourage their daughter's defiance).

Wonka likewise fails to address many of the children's queries and comments, insisting that he has "no time to answer silly questions!"[23] and warning them, "Don't argue, my dear child, *please* don't argue!"[24] This casual dismissal hints toward a traditional social dynamic in which the power of the sovereign is not subject to inquiry or debate: his word is law, and his punishments are vengeful rather than preventative. It is therefore not surprising that Wonka seemingly fails to achieve the primary goal of contemporary systems of punishment: preventing future transgressions.[25] Augustus's punishment for disobeying does not prevent Violet from disobeying, Violet's punishment for disobeying does not prevent Veruca from disobeying, and so on.

Still, it is vital to consider the fact that although the naughty children commit the exact same transgression—defying Wonka—they do so for very different reasons and under very different circumstances. Each child exhibits a specific type of bad behavior that results in a specific type of punishment. Returning to Foucault's rules, Wonka's tailoring of the punishments to fit the crimes epitomizes the sixth rule, "the rule of optimal specification,"[26] which stresses the need to individualize penalties based on specific transgressions. This rule is obviously of great importance to Wonka: the morbidly obese Augustus is squeezed thin; the rude Violet, who enjoys drawing attention to herself, is actually dyed violet; the snobbish and materialistic Veruca is sullied and humiliated; and Mike, the couch potato, is physically refashioned so that "every basketball team in the country will be trying to get him."[27]

Moreover, in spite of the commonalities between the naughty children, such as their disobedience and general impudence, Wonka adheres to the tenets of Foucault's rule, "tak[ing] into account the profound nature of the criminal himself, the presumable degree of his wickedness, the intrinsic quality of his will."[28] Notably, Veruca receives the least severe punishment, and this is due to the fact that her culpability for her crime is mitigated slightly; during the third Oompa-Loompa song, they question whether Veruca is "the only one at fault":[29]

> For though she's spoiled, and dreadfully so,
> A girl can't spoil herself, you know . . .
> Who turned her into such a brat?
> Who are the culprits? Who did that?
> Alas! You needn't look so far
> To find out who these sinners are.
> They are (and this is very sad)
> Her loving parents, MUM and DAD.[30]

Although the parenting skills of the Gloops, the Beauregardes, and the Teavees are questionable, this is the only song in which the parents are actually assigned blame for the child's bad behavior. It is therefore not surprising that Wonka spares Veruca the permanent alterations that he inflicts upon the other children and that he forces the Salts to share in their daughter's punishment. Veruca's chastisement is one of the strongest illustrations of a Foucaultian understanding of contemporary punishment; as per the rule of optimal specification, "the need for an individual-ization of sentences, in accordance with the particular characteristics of each criminal"[31] is acknowledged.

As for Foucault's other rules, it is important to note that the children are clearly discomfited by their peers' punishments, but, as suggested by the Oompa-Loompa songs, they associate these punishments with the specific bad behavior of that peer as opposed to the general failure to obey Willy Wonka. For example, following Violet's punishment (and the Oompa-Loompa song critiquing her bad habit), Mike reflects on the girl's gum chewing rather than focusing on her defiance of Wonka's instructions.[32] Consider also that the Oompa-Loompas' chants focus entirely on the punishable quality of each child's vice as opposed to the general problem with rule breaking: "Augustus Gloop" is a song about overeating, "Violet Beauregarde" is a song about gum-chewing, "Veruca Salt" is a song about spoiling children, and "Mike Teavee" is a song about watching television. As in the case of the punishments, there is specification.

Significantly, though the naughty children all disobey Willy Wonka, they do not inherit or adopt the vices of their predecessors: Violet does not become a glutton, Veruca does not become a gum-chewer, and so on. This suggests that Wonka has met two of the three remaining Foucaultian rules: "the rule of sufficient ideality"[33] and the "rule of lateral effects."[34] Both of these rules emphasize the notion that punishment is best used as a deterrent. The former asserts that the threat of pain is more important than the actual experience of pain, and the latter affirms that the penalty must exert its strongest effect, not on the transgressor, but rather on the general population so as to prevent future transgressions. Clearly, the idea of going up the pipe or being squeezed in the juicing room is enough to prevent Charlie and his peers from adopting the vices of Augustus and Violet. Furthermore, Charlie himself, who experiences none of the brutal punishments of the Wonka factory, repeatedly comments on how "terrible" it would be to suffer the fate of the bratty children.[35] While it would be inaccurate to suggest that Wonka's punishments affect Charlie more so than the other children, these chastisements certainly meet Foucault's criteria of leaving a permanent impression on the general public (as represented by Charlie). Regardless of the seemingly outdated nature of Wonka's physical punishments, the chocolate factory's system of chastisement strictly defines and promotes societal codes of behavior, underscoring Foucault's conception of contemporary punishment.

CHARLIE AND THE GREAT GLASS PANOPTICON

The previous two sections have focused on how, in spite of the physical alterations to the naughty children, the philosophy of punishment in *Charlie and the Chocolate Factory* reinforces Foucault's assertion that the body is an archaic target. As noted, the physical punishments are carried out, not by Willy Wonka, but rather by pieces of factory equipment. The use of mechanical devices at the precise moment that the child breaks the rules hints toward a punitive system that is automatic and functional as opposed to subjective and retributive. The former two adjectives are important to consider in the context of Foucault's analysis, particularly as they relate to one of Foucault's most noteworthy concepts in *Discipline and Punish*: the Panopticon. The idea of the Panopticon actually comes from the utilitarian philosopher Jeremy Bentham (1748–1832); it refers to "a circular prison with cells arranged around a central well, from which inmates can be observed at all times."[36] For Foucault, the Panopticon epitomizes the significance of observation and assessment in contemporary systems of discipline; it likewise reinforces the connections between the prison, the factory, and the schoolhouse, for all three institutions thrive on the concept of constant surveillance. If a person feels as though he or she is constantly being watched, that person will maintain the proper standards of behavior at all times, "assuring the automatic functioning of power."[37]

While the Wonka factory, with its innumerable twists and turns, seems antithetical to the set-up of the Panopticon, the most memorable means of transportation in Wonka's factory, the Great Glass Elevator, is a device meant to grant Wonka a complete visual perspective on any and every room in the factory: "The whole elevator is made of thick, clear glass! . . . Walls, doors, ceiling, floor, everything is made of glass so that you can see out!"[38] Furthermore, while the primary goal of the Panopticon is perpetual surveillance and observation (traits that are obviously important to Wonka in his monitoring of the children), Foucault notes that "the Panopticon was also a laboratory; it could be used as a machine to carry out experiments, to alter behaviour to train and correct individuals."[39] Here again, these descriptions seem strangely applicable to the Wonka factory, not just because of the wild experiments taking place within the various rooms but also because the visit of the five children to the Wonka factory is an examination in and of itself: Who is fit to be Wonka's heir?

When analyzing the various "instruments" used to promote the "system of discipline," Foucault cites the examination as one of the most important in that it combines "hierarchical observation" and "normalizing judgement."[40] In Dahl's novel, the excursion to Willy Wonka's chocolate factory proves to be an extended examination facilitated by the "Panopticon" and by Wonka's continuous observation and evaluation of the children. The factory owner eventually reveals that his primary goal in inviting five visitors to the factory was to find a young person to take over the running of his plant: "Mind you, there are thousands of clever men who would give anything for the chance to come in and take over from me, but I don't *want* that sort of person. I don't want a grown-up person at all. A grownup won't listen to me; he won't learn."[41] The 1971 film adaptation takes the matter even further, as Wonka informs Charlie, "A grown-up would want to do everything his own way, *not mine*."[42] Conversely, a *disciplined* child like Charlie will prove to be the perfect *disciple* by studying, adopting, and preserving Wonka's methodology. Dahl reinforces this notion in the sequel, *Charlie and the Great Glass Elevator*, as Wonka and Charlie develop a mentor/protégé relationship, with Wonka proudly noting, "You learn very fast. I am so pleased I chose you, my dear boy, so very pleased."[43] Throughout the sequel, Charlie repeatedly defends Wonka's methods (and the madness of said methods) to his parents and grandparents.[44]

While the notion of a child taking over the factory may hint at a subversive celebration of childhood on the part of the author, such a sentiment would contradict the moralistic components of the novel that have dominated the story up to this point. Notably, Wonka's primary interest in conferring the factory upon a child is based on the idea that a child is willing to learn, which is an ironic point when one considers that learning is the process by which people *attain* knowledge. Conversely, Wonka has spent most of the novel turning the children into *objects* of knowledge. Indeed, Wonka's study of the children through his examination epitomizes many of Foucault's assertions regarding the strictness of the contemporary "system of discipline"; in this system, "the child is more individualized than the adult" because the child is always under greater scrutiny.[45]

CONCLUSION: FAIRYTALE UNDERDOG OR
FOUCAULTIAN FRONTRUNNER?

Wonka's examination individualizes the four disobedient children based
on their unique quirks and foibles, and the fact that each of the naughty
children is eliminated based on his or her individual "quirks" returns us to
the point that initiated this inquiry: Charlie's comparative lack of vitality
and uniqueness. These same traits are what make Charlie the perfect
candidate to take over Wonka's factory, despite the sharp personality
differences between the shy, unremarkable child and the ostentatious,
eccentric candymaker. To become an individual in the Foucaultian sense
is to be closely scrutinized, labeled, and judged. Charlie's lack of individuality is what allows him to slip into the background, join Wonka in his
observation and judgment of the other children's failures, and then
emerge triumphantly as the winner. Charlie has demonstrated the discipline necessary to take on the running of the Wonka factory, and the
institution will thus be able to maintain its productivity. Ironically,
though the reader is tempted to rejoice at the triumph of the "underdog,"
Charlie was *never* the underdog, but rather the frontrunner. From the
moment the four naughty children were introduced, they were subject to
hierarchical observation and normalizing judgment in a way that Charlie
was not, and there is never any real question in Wonka's mind regarding
what the results of the examination will be.

Perhaps this is all for the best, especially in regard to the factory's
productivity. Augustus would likely consume the factory's output, Violet
would likely stick chewing gum on the buttons of the Great Glass Elevator, Veruca would likely whine every time she did not get her way, and
Mike would likely lock himself away in the TV room all day. Still,
though *Charlie and the Chocolate Factory* concludes with a child's triumph, the novel is not a rebellious celebration of childhood quirkiness
but a moralistic celebration (and preservation) of societal order.[46] Child-
ish rebelliousness is ultimately quashed by a Foucaultian system of discipline and punishment.

8

MATILDA AND THE PHILOSOPHY OF EDUCATION

or, What's an Education For?

John V. Karavitis

Roald Dahl's *Matilda* is the story of a precocious young girl, Matilda Wormwood, and the challenges she faces both at home and in school. Matilda is extraordinarily intelligent—preternaturally so. She teaches herself to read and do arithmetic in spite of being raised in a cruel and indifferent family environment. She is neither supported nor encouraged in her drive to learn. When not simply ignored, she is berated, especially when speaking up for herself. And her family sees no useful purpose served by the books she loves to read. When Matilda asks her father to buy her a book, he immediately expresses his disdain for them. "What's wrong with the telly, for heaven's sake?" he demands.[1] In spite of these obstacles, Matilda takes matters into her own hands. She finds more books to read by going to the village public library by herself. But when Matilda finally enters Crunchem Hall Primary School at the age of five and a half, she finds herself in a hostile environment that will do nothing to help further her learning. The headmistress of Crunchem Hall, Miss Agatha Trunchbull, "was a gigantic holy terror, a fierce tyrannical monster who frightened the life out of the pupils and teachers alike."[2] The only person who sees and appreciates her unique talents and good nature is her teacher, Miss Jennifer Honey. Matilda eventually escapes from her abusive family environment and ends up in a supportive one in which her teacher also becomes her guardian.

Much of Dahl's story focuses on Matilda's learning experiences, first at home and then at Crunchem Hall. Matilda begins her journey outside her home by reading books she discovers in the public library. There, she is helped by Mrs. Phelps, the librarian. Once Matilda exhausts the books in the children's section of the library, Mrs. Phelps introduces her to the works of authors like Charles Dickens, Jane Austen, Ernest Hemingway, and William Faulkner. At the public library, Matilda reads what she wants to read, and she learns a great deal about the world. When Matilda learns from Mrs. Phelps that she can sign books out of the library, she finds herself able to travel "all over the world while sitting in her little room in an English village."[3] Unfortunately, books can only take Matilda so far.

Entering school seems inevitable. School plays an important role in society. Each succeeding generation must be fully prepared to assume its responsibilities so that society can continue to function. In order to produce well-rounded, fully functioning future citizens, both social skills and the moral values society deems important must be learned alongside factual knowledge of the world. School is traditionally where this education takes place. In his *Politics*, Aristotle (384–322 BCE) acknowledges both the importance of education for society—"for the neglect of education does harm to the constitution"[4]—and that education is a matter of public responsibility: "It is manifest that education should be one and the same for all, and that it should be public, and not private . . . the training in things which are of common interest should be the same for all."[5] Thus, Aristotle acknowledges that a society needs its members to hold a common set of beliefs, a common culture, in order to make the city-state function optimally.

But what exactly should be taught, and how, has always been the subject of debate. This debate over the content, structure, and delivery of education to the young is nothing new. In *Politics*, Aristotle avers that "education should be regulated by law and should be an affair of state . . . but what should be the character of this public education, and how young persons should be educated, are questions which remain to be considered. As things are, there is disagreement about the subject."[6] Here, the present resembles the past.

There are many schools of thought regarding the purpose or goals of education, the content to be taught, and the method of providing it. As Matilda travels on her childhood journey of discovery, the reader is introduced to three alternative philosophies of education. Throughout her self-directed learning efforts, Miss Trunchbull's oppressive and severe disciplinarian style of schooling, and Miss Honey's attentive, understanding, and individualized guidance, Matilda faces and overcomes many challenges. Her challenges and how she overcomes them shed light on current issues in education.

LESSONS AT CRUNCHEM HALL: SOCIETY AS TEACHER

Matilda's parents "weren't very concerned one way or the other about their daughter's education,"[7] and thus she started school late, at the age of five and a half. When Matilda enters Crunchem Hall, she finds a strict, regimented environment. Each grade level is an age cohort, and all that matters are learning one's lessons by rote and behaving oneself. Miss Honey warns her pupils that their first day in school marks "the beginning of at least eleven long years of schooling that all of you are going to have to go through." She warns the children that they must behave, as "Miss Trunchbull deals very very severely with anyone who gets out of line." Indeed, Miss Honey graphically describes how Miss Trunchbull "can liquidize you like a carrot in a kitchen blender."[8] No mechanisms exist to accommodate the very bright or those who are struggling. For example, on the first day of class, when Miss Honey sees how bright Matilda is, she recommends to Miss Trunchbull that "Matilda should be taken out of my form and placed immediately in the top form with the eleven-year-olds." Miss Trunchbull refuses, stating, "I have a rule in this school that all children remain in their own age groups regardless of ability."[9] With regard to discipline, the children soon learn about "the Chokey." The Chokey "is a very tall but very narrow cupboard" that Miss Trunchbull will put a child in to punish her. "Three of the walls are made of cement with bits of broken glass sticking out all over, so you can't lean against them. You have to stand more or less at attention all the time when you get locked up in there."[10]

The strict, regimented learning environment of Crunchem Hall is one that is familiar to almost everyone reading this chapter. Classes are divided by age. Children's desks are arranged in a grid of rows and columns, all facing the teacher's desk. The material to be taught is determined by grade level. Learning is mostly accomplished by repetition and rote memorization. Discipline is strictly enforced, and everything is structured around the calendar and the clock. The learning environment of Crunchem Hall provides a clear example of an essentialist philosophy of education.

Essentialism, articulated by William C. Bagley (1874–1946), a professor at Columbia University,[11] maintains that everyone must possess the same education and acquire the same basic knowledge in order to become citizens who can actively and fully participate in society. The teacher plays the role of a knowledge expert,[12] directing daily learning activities so that critical knowledge and the "ideals of the community"[13] may be imparted and discipline maintained. The student is expected to listen attentively, to take direction well, and above all to learn.[14] In effect, learning and discipline go hand in hand. What Crunchem Hall teaches and how students are expected to behave parallel real-world expectations: obedience, conformity, and functionality. In essentialism, education exists to serve the demands of society.

Although Bagley wrote in the early twentieth century, the idea that education serves the needs of society is not new. Indeed, we see such a philosophy of education presented in Plato's *The Republic*. In this work, Plato (427–347 BCE) describes the ideal form of government for a just society. Toward this end, the education of the citizens, both male and female, is of paramount importance. There are two educational systems described in *The Republic*. One system educates the guardian class; the other identifies the "philosopher-kings," those who would rule the just society, and also develops their skills. The guardian class is educated through music and gymnastics,[15] and tales told to those in this class are heavily censored.[16] For the philosopher-kings, education is structured in stages and takes decades. In the beginning, the focus is on basic study and physical fitness. This stage lasts until the age of eighteen. This is followed by two years of military service. After military service is completed, candidates study mathematics for ten years. Successful completion of this stage is followed by the study of dialectic for five years. After this, candidates study leadership for fifteen years. Thus, by the age of fifty, the philosopher-kings who will be leading society have been identified and properly trained.[17]

The importance of education in serving the needs of society was also acknowledged by Immanuel Kant (1724–1804). In *On Education*, Kant notes, "Man needs nurture and culture. Culture includes discipline and instruction."[18] Kant would surely have understood and supported the goals of Crunchem Hall. Comparing home education with public education, Kant believed that "as a preparation for the duties of a citizen . . . public education is the best."[19] Kant would also, to some small degree, have supported Miss Trunchbull's disciplinary efforts, for "a child must become accustomed to work, and where can the inclination to work be cultivated so well as at school? School is a place of compulsory culture."[20]

In the world of *Matilda*, society expects its citizens to have learned not only basic skills such as reading, writing, and arithmetic but also how to behave properly. Children acquire both the basic skills and an understanding of how to behave over many years of compulsory schooling. Proper behavior is reinforced at Crunchem Hall partially by example: each teacher acts as the students' boss, and the headmistress is the "head teacher, the boss, the supreme commander."[21] This daily example reinforces the hierarchical structure that children will be expected to follow in the real world. Conformity and obedience are valued, whereas creativity, independence, and free thinking are condemned. Proper behavior is also reinforced through the threat of punishment. Disobedience is punished severely, and children are constantly reminded to behave. Miss Honey warns her pupils prior to Miss Trunchbull's arrival for her weekly lesson that they need to be on their best behavior: "Speak only when spoken to. When she asks you a question, stand up at once before you answer it. Never argue with her. Never answer back. Never try to be funny. If you do, you will make her angry."[22] Such an oppressive environment takes a psychological toll on the children. As Matilda observes, "Being in this school is like being in a cage with a cobra."[23] And the psychological toll doesn't end when school does. Although she doesn't explicitly invoke memories of her school days, when Miss Honey tells Matilda that "any courage I had was knocked out of me when I was young,"[24] the presumption is there.

Matilda is clearly ill served by the essentialist philosophy of education. Rather than recognizing that she possesses a unique constellation of strengths and weaknesses and modifying her lessons accordingly, Crunchem Hall's plan is to shoehorn her into a preordained, unyielding mold and to use harsh discipline when necessary. Although school does provide Matilda with opportunities for social interaction with members of her own age group, her academic growth has come to a standstill. Her relationship with Miss Honey, however, points the way to an alternative.

LESSONS WITH MISS HONEY: MOTHER NATURE AS TEACHER

Matilda experiences another approach toward education through her interaction with her teacher, Miss Honey, both inside and outside the school environment. Here, the interaction between teacher and student is personalized, geared toward understanding Matilda as a person and exploring her abilities and limitations. In school, Miss Honey gives Matilda books on algebra and geography, subjects that are far beyond the reach of her classroom peers, and allows her to study them during class. At the end of the book, after Miss Trunchbull leaves forever and Miss Honey reclaims ownership of the Red House, "Matilda was a welcome visitor to The Red House every single evening after school, and a very close friendship began to develop between the teacher and the small child."[25] The relationship between Matilda and Miss Honey illustrates the philosophy of education called progressivism. It is a philosophy famously espoused by French philosopher Jean-Jacques Rousseau (1712–1778) in *Émile*. Rousseau did not favor the school system of his day. The strictures and harsh punishment of the French school system made no sense to him. In *Émile*, he proposes a system of education that he claims is superior. For Rousseau, nature is the best teacher, and the student must actively interact with the environment to learn effectively.

Rousseau believed that it made no sense to teach children material that they were not ready to learn. Forcing a child to learn means that the child ceases to think. Instead, the child merely repeats what she is taught, without necessarily understanding. In Miss Honey's class, the first lesson we observe is the recitation of the "two-times" multiplication table by the entire class en masse. But do they really understand what they are reciting? Are they reciting from their understanding of the material or merely parroting? When Miss Honey tells Miss Trunchbull about Matilda's great skill with arithmetic, Miss Trunchbull refuses to believe that Matilda truly understands the material: "'So she's learnt a few tables by heart, has she?' Miss Trunchbull barked. 'My dear woman, that doesn't make her a genius! It makes her a parrot!'"[26] We see another example of this lack of understanding when Miss Trunchbull challenges one of Miss Honey's students, Nigel, to give an example from their spelling lesson. To spell the word "difficulty," Nigel bravely sings, "Mrs D, Mrs I, Mrs FFI / Mrs C, Mrs U, Mrs LTY. / That spells difficulty."[27] But is this really anything more than parroting? Rousseau understood that lessons that are not geared to a child's stage of development will not be understood and internalized. Instead, the lessons will simply be repeated on command. For Rousseau, "Childhood is the sleep of reason."[28] By this he means that it would be best for a child to remain ignorant of any ideas that are beyond her current grasp. Rousseau proposed that it was better to let children "run, jump, and shout to their heart's content"[29] than to force them to learn when they are not ready.

Rousseau counsels tutors to not struggle against nature. Children learn when they have to, when they want to, or when it's fun. Reading is of special concern for Rousseau. He refers to it as the "curse of childhood,"[30] and he questions the wisdom of forcing a child to learn how to read when she hates the activity. Rousseau could not see how a child could be expected to learn from a lesson she detests, and he felt that the way reading was forced on children distorted its benefits. "What is the use of inscribing on their brains a list of symbols which mean nothing to them? The first thing taken for granted on the word of another person . . . is the ruin of the child's judgment."[31] Indeed, Rousseau observed that, in his age, "Too much reading only produces a pretentious ignoramus. There never was so much reading in any age . . . and less learning."[32] Yet again we find another parallel between the present and the past.

Since he maintained that society and its rigid rules are the problem, Rousseau looked to nature for how best to educate children. Since we learn from experience, Rousseau saw experience as the most effective method of teaching and learning. Doing is more important than reading. Children should learn nothing from books that they could instead learn from experience. The student should explore and discover and figure things out independently. "Nature should be his only teacher."[33] Rousseau saw play as being an excellent tool for encouraging children to explore their world and in the process learn from it. He understood that when children see an activity as play, they "endure without complaint."[34] Also, if the child sees an activity as being in her interest, she will pursue that activity with vim and vigor. A student must want to learn and be ready to learn, as Matilda shows herself eagerly doing throughout the novel. We see this when the village librarian, Mrs. Phelps, guides Matilda in selecting books to read once she has exhausted the books in the children's section. We also see this when Miss Honey selects textbooks from the senior class to give to Matilda. The child is directed to learn new material when it is perceived that she is ready.

Thus, when the pupil is perceived ready to learn, the tutor provides guidance. This is quite different from daily life at Crunchem Hall. However, with progressivism, Matilda's learning is dependent on the efforts of her tutor. Will this educational model afford Matilda a diversity of learning opportunities? And can we be sure that the tutor will know when Matilda is ready to move on to more difficult material? Or could this philosophy of education be just as bad, in its own way, as that of Crunchem Hall?

NO CLASSES, NO TESTS, NO GRADES: MATILDA THE EXPLORER

There is a third philosophy of education presented in *Matilda*. If essentialism is education by society's fiat, and progressivism is education by nature, then the third philosophy of education is romanticism.[35] It is represented in modern-day schools such as A. S. Neill's Summerhill School in Suffolk, England; Sudbury Valley School in Framingham, Massachusetts; and the Fairhaven School in Upper Marlboro, Maryland. These schools are also referred to as "democratic." This educational philosophy has no set curricula, no formal classes, no tests, and no grades. Students decide what they want to study and when. Teachers are available on demand, and they are there to assist, not direct or control. Indeed, at such schools, staff and students are viewed as equals. When Matilda begins her journey of learning, she first goes to the public library on a daily basis and reads whatever books she decides to. She also teaches herself arithmetic. No one forces her to learn, no one monitors her progress, and no one tests her efforts. When Matilda decides she wants to practice her telekinetic powers, she does so on her own with great success.

This educational methodology is quite rare, although schools that subscribe to this philosophy of education do exist around the world. It is a methodology that raises concerns in those familiar with traditional schools. The most obvious concern is that students at such schools will learn nothing and that they will simply play all day long. It is also difficult to see how a student in this environment could ever hope to one day enter a profession such as engineering, mathematics, or medicine without years of formal schooling. Certain fields demand tremendous amounts of foundational knowledge that can only be acquired over many years of study. There is also the problem of accurately measuring the effectiveness of these schools. As many more students attend traditional, institutional schools than do democratic schools, can the achievement of students from both types of schools be accurately compared? Democratic schools, by their very nature, may not be able to handle large numbers of students without formal discipline. For example, Summerhill reports that it has less than one hundred students attending at any given time.[36] The only way to quickly compare students of democratic schools with students of traditional schools is through their performance on standardized tests. In England, where Summerhill is located, students ages fourteen to sixteen may take GCSE (General Certificate of Secondary Education) exams. About 46 percent of Summerhill's students taking the GCSE exams score grades of C or higher, including in English and mathematics, compared with almost 59 percent of students nationally.[37] Although one might think that this philosophy of education could only lead to anarchy, students from these schools tend to express positive feelings regarding their experiences, and many do end up going to college.[38] The Sudbury Valley School reports that 82 percent of its students have graduated from college.[39] Matilda follows this path at the beginning of her story. Although she learns a lot from the books she reads, how would she have eventually chosen a specific direction in her life? Given a lack of formal education, would certain career paths be forever out of her reach? Could this philosophy of education in fact be worse than Crunchem Hall's over the long run? But beyond Matilda, what can the real world teach us about education? Is there in fact a best way to teach our children? Or is every method of education equally damaging in its own way?

THE PROBLEM WITH CRUNCHEM HALL

The idea that traditional, institutional schools are the source of more harm than good is a popular view in some segments of the population and is

well articulated by American educator John C. Holt (1923–1985). Drawing on his observations of classroom activities and his experiences as a
teacher, Holt came to believe that "to a very great degree, school is a
place where children learn to be stupid."[40] Holt maintained that American
public schools create a hostile and intimidating environment in which
children are "afraid, bored, and confused."[41] This leads children to develop neurotic behavior and self-destructive strategies for coping with the
confusion and uncertainty of the school environment. We see this destructive behavior throughout *Matilda*. Hortensia regales Matilda and
Lavender with stories of the pranks she pulled on Miss Trunchbull: pour-
ing half a tin of syrup on the seat of her chair and putting itching powder
in her knickers. When Miss Honey announces that Miss Trunchbull
would be teaching a class for one period every week, she asks for a
volunteer to make sure that a jug of water and a glass would be available
for her. Lavender volunteers immediately. "Already Lavender's schem-
ing mind was going over the possibilities that this water-jug job had
opened up for her. She longed to do something truly heroic."[42] Lavender's prank was to put a newt in the jug of water from which Miss
Trunchbull would drink. Overbearing teachers who force students to
learn even when they are not ready drive children to anxiety and frustra-
tion, ultimately resulting in destructive behavior and failure. Is it surprising that the lesson that Matilda and her peers learn is revenge? "It's like a
war,"[43] says Matilda.

Holt was concerned with the goal of education, which he believed
should be to foster the ability to think independently and to understand.
Holt doubted very much whether it was possible to truly teach anyone
how to understand anything. Instead, a student must come to an understanding of how the world works on his own. Knowledge that a student
does not discover on her own is very likely not only useless but also
quickly forgotten. Holt wrote of his observations and experiences from
the late 1950s. Over the ensuing decades, nothing appears to have
changed in the basic structure of American public schools.

John T. Gatto, an award-winning educator from New York State with
decades of teaching experience, has written extensively on education in
the United States. His view of the development of American schools
since the Civil War is that they represent forced schooling that does more
harm than good. Gatto, therefore, echoes Holt's sentiments regarding
American schools: "Ordinary people send their children to school to get

smart, but what modern schooling teaches is dumbness."[44] "Dumbness" for Gatto isn't ignorance—it is a form of indoctrination that substitutes for understanding. People "are certain they must know something because their degrees and licenses say they do," and they remain certain until they are faced with a catastrophic event that destabilizes their pre-packaged view of the world, an event for which they are unprepared and cannot resolve on their own.[45]

Gatto, like Holt, believes that having students develop understanding is the proper goal of education. But Gatto does not see schools as rising to the challenge. Rather, for Gatto, "Growth and mastery come only to those who vigorously self-direct."[46] To self-direct is to be self-propelled in life, to think and to create, and to make informed choices about the direction of one's life. Matilda does this, whether it's reading at the public library or practicing her telekinesis at home. Indeed, although Miss Honey suggests that the two of them together explore her power very carefully, Matilda decides to forge ahead on her own and to push her power to its limits. And this turns out to be the best course of action.

CAN WE FIX CRUNCHEM HALL?

The current focus on improving educational results in the United States is on testing, and this has been driven by the federal No Child Left Behind law. Studies show that the extensive annual testing mandated by this law has "failed to significantly increase average academic performance and significantly narrow achievement gaps."[47] If traditional, institutional schools have continually failed, and mandatory annual testing has also failed, can our schools be reformed? Perhaps traditional, institutional schools have failed because they treat every student the same.

As the narrator of the movie version of *Matilda* tells us, "Everyone is born, but not everyone is born the same. Every human being is unique."[48] Howard E. Gardner would agree. Gardner developed the idea of multiple intelligences, and he sees each individual as possessing a unique constellation of these. In *The Unschooled Mind: How Children Think and How Schools Should Teach*, Gardner reviews the current state of education in the United States and discovers that most students leave college with very little understanding about how to approach, understand, and solve real-world problems. Gardner has observed that, when faced with novel problems, people tend to fall back on scripts used to solve canned example problems they learned while in school. This is partly the result of having an educational system that teaches everyone the same way, regardless of individual abilities or inclinations.

For Gardner, the goal of an education should be to foster an ability to understand the real world and not to simply apply learned algorithms. An education should focus on the process or learning, not simply the production of correct answers to a bank of standardized questions. The learning environment should be project-oriented, not "right answer"–oriented.[49] Differences between students should be acknowledged and taken into consideration, and high standards should be articulated and maintained. Toward this end, Gardner believes that an apprenticeship model of learning is best.

Matilda is presented as a child prodigy in order to reinforce the idea that each child is different and that it is nonsensical and counterproductive to teach all children at the same pace. Gifted children will become bored, and children who need help will fall further and further behind. Gardner's apprenticeship model, which considers each student as unique, closely resembles the spirit of the student-tutor relationship between Matilda and Miss Honey.

The real world and Crunchem Hall clearly have much in common. What we see in the real world is that an essentialist philosophy of education, in which expectations are mandated and then tested, has not worked. Absolute control of education applied from the top down has continually failed. The results have been disastrous, with students miserable and prone to destructive behavior. Contemporary educators who have investigated education in America all appear to agree that the goal of education should not be to shoehorn every student into the same mold. Rather, the goal should be to foster a student's ability to understand.

IF NOT CRUNCHEM HALL, THEN WHERE IS SCHOOL?

Alternatives to traditional, institutional education do exist: homeschooling and unschooling. Both of these alternatives take control of a child's education away from society, and they have arisen as the result of grassroots efforts on the part of concerned parents. Homeschooling is exactly as it sounds: children stay at home during the day instead of attending a public (or private) school, and they are often taught by a stay-at-home parent. Although the actual criteria to qualify for homeschooling vary by state, a lesson plan is typically filed with the local school district,[50] and the subjects taught at home are those that would be covered at a public school. The advantages of homeschooling are many. For example, the individualized attention students receive can take into account each student's particular constellation of talents and deficiencies. Students will not feel the pressure and anxiety that flow from uncertainty in a school environment, and there are no opportunities for children to be bullied, either by peers or by teachers. (Being bullied is still an all-too-common experience in American public schools.[51]) *Education News* reports that, since 1999, the number of children being homeschooled in the United States has grown at a rate seven times faster than that of children enrolling in school from kindergarten to high school. Homeschooled children have demonstrated that they can score as well on achievement tests; indeed, they score better than children in traditional academic settings. And this accomplishment is achieved at an average annual cost per child of only about $500, compared with $10,000 per child per year for public school (though the stay-at-home parent is forgoing the salary of a full-time job outside the home). Homeschooled children go to the best colleges; indeed, many colleges actively recruit them. As for concerns about socialization skills, homeschooled children appear healthy and well balanced.[52]

Another alternative approach to traditional schooling is unschooling.[53] Here, parents neither send their kids to school nor actively homeschool them. Unschooled children are allowed to spend their time as they wish. Parents who unschool their kids and the children themselves praise it as being superior to traditional public schools. The closest analog to unschooling would be schools that follow the romantic philosophy of education, like Summerhill and Sudbury. The Wormwoods' neglect of Matilda unwittingly provides this type of environment at the beginning of her journey. It's an environment that, ideally, imposes no undue stress on the child. However, there is no direction either. And as we saw with Matilda, her self-directed book learning only took her so far.

GOODBYE FOREVER, HEADMISTRESS TRUNCHBULL

Kant states, "Man can only become man by education. He is merely what education makes of him."[54] So what do we want to make of our children? As we have followed Matilda on her journey of intellectual discovery, what have we learned? What's an education for?

Obviously, society has a vested interest in the education of children. Each succeeding generation must be ready and capable to assume their responsibilities as well-rounded, fully functioning future citizens. The goals of education, the content of the material taught, and the method of providing it are all important factors that must be considered and addressed in any educational system. As Roald Dahl's *Matilda* shows, there is a spectrum of ideas regarding how best to provide a child's education. Perhaps the best way to educate the young would be a judicious blend of all of these approaches. Essentialism holds that some material must be learned by all students in order to provide a common ground, a common culture for all members of society so that they are able to communicate with each other. Progressivism holds that students learn by doing, that knowledge about the real world must come from lived experience. Romanticism holds that students can be self-propelled explorers, charting their own path in life, and still become well educated.

Each of these philosophies of education possesses some wisdom. But as long as we acknowledge that getting students to develop their understanding is more important than forcing them into the same educational mold, there is the possibility to make each child's school years productive, enjoyable, and memorable. Regardless of educational approach, the goal must be a child who can understand, not merely parrot his lessons—a child who has learned how to learn. Toward this end, let us proceed like Matilda. When she became aware of the possibilities that her telekinesis afforded her, she made a plan to help Miss Honey: "Her plan . . . was beginning to form beautifully in her mind. She had it now in almost every detail. . . . She knew she wouldn't manage it right away, but she felt fairly confident that with a great deal of practice and effort, she would succeed in the end."[55] Let's plan to start getting better at educating our children—right now.

9

SHATTERING THE GLASS ELEVATOR

Authenticity and Social Order in
the Works of Roald Dahl

Joseph J. Foy and Timothy M. Dale[1]

The world is so vast. Children are so small. The world can be quite cruel. Children are so vulnerable. The world imposes order. Children are so full of unique potential.

The works of Roald Dahl are classics of children's literature, passed on from generation to generation and across the globe because they speak creatively to the world in which children actually live—a world of imagination that is beset on all sides by hierarchies of power and control. Rather than working to liberate children and inspire their lives, these hierarchies attempt to regulate them by imposing forms of order. From the limitations that are forced on children by adults and institutions of education that stifle their creativity to the more complex structural problems of socioeconomic inequality and the violence of abuse and neglect, Dahl weaves tales of philosophic importance that confront principles of power and the possibility of salvation. From the heroic adventures of the orphaned Sophie and James Henry Trotter to the virtuous triumph of the starving Charlie Bucket and Mr. Fox, Roald Dahl's works feature protagonists that are among the most disempowered and marginalized members of society who overcome various forms of oppression through a commitment to justice and virtue in the face of structural, physical, and psychological violence. In doing so, he helps children realize the power of their own self-worth and the incredible possibilities that lay before them.

WE ARE THE DREAMERS OF DREAMS

In *The Twits*, Dahl suggests that if a "person has ugly thoughts every day, every week, every year, the face gets uglier and uglier until you can hardly bear to look at it." However, "if you have good thoughts it will shine out of your face like sunbeams and you will always look lovely."[2] His humorous description of the self, both good and bad, showing through in one's actions reveals something important about Dahl's writing and characters. For him, there is a true "inner core" that defines the person (or person-sized insect, in the case of James's friends in the peach). Dahl's heroic characters are those whose inner core is one of goodness that is also projected onto their interactions with others. His antagonists, like Aunt Spiker and Aunt Sponge, who are described when we first meet them as "both really horrible people" and "selfish, lazy, and cruel,"[3] are defined by the ugliness of their looks (Sponge, for example, is described as being "enormously fat and very short" with "small piggy eyes, a sunken mouth, and one of those white flabby faces that looked exactly as though it had been boiled"[4]), the ugliness of their thoughts (their terrible and unfounded vanity, "each one saying how beautiful she thought she was"[5]), and the ugliness of their behaviors ("They never called [James] by his real name, but always referred to him as 'you disgusting little beast' or 'you filthy nuisance' or 'you miserable little creature,' and they certainly never gave him any toys to play with or picture books to look at"[6]).

Dahl's heroes often encounter choices that require them to make decisions between who they are and what society expects them to be. Their inner core tells them one thing, but society tells them another. In that respect, they have to choose between being who and what they are, pursuing what their values tell them, or compromising themselves to conform to social expectations. What often saves them is a commitment to their true being, as it is often the external world that needs to be cleansed of injustice rather than the virtuous souls of our heroes.

Being true to oneself suggests acting in a way that reveals who a person truly is and desires to be. When we interact with others in a way that doesn't require that we change who we are in order to fit in or deceive others about how we feel or what we like in order to be accepted, we are being true to ourselves. Of course, this also suggests that we might act in ways that are *not* ourselves. But how can that be? How can I be anyone but me? Such considerations are important and not just a matter of, as the BFG might suggest, "gobblefunking" around with words. They mean a lot when we think about who we choose to be and who we feel we must project around others in order to be accepted.

Martin Heidegger (1889–1976), a German existentialist philosopher, suggests that most people are essentially shaped by the world around them. They don't spend very much time critically reflecting on who they are and what they want to be. Instead, they exist in the world as a projection of their history and environment—and, as in the case of someone like Mike Teavee, as a projection of consumable forms of entertainment and commercials. As Heidegger describes it, a human being "expresses itself not because it has in the first instance been encapsulated as something 'internal' over against something outside, but because as Being-in-the-world it is already outside when it understands."[7] Heidegger suggests that most people will never think all that much about their values or their place in the world. Attached to our history and our surroundings, we end up pursuing goals and valuing outcomes without ever really questioning if that is what we want to be doing, and we assume we have either achieved great things or failed in our pursuits based on our relative success in relation to society's values. As Zinnia Wormwood puts it, "Take a look at you and me. I have a nice house, a wonderful husband . . . and you are slaving away teaching snot-nosed children their ABCs."[8] Sure, she has nice things, but what are we to make of her rather shallow view of success or her estimation of herself as a person? When we take on, without question or freely choosing, the values and standards of the larger society, we become, according to Heidegger, "inauthentic."

But if being inauthentic means uncritically allowing ourselves to become shaped in terms of values and preferences imposed on us by the external world, what does it mean to be "authentic"? According to Heidegger, authenticity is the understanding that we have the ability to make choices in the face of all that determines us. As Heidegger puts it, this understanding is a person's "own potentiality-for-Being," and with this understanding a human being is able to disclose "in itself what its Being is capable of."[9] Being authentic, or being oneself, means taking responsibility for choices that one makes, even when there are many factors that influence the choice being made. In Heidegger's account, being human essentially means asking questions about our own existence and understanding that we can play a significant role in shaping that existence.

Another existentialist philosopher influenced by Heidegger is Jean-Paul Sartre (1905–1980), who suggests that freedom is the essential characteristic of being human. Ultimately, who we are as individuals is the result of the free choices that we make. The authentic person is one who understands her freedom and therefore accepts that she is responsible for her decisions and actions. A person is inauthentic if she blames decisions on other value systems or social pressures for which she is not responsible. An inauthentic person will avoid facing difficult information or facts about herself because facing such facts would be too painful, and accepting responsibility for those acts would require she do things differently. Sartre describes this condition as one of "bad faith," because "in bad faith it is from myself that I am hiding the truth."[10] Sometimes it is easier to deceive ourselves into believing we have no freedom to make choices, because it allows us a way out of being responsible for our actions. Sartre argues that the peace of mind gained from this form of dishonesty is a problem because it denies us the freedom to make choices for ourselves and the very truth of our existence in "fleeing what it can not flee, to flee what is."[11] The inauthentic person makes a bad-faith attempt to avoid reality by refusing to take responsibility for her choices.

Dahl's heroes, whether they are the abused but indomitable James Henry Trotter or the impoverished but always caring and giving Charlie Bucket, encourage us to "be ourselves" despite pressures we might feel from others, and this message is linked to the philosophical argument that to determine our own lives is what makes us human. We should endeavor to understand our place in the world so that we can choose for ourselves what we want to be within it. Likewise, we should allow others to choose their lives for themselves, because being human also means equally allowing everyone to make those choices that give life meaning.

THOSE WHO DON'T BELIEVE IN MAGIC WILL NEVER FIND IT

Apart from his approach to his characters, Dahl often situates his stories in social settings that are distorted in ways that actually reward the "bad nuts," with their twisted souls, while punishing or mistreating those with a good inner core. Take the children from *Charlie and the Chocolate Factory*. Violet Beauregarde smacking around on her gum is actually praised and lauded in the form of records and honors for the meaningless achievement of chewing the same piece longer than anyone else in the world. Veruca Salt is handed anything she wants whenever she wants it, no matter how much of a brat she is. And the gluttonous Augustus Gloop devours more and more, while other children (like poor Charlie Bucket) have almost nothing. As readers, we get to see these characters for what they are, described so brilliantly by the magical pen of Dahl to have their outer appearance align perfectly with their inner core.

And yet what of our own world? Unfortunately, we do not have special squirrels that can help us know whether we are dealing with a good nut or one that should be tossed down the garbage chute. Society often seems to praise those who possess the most money or power or fame, allowing wealth and power to be transvalued from those things that have extrinsic worth (a tool for achieving other ends) to something that is seen to have intrinsic value (a good in itself). In such cases, wealth or status become a benchmark for what is praiseworthy, rather than evaluating individuals based on other traits like kindness, compassion, honesty, and altruism. One need only turn on the television to see that we have plenty of Veruca Salts and Augustus Gloops in the world capturing attention, but very rarely does a good-hearted Charlie Bucket make headlines.

So what is to be done? Should we conform to the standards and interests of the world, regardless of how twisted we might personally find its values? Do we risk being marginalized, made fun of, or punished if we don't? For some, it's easier to simply adopt the values and standards society has established rather than follow an internal set of values they might personally hold. Living in Sartrean bad faith, these individuals convince themselves that they have no other choice but to buy trendy clothes, befriend popular peers, get a respectable job, choose the "right kind" of spouse, buy a house, live in the suburbs, drive an SUV, and raise their children to believe that these are the things they also need to live for. But what do we sacrifice of ourselves in an effort to fit in? If we do hide our true selves, or compromise what we know to be right because we convince ourselves we have no choice in the matter, aren't we lying to the world and, worse, to ourselves? What are we living for if not a life of our choosing?

Matilda is a perfect case in point. At a young age it is already obvious that Matilda is a unique young lady. Her precocious nature and penchant for the magically fantastic set her apart from her peers. Her parents, both of whom seem to revel in their own dimwittedness, actually mock Matilda as foolhardy and dense. Matilda does not have an easy childhood because she remains authentic and true to her inner self. It's only when she meets Miss Honey, who reveals that she was abused as a girl by her aunt (Headmistress Trunchbull), that Matilda encounters an adult who sees her for who she truly is. Miss Honey helps Matilda empower herself and ultimately provides her a genuine and loving home when Matilda's parents have to cheese it to escape law enforcement officials who are after them for illegal dealings in their auto business.

For children the question of authenticity is problematized by the additional forms of authority imposed on them that force them to act in ways they may not freely choose. Children lack a form of personal empowerment, as they are often dependent on adults for food, shelter, and protection. They are physically unable to assert or defend themselves when confronting authority figures, and there are methods of monitoring and controlling the behavior of children in ways that are not acceptable for adults. This might be the verbal insults or screeching some adults direct at children to modify their behavior (Grandma Kranky) or, in the worst possible cases, the torturous treatment some children are forced to endure in the form of corporal punishment and abuse (Aunts Sponge and Spiker or Miss Trunchbull). Their physical and mental development prevents children from being fully autonomous, which means that they must rely on adults for help. Such an imbalance of power can unfortunately yield an unjust relationship in which authority is wielded not for the sake of helping a child realize her potential, but instead to establish a hierarchy of power. As Harry Wormwood aggressively lords over Matilda, "I am right and you're wrong, I am big and you are small, and there's nothing you can do about it."[12]

Dahl's presentation of society in many of his works calls to mind the writings of French social theorist Michel Foucault (1926–1984). Foucault argues that society removes possibilities and genuine choice from individuals through collective norms and values that are socially and politically enforced. As Foucault describes them, these forces "centralized humanity, the effect and instrument of complex power relations, bodies and forces subjected by multiple mechanisms of 'incarceration.'"[13] These mechanisms are used to categorize and control individuals, as they define what society will accept as normal or appropriate behavior and identity. We are monitored, Foucault suggests, at all times, with society and the state acting like George Kranky's grandmother, ever watching us with a skeptical "wicked eye" and wondering "what are you up to?" In order to conform, and therefore be accepted and rewarded by society, the masses will adopt the standards and values of the broader social order. The individual that attempts to deviate from those conventions and standards runs headlong into the systems of conformity that maintain social order. When someone adopts an identity or a course of action that is perceived to be deviant (meaning it falls outside the normalized prescriptions of behavior), the individual is confronted and corrected by either formal sources of power or informal pressures from society.[14] Foucault uses the example of government-run asylums to represent the way that "institutions of morality are established in which an astonishing synthesis of moral obligation and civil law is effected."[15] A person is either cut off from society or marginalized through isolation or prescribed some type of treatment to correct their "abnormal" behavior, such as psychotherapy or medicine (not of the "marvelous" kind).

This is not to say that social conventions or norms of behavior in a public setting are not good. Distinguishing between public and private forms of behavior reveals an understanding of civility and mutual respect that are important for us to live among one another. After all, in the immortal words of the Greek philosopher Aristotle (384–322 BCE), the "human being is by nature a political animal."[16] In order to get along, we must adopt common understandings of how we ought to behave within social settings that allow for interaction and cooperation. If we were constantly offending and insulting and attacking one another, we would be more like the Fleshlumpeater and Bloodbottler and the other nasty giants than we would be like the goodhearted Sophie.

Society requires mutual toleration and respect. However, what is important for the philosophers who consider authenticity is that individuals be allowed to genuinely choose to behave in ways that are to the benefit of all because they understand the importance of doing so and because they morally own their actions. The authentic person does not just uncritically accept social norms; she embraces them because she authentically chooses to behave in such a manner because she knows it is right. And when, through an examination of her conscience, she is unable to accept the social standards imposed through collective acceptance, she must be allowed to openly express herself and challenge those conventions.

Let's take, for instance, the BFG's love of whacking back some delicious "frobscottle" and letting loose a good, wall-shaking "whizzpopper." Partaking in the release of this malodorous gas helps avoid painful bloating, and the sounds can sometimes even elicit a giggle or two; exceptional examples even get one airborne. When you are by yourself, or with friends or family, there is nothing wrong with a left-cheek-sneak. However, when breakfasting with the Queen of England, there are different standards of behavior that establish an air of civility and mutual respect. In those latter instances, or when in public settings, one may need to politely excuse oneself or hold in one's flatulence. What is important here, even in such a whimsical example, is that the individual understand and accept the choice of how to behave, owning that choice as one she makes freely for the sake of advancing other values that are of equal or greater importance. Being authentic does not mean one should strive to offend others or be unconcerned with the feelings of others. It does, however, require a critical reflection on why we behave, think, and act as we do. And if we decide that ultimately society is in the wrong, and that we cannot in good conscience hold back from an action, or that conformity would require cutting ourselves off from who we are, we must follow our conscience and accept that there may be consequences to our actions for which we are responsible.

DREAMS DON'T WORK UNLESS YOU DO

It is on that last part that the discourses on social control and identity in Dahl's work come full circle. Through his discussions of the tensions that exist between the authentic self and social order, Dahl seems to be raising the critical question of what is required from society in order to allow authentic individuals to exist among one another. Moreover, Dahl's work suggests that the morality we choose makes up who we are. In that sense, a person's understanding of the good life is a constitutive part of her identity. To try and impose upon her the kind of life or moral code chosen by society through systems of discipline and punishment is akin to trying to eradicate her identity. A moral code we genuinely adopt and embrace for ourselves is part of who we are, and we must have the freedom to pursue our conscience. The only limitations we ought to place on this choice are those that ensure the principles of justice—that is, those that maximize the opportunities for others to pursue their understanding of the good as well.

John Rawls (1921–2002), a modern American political philosopher, suggests that the just society is one that is based on principles of fairness. As articulated by Rawls there are two basic principles of fairness. The first principle of fairness is that "each person is to have an equal right to the most extensive basic liberty compatible with a similar liberty for others" (like freedom of speech, freedom to assemble, and freedom of beliefs).[17] The second principle of justice is that any inequalities in society be arranged to the benefit of the least advantaged and that positions of power be open to all under conditions of equality of opportunity.[18] Rawls's theory of justice is thus based on the idea that society should be a place in which individuals can openly pursue the life they wish under conditions in which they are free from restraint, and also equal to everyone else in society. Such a conception means that justice includes protection from threats (no giants gobbling us up in the night!) and also that we be allowed to make truly free choices about what to do with our lives.

It's important to notice that according to the principles of justice listed above, freedom and equality have a close relationship. It is not enough simply to have a freedom to do something; freedom also might mean having the resources to accomplish that thing. For example, we might have the freedom to eat what we choose, but until we actually have equal access to food, our choice to eat might not be a choice at all. For example, we might think it is unjust for Boggis, Bunce, and Bean to own so much that no one else can get a share and thus prevent Mr. Fox from eating and feeding his family. Does this mean that it would be just for Mr. Fox, who is otherwise on the brink of starvation, to have a legitimate claim to some of the surplus Boggis, Bunce, and Bean grow on their farms? In a just society, Rawls would argue, there must be a mechanism for redistributing resources to give everyone the same basic set of rights. Equality of opportunity is not just about what is required to protect people (or anthropomorphic foxes) from mistreatment, but also about what is required to help people have meaningful choices by providing for their basic needs.[19]

Rawls's notion of justice does not call for an end to inequality—only that where inequalities exist, they be to the benefit of those in society with less. Mr. Fox is not entitled to the exact same things as the farmers; nor is Charlie Bucket's starving family entitled to the same resources as the wealthy Salts. Rawls's theory of justice does, however, require that inequalities exist to promote the well-being of all in society. The farmer can have more, for example, to reward industriousness and promote the production of more food. But if we are serious about maximizing freedom, we must recognize that no person is truly free to make meaningful choices if they are destitute or concerned only for whether they can afford their next meal. As Amartya Sen describes it, poverty is thus a deprivation of basic capabilities, and not merely a description of low income.[20] Put simply, poverty means more than simply not having money. It means not having substantive choices to pursue a life of one's choosing, as a lack of access to resources like food, shelter, clothing, health care, education, and more means limiting freedom for those who live in poverty. It is obvious that Charlie Bucket has a lot less freedom to do as he wants, or to craft a life of his own choosing, than the children of means he sees every day and on television, and when Mr. and Mrs. Fox's children are starving they can think of nothing other than their hunger. These are descriptions of poverty that reveal how limiting it can be on anyone experiencing such an extreme state.

But why focus on the least advantaged? One can ask this not only of Rawls but also of Dahl. Many of Dahl's protagonists are children who come from backgrounds of poverty (or at least of simple means), are orphans, or suffer physical and emotional abuse. Among his other heroes are anthropomorphic bugs or animals that are usually looked down upon (or with fear—imagine falling into a room with human-sized spiders and centipedes!). These are not what are commonly thought of as heroic figures. Yet, by focusing on the least advantaged members in a society, Dahl causes us to truly reflect on how just and fair our rules are. We cannot evaluate fairness by asking how it is working out for the most privileged and advantaged individuals in society. We must look at those who lack the greatest advantages to see how fair an opportunity they have to define and pursue their life goals and dreams.

Rawls's theory of justice as fairness requires that we adopt a similar framework to Dahl's stories. Rawls understands that economic and other advantages within a society are inevitable, and so he does not try to impose a singular equality of outcome for all. Not only is this impractical, but it also may not actually be the best way to meet the diverse needs of a society. Instead, he evaluates the justness of inequality based on how it impacts the least advantaged members of society. Inequality is okay, he argues, so long as the least advantaged are better off than they would be in a situation in which there was more equality of outcome. For example, let's assume that chocolate is the most valuable resource in society (not a difficult assumption for many of us). If in one society the person with the most chocolate has ten Scrumdiddlyumptious Wonka Bars and the person with the least has one, there is an inequality of resource distribution. If in another society the person with the most chocolate has twenty Scrumdiddlyumptious Wonka Bars and the person with the least has two, there is also an inequality in terms of distribution. In the first society, there is an inequality of nine chocolate bars. In the second society, there is an inequality of eighteen. The inequality doubled between the two societies. However, according to Rawls, the principle of fairness would not examine the relative difference between folks within society, but the difference across the societies for the least advantaged. In this case, the second society is arguably more just than the first because the person with the least resources in that society is better off than the person with the least resources in the first. Applied to any policy choice, then, if we look to the policy that provides the most relative benefit for the least advantaged, that policy is the most just.

ADULTS (AND KIDS) ARE COMPLICATED CREATURES

Of course, not all of us share the same understanding of what it means to lead a good or fulfilling life, which is why we need to separate our notions of justice from our moral conceptions of what is good. If we all simply came to the same conclusion about what is best in life, and if we all shared the same beliefs and opinions, living among one another would involve less conflict. However, as previously discussed, that would also mean displacing our individual identity and authentic selves. Therefore, what is required from the rules that govern society is a commitment to establishing a playing field for all that allows for equal opportunity to pursue an authentic existence. The state must be protective of our rights to pursue the good life without, to the greatest extent possible, privileging one view over another. If I choose to make exotic candies and express myself through confectionary, or work in a factory twisting caps on toothpaste tubes, or use my immense princely wealth to build a grand castle out of nothing but chocolate, no moral judgments ought to be imposed by society that would ultimately restrict me from doing any (or perhaps all) of these things. The life that is meaningful to me may not be meaningful to you. The goal of our politics, then, is to protect our abilities to define what we believe to be the good life and to pursue it.

It's with those principles in mind that Rawls argues that we must separate notions of justice, which are public and universal, from our moral conceptions of the good, which are personal and subjective. As Rawls describes it, "it is not our aims that primarily reveal our nature, but rather the principles that we would acknowledge to govern the background conditions under which these aims are formed."[21] That is, we choose what is good for ourselves on a background set of conditions, and it is these conditions for which justice is primarily concerned. We will not all agree on principles of morality and what it means to live a good life, but we are able to agree on a set of conditions that make our pursuit of the good life possible. This means that a just society cannot contain systems of control coercing us to adopt moral codes that are not of our own choosing.

Dahl's work suggests a similar reflection on society. We ought to be allowed to be our authentic selves within the rules of society structured in a manner that maximizes our opportunities. We must not allow the powerful to monitor and enforce discipline on "deviant" behavior deemed immoral or unacceptable (Grandma Kranky, Boggis, Bunce, Bean, Aunts Sponge and Spiker, Zinnia and Harry Wormwood), or structural barriers that eliminate choice by denying access to opportunities (the poverty of the Buckets, the abuses exercised upon James Henry Trotter, the hunger of Mr. Fox). We must commit ourselves to creating a just society that unites us by allowing difference; bringing us together in our pluralistic quest for our own versions of the good life. The political philosopher Iris Marion Young (1949–2006) articulates this theme we find in Dahl's work by arguing that an inclusive society requires "explicitly acknowledging social differentiations and divisions and encouraging differently situated groups to give voice to their needs, interests, and perspectives on the society."[22]

ENTERING A WORLD OF PURE IMAGINATION

We learn not only from children's stories but also from children themselves. More important, if we think about the rules and pressures and intimidations they confront every day, ranging from social pressures forcing them to adopt to consumerist standards of self-worth to stifling their creativity and exploration by imposing identities, we might ask ourselves whether those mechanisms of control are designed to unlock a child's authentic inner core or to destroy it in the name of conformity. Are we empowering our children with our instructions and disciplinary methods, or are we trying to force them to become another vessel to merely accept and uncritically fall in line with the values and norms of society? Are we protecting children, who themselves are already so vulnerable and helping them to maximize their full potential? Or are we training them to be functional consumers who will go on to uphold the status quo and have children whom they, too, can mold and shape and force to conform? If we truly thought that what we were doing through the monitoring and disciplining of our children was not protecting them and ensuring their safety and development, but rather destroying their identities, wouldn't we agree that we are creating a "trogglehump" of a nightmarish world for them? And what of the ways that we also try to categorize and correct the behavior of adults who refuse to conform to our moral frameworks?

Beyond addressing the social rules and cultural forces that impose limits on the ability of children to explore their identities and to dream and create fully, Dahl's works challenge us to think about the world so many children grow up in—a world of poverty in which hunger, poor health, and a lack of other necessities consume them. It is not enough to merely say "you are free to go and be yourself"; as a society we must work to promote access to basic needs and work to positively promote options for all. In this respect, Dahl's works illustrate the importance of both negative freedom (freedom from intervention) and positive freedom (freedom to engage in an action) as it relates to identity. It is only when we are free from the control and forced imposition of others, and have access to the material resources that enable us to positively pursue a variety of options, that we are free to be who we truly want to be. Dahl's work reminds us that sometimes we need a "world of pure imagination" to shine a light on our own. And perhaps that is why, in the words of Willy Wonka, "a little nonsense now and then is relished by the wisest man."[23]

10

THE FANTASTICALLY JUST MR. FOX

Property and Distributive Justice According
to Foxes and Other Diggers

Jacob M. Held

Mr. Fox is a thief. He is a con man, a liar, and a parasite living off of the work of others. He steals for his survival and his family's survival, but he also steals hard cider for his pleasure. Mr. Fox is also fantastic, and he is our hero. Farmers Boggis, Bunce, and Bean are landowners. They are entrepreneurs, business owners who profit through their own hard work and ingenuity. They cultivate the land, raise chickens, ducks, turkeys, and geese, bring these items to market, and amass great wealth doing so. They are also greedy, gluttonous, and spiteful. They are the villains. In Roald Dahl's *Fantastic Mr. Fox*, the thief is the hero, and the businessmen are the villains. This simple inversion of traditional values demands that we question them, that we rethink things like the morality of theft as well as the right to own property and the justice of distributing, or redistributing, resources.

The lesson of *Fantastic Mr. Fox* seems simple enough. Mr. Fox must steal to feed his family, and he overcomes great obstacles, the loss of a tail, and the possibility of further mutilation or death to do so. He is a provider pushed to extremes who overcomes adversity through bravery and cunning to provide a living not merely for his family but for all the diggers. The farmers are disgusting, selfish, loathsome, hateful men who seek to kill Mr. Fox and his family as well as anything else that gets in their way. We know we are supposed to dislike the farmers. Dahl makes this clear through his descriptions of them. Boggis is enormously fat, a glutton who devours three chickens at every meal. Bunce is a potbellied dwarf who eats doughnuts stuffed with goose livers. And Bean is a drunk-ard.[1] If these descriptions weren't enough, the sentiment of the local children should be: "Boggis Bunce and Bean / One fat, one short, one lean. / These horrible crooks / So different in looks / were nonetheless equally mean."[2] So we know we are supposed to root for Mr. Fox and cheer when he gets one over on Boggis, Bunce, and Bean.

In terms of philosophical issues, obviously there are problems sur-rounding the morality of theft. And we could parse out whether, or rather when, it's okay to steal. In the case of Mr. Fox (for whom it is steal or starve), when he steals from those with so much, such greedy and glutton-ous creatures like Boggis, Bunce, and Bean, it seems easily justifiable. His theft causes the farmers little loss and spares his family the fate of starving to death. Clearly a greater evil is prevented through his minor infraction of taking a handful of chickens now and then. It would be easy enough to quickly throw together a chapter on the ethics of theft or ethics in extreme cases, the ethics of disasters. But to do so would ignore a more interesting topic. What is fascinating about *Fantastic Mr. Fox* isn't whether one can justify theft, but whether it is just to organize society in such a way that some are forced into such a state of deprivation, such as Mr. Fox and his fellow diggers, that drives them to extremes like theft. That is, is it just to organize a society so that a few—Boggis, Bunce, and Bean for example—own everything and thereby force the rest to beg, borrow, or steal merely to eke out a living? This issue is not about theft; it's about distributive justice, about how we organize the distribution of resources in society. If we look at Mr. Fox and the rest of his woodland friends, we see an interesting problem. Instead of asking whether the poor can justify stealing in extreme cases, we can instead ask how they became poor. How is society structured such that some can have so much and some so little? Should we rethink how we distribute property and wealth to make sure that we don't drive the poor, the Foxes, to a choice between starvation and criminality?

In order to investigate this issue we should begin by understanding the background conditions of Mr. Fox's world. First, it appears as though Boggis, Bunce, and Bean own all the land surrounding Mr. Fox so that he can't hunt or scavenge outside of what they own. Dahl's story seems to imply that the farmers own everything, so either you get it from the farmers or you get nothing at all. But the farmers seem to be honest men. They didn't steal their farms; they merely run agriculturally based businesses. So even if the local children want to call them "crooks," they own their land, farms, and wealth honestly. In fact, they are quite successful at running their businesses, which explains how they can own so much and employ so many. Regardless of their greedy, selfish, despicable dispositions and lack of personal hygiene, they do rightfully and legally own their property and the fruits of their labor. And Mr. Fox is a thief. He is taking what is not his; he is violating the property rights of the lawful owners when he steals chickens, geese, ducks, and hard cider. Thus, if we are going to exonerate Mr. Fox, it will have to be related to the fact that the structure of the world in which he finds himself is somehow unjust, thus legitimating his violation of the farmers' property rights. Although they own their farms legally, they are still in some way "crooks," and Mr. Fox is justified in stealing from them.

LIFE, LIBERTY, AND PROPERTY ... EVEN FOR FOXES!

Let's begin simply. What is property? Well, claiming something as your property is about claiming exclusive rights to it. That is, when you claim an object or piece of land as yours, you are claiming that you have exclusive right to its use; you're excluding others from it. This is simple enough. And if something is your property, then when someone uses it without your permission or takes possession of it against your will they have stolen it—they have violated your right to property, your right to its exclusive use. In this regard, Mr. Fox is a thief and a vandal without question. In this regard, Boggis, Bunce, and Bean own their farms, their chickens, geese, ducks, and cider, without question. So the farmers have the right to exclude others, like Mr. Fox, Badger, or Mole, from trespassing and taking what they please. But simply pointing out what property is, is a far cry from justifying it. We should ask not simply what property is, but also why property in this sense exists at all. Why should anyone have an exclusive right to an object or land? Where does this right originate from? Are there limits to ownership, to one person's right to exclude others from certain objects or parcels of land?

In the history of political thought arguably the most influential theory regarding property is that of John Locke (1632–1704). His theory continues to be influential, often serving as the starting place for any contemporary discussion on the nature of property, property rights, and distributive justice. Locke's theory of property begins with the individual person. He recognizes that self-ownership is the first and fundamental form of ownership: "Every man has a *property* in his own *person*: this no body has a right to but himself."[3] We each own our own bodies, our selves. And this ownership of our self is inalienable: we can't sell ourselves—we can't alienate or get rid of our property rights in our selves. We are always and forever our own property.

Likewise, since we own ourselves, we also own all of our capabilities, all of those things that stem directly from ourselves. So Locke's theory of self-ownership leads to a labor theory of property. Since I own myself, I also own all the products of myself. As a self-owner, I therefore own my labor power. So however I direct this power, however I use it to acquire objects in the world, or cultivate and alter the world, my labor power puts my own unique stamp on whatever it touches; I own things by virtue of having marked them out as mine. "He that is nourished by acorns he picked up under an oak, or the apples he gathered from the trees in the wood, has certainly appropriated them to himself. . . . I ask then, when did they begin to be his? When he digested? Or when he eat? Or when he boiled? . . . it is plain, if the first gathering made them not his, nothing else could. That *labour* put a distinction between them and common . . . and so they became his private right."[4] The same goes for land ownership. Although we can't pick or physically hold land the way we can acorns or apples, we can till it, mix our labor with it, and so distinguish it from the commons, thus making it ours. *"As much land* as a man tills, plants, improves, cultivates, and can use the product of, so much is his *property*."[5]

So when Bean claims a parcel of land as his and then cultivates it by planting apple trees, it becomes his. The trees are his. When he plucks ripe apples from the trees they are his. And when he turns them into mash, puts them in casks, and ferments them into hard cider, that cider is his. He claimed the land, cultivated it, grew the trees, harvested the apples, and processed the cider. In each of these activities he marked out these things as exclusively his insofar as he imbued them with his labor. Doing so distinguished them from objects found in nature. They are uniquely invested with his labor, his essence. Even when he employs others and they are the ones working the land, the product is still his by virtue of having formed a labor contract with his employees. He purchased their labor power for a wage, and so he owns the product of their labor. The same goes for Boggis and Bunce.

According to Locke, this is the only theory that seems to make sense. If one is going to have a moral right, a moral claim to property, then it has to stem from that individual and his labor power. This is the obvious stage at which a thing is marked out as distinct from what is held in common, and that stems directly from the one inalienable claim to property all men have—namely, self-ownership. If we are going to maintain that there is a right to property—that is, that there is a moral, natural basis to the claim of exclusive access or use to any particular thing—then the fact that I made it or cultivated it through my labor seems a reasonable account. Any other option smacks of arbitrariness. What else could be the justification for claiming ownership? Consider Bean's cider. If he can't claim that he owns it because he made it, what other type of claim could he make? Perhaps that it is in his possession. Well, when Mr. Fox steals it, it changes possession. Is it then rightfully Mr. Fox's? That would be an odd theory of property, a finders-keepers theory of ownership. Or perhaps it's just that he can retain ownership by force. Bean's cider is his because he has the power to claim it as his own. But then the most powerful thief would own everything. So Mr. Fox, who can circumvent all the farmers' security measures, does own everything. He has the power or cunning to take possession of it all and hide it underground. Or maybe property rights are merely conventional—a fabrication of the government, the result of arbitrary laws.

One of the values of property is that it is necessary for our survival and development. We need to be able to exclude others from our goods so that we have enough to eat and are secure in our homes. To allow convention or the government to dispense with property as it sees fit would be to put our livelihood in the hands of the government; it would actually be to put our entire welfare into the hands of the state. Thus, we'd be beholden to the government when it comes to claims regarding our property. No longer would it be ours by virtue of the labor we invested in it; instead, it would be granted to us by the government, which could rescind our rights as readily as it granted them. In effect, all people would be left to the caprice of the government, and this would circumvent the idea that we owned ourselves, our means to survival, and life—the necessary preconditions of liberty. If we are self-owners, if we have a right to liberty, the government can't rule absolutely over our lives in this way.

Governments are not forces of nature that exist in virtue of themselves. Rather, governments exist at the behest of the governed. They only exist so long as those who make them up, the people, decide they should exist, and they exist as a result of an implicit or hypothetical contract between all participants. Locke is a social contract theorist. He believes that governments get their power and are legitimated by the consent of the governed. We begin from a state of nature in which we are all on our own, striving for survival. But we quickly seek community with others for the benefits, safety, and security it confers on us. "The only way whereby any one divests himself of his natural liberty, and puts on the *bonds of civil society*, is by agreeing with other men to join and unite into a community for their comfortable, safe, and peaceable living one amongst another, in a secure enjoyment of their properties."[6] But we form these communities in a way that benefits us. "The great and chief end, therefore, of men's uniting into common-wealths, and putting themselves under government, *is the preservation of their property*. To which in the state of nature there are many things wanting."[7] We want to preserve our "lives, liberties, and estates,"[8] our property. But in a state of nature we are limited in our ability to be productive and secure our goods against others. We can't enforce and maintain our exclusive property rights in lawlessness, so we enter into a social contract, the formation of a government, to do so for us.

Consider if Boggis, Bunce, and Bean lived in a state of nature. Here they would all be competing for survival, but since there would be no government, there would be no publicly funded infrastructure, no police, no army, no legal system. For a while they might think this was ideal, as they could do as they wished without being hampered by governmental regulations. But eventually they would want to be able to guarantee the security of their goods, their chickens, geese, ducks, or cider, or they would have to resolve a dispute about borders and who owned what land. If Boggis were to claim that Bunce encroached on his land, or overextended his farm, to whom could he appeal? He could appeal to Bean, but what authority does Bean have to resolve this dispute? He could appeal to Bunce, but Bunce is the one whose land is in question. Could Bunce or Bean trust Boggis's judgment in this matter? After all, Boggis and Bunce have ulterior motives for promoting their own positions. This dispute would be irresolvable and most likely result in a show of force. All the theory in the world about who imbued what with whose labor wouldn't settle this dispute. Each person will seek their own favor, and at the end of the day force would win out unless there were an objective arbitrator who could enforce his or her final decision.

The state of nature devolves into a state of war, as Thomas Hobbes (1588–1679) so rightly noted.[9] A government, publicly formed and supported by the people, formed to ensure their welfare, rights, and liberties, is the best solution. So Boggis, Bunce, and Bean will enter into a contract to form a government that will promote their interests by protecting their rightful property claims. But property came first, and the government came after the fact to secure it. There was no need, no point to form a government, until there were interests like safety, security, and property, or "life, liberty, and estates," to be protected. So the idea that property is conventional and the product or invention of the government, for Locke, gets things backward. Property is the reason the government exists, and property exists as a moral right independently of the government. Property is a natural right we claim based on our labor, and the government is set up to protect our rightful property claims. But does this mean I can own whatever I want, and however much I want? Are there limits to ownership?

ENOUGH, AND AS GOOD . . . EVEN FOR FOXES!

When it comes to property, everybody needs some or at least the right to acquire a portion that affords them the ability to survive, to function as a free, self-determined being. And since originally all property belonged to no one in particular (or, rather, it belonged to all of us in common), there should be enough property to go around (or, rather, everyone should be able to exercise their equal right to accumulate property). At least, any distribution of actual property rights or claims to ownership shouldn't allow anyone to own so much as to deprive others of their right to acquire and utilize property. Locke states, "The same law of nature, that does . . . give us property, does also *bound* that property too."[10] Nobody should own so much that others have no chance to own property themselves. Now there are a lot of assumptions at work here. There are the assumptions that there is enough to go around, and that all people have equal access or opportunity to make use of this equally accessible property. But the basic idea is that given how fundamental land and property is, and given that we enter into a contract for our mutual benefit, property ownership should be regulated in a way that we as self-interested, rational people would think appropriate, so that everyone can acquire property and reap the benefits. No one should be left to starve because of someone else's greed, nor should anyone be forced to indenture themselves to another because there is no other way for them to make a living. With respect to property and land, you can take what you please, whatever you can invest with your own labor, with one simple limitation: you must leave "enough, and as good,"[11] for others beyond what you yourself can utilize.

Here is the problem that Boggis, Bunce, and Bean pose. At some point they were allowed to own too much land: they were allowed to own it all, and so exclude all others from the very means to survival. They ended up owning the wilderness entirely and turning it into private farms for their own profit. Although they have a right to property, property that is the result of their own labor and ingenuity, they don't have a right to force others into poverty, destitution, and ultimately death. This is where we find Mr. Fox. The farmers own so much that to eke out a living he must steal, as must the other woodland creatures. There simply isn't enough, nor as good, left in the wild given the encroachment of the private farms into formerly wild areas. The foxes, badgers, and others must then either starve or implement a solution (in this case, theft, a radical redistribution of resources). This condition is exacerbated once everyone is forced underground due to Boggis, Bunce, and Bean's desire to kill Mr. Fox.

The farmers seem to own too much; that is why they are "crooks." By exercising their right to own land and private property, they ended up acquiring all of it, thus denying others the right to as much and as good. Everyone else then must get their food from the farmers or starve; they must live according to their rules and regulations or risk death. They own the world around Mr. Fox and the other creatures and, insofar as they own the resources necessary for life, resources like food, they own life itself. They thus hold the lives of Mr. Fox and all the other diggers hostage, all under the claim of property rights. They have overextended their right to property to the point that it infringes on Mr. Fox and his family's right to life and liberty. So the farmers' right to property must be restricted.

What the relationship between the farmers and the diggers seems to indicate is that ownership itself is coercive—that is, owning something to the exclusion of others limits those others in how they can interact with the world. Ownership is exclusion, and exclusion from goods necessary to survive is a form of coercion, or violence, that needs to be justified in order for it to be anything other than brute force. The moral right to own property does not include the right to harm others or force them into destitution or subjugation. Property needs to be regulated.

THE FAR TOO RESPECTABLE MR. BADGER GETS A LESSON IN JUSTICE

Once driven underground, Mr. Fox devises a plan for raiding the store-houses from underneath. He burrows to each storehouse, taking what he wants without having to surface and risk being shot, yet again, by the farmers. On his last errand, as he is burrowing to Bean's secret cider cellar, Mr. Badger expresses doubts. He asks, "Doesn't this worry you just a tiny bit, Foxy? . . . All this . . . this *stealing*?" Mr. Fox responds, "You are far too respectable."[12] Fox makes his case that they are simply stealing enough to feed their families, and who wouldn't steal to do so? In addition, Boggis, Bunce, and Bean want to kill them, and all they want is a bit of food. At least they are not stooping to the level of the murderous farmers. Badger seems reassured, or at least contented enough to continue with the plan. After Fox's short demonstration of the morality of their actions, "Badger laid his head on one side and smiled at Mr. Fox. 'Foxy,' he said, 'I love you.'"[13] So why is Badger "far too respectable," and what exactly is Mr. Fox arguing for here? Is it the morality of theft in extreme cases, or the injustice of ownership on the scale of the farmers?

Mr. Badger's doubts, arguably, stem from the fact that he accepts the status quo; he accepts that the farmers own their land and goods legally and so their rights must be respected. Their property claims, their rights, are predicated on the idea that it's their land they work, and their goods they amass, so they deserve exclusive rights to them; thus, when Mr. Fox and his comrades steal, they are in the wrong because they are unduly violating the farmers' legitimate claims to private property. To put it another way, Mr. Badger accepts the libertarian ideology that you may own whatever you like, so long as you acquired it justly, without regard for the effects such ownership has or the reciprocal claims of others to an equal right to property and survival. This is why Badger is "too respectable." He upholds this system unthinkingly, uncritically, even as the system itself drives his family underground and to the brink of starvation. As he and the other diggers die because of the farmers' property rights, he still maintains their right to drive the diggers to starvation, because he accepts without question and without doubt the right to own property. Mr. Fox, on the other hand, has doubts. It's not about stealing for Mr. Fox. Instead, it's about who has a right to own what and whose rights are infringed upon by claims to ownership. For Mr. Fox, property is not a good in and of itself; instead, it is a right that must be respected, since it promotes our good and our freedom. But when one man's, or three farmers', right to own land begins to encroach on everyone else's right to life and liberty, then property becomes coercive—it becomes violence, and something must be done about it.

If we recognize that everyone has an equal right to life and liberty—and, with Locke, property—and we recognize that there is only so much stuff to go around, so many apple trees, so much land, and so forth, then we have to acknowledge that we are faced with a problem. How do we hand out or distribute these limited resources to all the people who have an equal right to them, all those people who have an equal right to life and liberty? Clearly we can't just do it first come, first served. In that case, the first person to show up might claim all the land for himself or all the trees. This is why, as noted above, Locke says we need to leave enough and as good for others. This is a theory of distributive justice. Goods and land are distributed according to the labor theory of property up to the point at which your acquisition prevents others from acquiring property or land for themselves. And since we're all morally equal, you're not allowed to restrict my rights because of your greed. It's all about equal rights and maximal freedom; it's a liberal political philosophy that emphasizes individual liberty while recognizing limits on each individual consistent with other people exercising their equal, individual liberties. Just as I can't have a right to own you, so I can't have a right to own so much stuff that you're forced to work for me or become my servant.

But this is exactly what the farmers have done. They have a monopoly on the land, on food, and so they have a monopoly on life. Either you buy from them or you starve. Or steal! There is no freedom for Mr. Fox, no liberty for the woodland creatures. Boggis, Bunce, and Bean have exercised their rights to the point that they've effectively denied the same rights to everyone else. Locke's theory is quite clear on this point. You have a right to own stuff, but not too much, because ownership is a form of coercion, a form of limiting the world for others. So how should Boggis, Bunce, and Bean be regulated? What can Mr. Fox and the others reasonably and justifiably claim as their own against the property claims of the farmers?

BEYOND "RESPECTABLE": A DIGGER'S THEORY OF DISTRIBUTIVE JUSTICE

Perhaps the most influential contemporary theory of distributive justice is that of John Rawls (1921–2002). Rawls is famous for having authored a theory of justice as fairness, a distributive justice paradigm that emphasized individual liberty while recognizing the need to redistribute goods to assure liberty for all participants by guaranteeing a minimal level of primary (necessary for proper function) goods and equal opportunity for all. Rawls began with a thought experiment, the idea that we bargain for principles of justice in an original position. Imagine you were behind a veil of ignorance—you didn't know anything about yourself, factors such as your race, gender, ability level, or any other non-moral factor, those things that you don't control about yourself but that impact your chances of success in the real world. But imagine you were still self-interested—that is, concerned primarily with your own well-being, and rational. How would you want to distribute the limited resources of society? It's like cutting a cake. Imagine you have to cut it, but you don't know whether you'll get to pick a piece of cut cake first or last. A rational person, one who doesn't gamble recklessly, would cut the cake fairly to guarantee he got a decent-sized piece no matter when his turn to pick came. In the case of cake, that'd probably be equally sized pieces. But in distributing goods in a political system, pure equality probably won't be best. We want to incentivize hard work, so workers keep working hard and producing awesome hard cider and cheap, meaty chickens. (Ideally, these would also be produced morally—that is, in an environmentally sustainable fashion.) But we would make sure that however we distribute goods, however we "cut the cake," everyone would get enough to do well. We wouldn't cut the cake so no one got a piece, because we might be that person. Nor would we cut it so that the least well-off starved to death, since that might be us as well. Our self-interest, paired with our rationality and ignorance, would motivate us to select a distributive paradigm in which even the least well-off did fairly well. So in the original position, "[the participants] know that in general they must try to protect their liberties, widen their opportunities, and enlarge their means for promoting their aims whatever these are . . . they do this by trying to win for themselves the highest index of primary social goods . . . the parties do not seek to confer benefits or to impose injuries on one another; they are not moved by affection or rancor . . . they are not envious or vain."[14]

We all seek what would be best to promote our ends, whatever they might be, regardless of where we might find ourselves in society. All positions in society are thus advocated for in a delicate balancing act of distributing resources to maximize liberty, choice, and opportunity. This is what the farmers never consider. They claim a right to their farms and all their goods without recognizing that the other animals also have an equal right to live. The distributive paradigm the farmers impose on everyone else would not pass Rawls's original position test; it favors their position simply as theirs. "The reason the original position must abstract from and not be affected by the contingencies of the social world is that the conditions for a fair agreement . . . must eliminate the bargaining advantages that inevitably arise within the background institutions of any society from cumulative social, historical, and natural tendencies."[15] The farmers promote their advantage out of pure egoism, without consideration of where that advantage arose from or its impact on others. They never consider whether it's fair. The way property and land is distributed by the farmers is a problem not only because it wouldn't be chosen by rational, self-interested participants and is instead merely about promoting their own self-interests above and even against the interests of others, but also because it outright deprives everyone else of equal rights and equal opportunity. As Rawls states, "The fact that we occupy a particular social position is not a good reason for us to propose, or to expect others to accept, a conception of justice that favors those in this position."[16]

Imagine if we put the farmers behind the veil of ignorance in the original position. Boggis would not accept being in Mr. Fox's position. He would not accept being forced into poverty by greedy landowners. So he can't claim that the current distribution is fair. If we asked him to consider a distribution in which some must steal to stave off starvation, and he knew he might be in this position, he couldn't reasonably support such a distribution. If he, as a self-interested and rational individual, wouldn't accept a world in which he was the fox, then he has to admit that this paradigm doesn't treat all participants fairly. Rather, it unfairly privileges the farmers over the others.

But beyond this problem we can see that this very idea points out that property itself may need a further justification since it is the root of the problem. Maybe, given that property is coercive, we need to justify the very right to property, the right to coerce others and shape their world through the process of property and land acquisition. Contemporary political philosopher Jeffrey Reiman makes this case.

Reiman points out that private property leads to structural coercion. That is, the process of ownership results in a situation in which some have too much and others not enough, such that those without, through no fault of their own, are forced to work for others and effectively have their liberty unduly limited. This fact is obscured by the ideology of private property, a set of beliefs regarding property that masks its coercive nature. "Libertarian defenses of capitalism characteristically fall prey to this ideology. Seeing no special power in great property-holdings, they think that all that is necessary for justice is that transactions be free of violence or fraud."[17] But all transactions occur within a system that privileges some and disadvantages others, in which great property-holdings do lead to destitute poverty, thus driving foxes to extremes. This ideology seeks to rationalize poverty with reference to laziness. And it justifies unfettered ownership as if it resulted from effort alone and was necessary to motivate innovation, neither of which is true. But Reiman points out that "people come to take the institutions in which they grow up as natural, structural force tends to be invisible . . . libertarians . . . who defend capitalism as a purely free system fail to see the force built into the structure of property ownership."[18]

The force of ownership is seen in the case of Mr. Fox and his friends. Owning all the land, owning food production itself, makes all others beholden to the landowner, to the producer. The farmers own everything at the expense of the freedom and well-being of all the other occupants of the land. This is why Badger is "far too respectable." He buys into this ideology. He accepts the right of the farmers to own everything even in the face of his own starvation because he buys into the idea that this type of "free" market is natural. But Fox sees through this illusion. He sees their ownership for what it is: force, violence. In arguing with Badger, he claims, "Boggis and Bunce and Bean are out to *kill* us . . . but *we're* not going to stoop to *their* level. We don't want to kill *them*. . . . We shall simply take a little food here and there to keep us and our families alive. . . . We down here are decent peace-loving people."[19] The farmers want to kill the animals because the animals' thefts violated their property claims. They have a right to defend their property and their farms. The farmers thus want the right to either force the diggers into poverty and starvation or murder them when they steal out of desperation. They are crooks, morally speaking, even if the legal system backs them up under a particular system of private property. So Mr. Fox questions the system itself, finds it to be flawed, and institutes a radical redistributive paradigm. Why shouldn't they have enough to eat? Why should others through claims to land be able to starve whole populations? Boggis, Bunce, and Bean are horrible crooks. Fox and his comrades are peace-loving folk. Once we (or Mr. Fox, in this case) unmask this ideology and see that property is coercive, we recognize that it needs to be justified. If we take liberty seriously, then we should take its limitation seriously, and property limits liberty. So these limitations need to be justified in some way and not merely with reference to a natural right to property.

Unlike John Locke, Reiman begins from a natural right to liberty, not property. This right leads to a theory of justice, and property has to be justified within this broader theory. Liberty is essential, and property is merely a means to it. "Private property starts by limiting the liberty of nonowners. That is what makes it necessary for private property to be consented to in order to be moral . . . that larger right to property needs to be consented to for the same reason that the authority of the state over its subjects needs to be consented to."[20] If we take individual liberty seriously, then those who wield significant power over us need to be answerable to us, and that includes not simply political power like the government, but also the power of property owners who own food production, land, and all the other resources we require in order to live our lives. Mr. Fox knows the score. Boggis, Bunce, and Bean—by virtue of owning everything—limit his family's ability to live. When he steals as a necessary response to the coercive relationship the farmers impose on him and the other diggers, the farmers seem justified in hunting and attempting to kill him because of the ideology that privileges private property above all else. But this ideology doesn't recognize that their ownership drives the foxes to desperation; instead, it sees them as petty thieves and parasites, not victims of gluttonous farmers infringing on Mr. Fox and the diggers' equal right to liberty.

What this focus on liberty suggests is that there is no natural right to property as Locke suggested. Instead, given that property is coercive, that it limits our natural right to liberty, any property relationship needs to be justified under an overarching theory of justice. Such a theory might be reminiscent of Rawls's, in which one might ask about how to limit property to maximize the benefits for even the least well-off under any distributive paradigm. Regardless of the particulars, property should be seen for what it is: a potentially liberty-threatening institution that needs to be regulated in a way to maximize the freedom of all. Property isn't a good in itself; in fact, it's a threat to liberty if left unchecked. In this regard, Mr. Fox's solution seems eminently reasonable. He and the rest of the diggers create a system of tunnels through which they can forage from the farmers' storehouses without risk of detection or death. They steal, but they don't take so much that the farmers will notice.

So let's consider the original position and ask about this distributive framework. The farmers are still wealthy and successful; they won't even notice that they are missing anything. But the diggers are able to live contented lives. Anyone would be happy in either position being afforded the liberty to live their lives with the least well-off, the diggers, still being afforded a desirable form of life. From this perspective, Mr. Fox's underground village is preferable to the farmers' libertarian dystopia. It is just and fair and seems to be desirable from any position within society, or at least more desirable than the alternative.

AS FAR AS I KNOW, WE'RE STILL WAITING

Mr. Fox's predicament raises many more issues than simply whether it's okay to steal in extreme circumstances. The heart of the matter isn't about theft, but rather the conditions of the basic structures of society, how we choose to distribute property and how this very structure may be unjust if it forces others into poverty and deprives them of basic liberties and equal opportunity, conditions we wouldn't accept for ourselves as rational, self-interested people. Mr. Fox has no real option. In this respect many of us are in a similar position. No, we often don't resort to theft. Most of us are law abiding. But our lives are driven by necessity. We can't buy land and become self-sufficient. Most land is owned or priced beyond the reach of the average person. In addition, we can't all run our own businesses or be independently wealthy. At the end of the day most of us have to get jobs. We have to sell the greater portion of our lives, our energy, and our freedom to another person for a paycheck, so that we might have enough money to pay our bills and perhaps buy a few toys along the way. But ultimately we will spend our lives working for others, doing as we are told for enough money to survive, while those who own our jobs—who own the means to our survival, our health care, our retirement, who own us—are able to do more and are more effectively free because we do their work for them.

If this sounds like servitude, that's because it is. Private property is a coercive relationship, perhaps more so than governmental institutions and regulations. In this regard, it should be accountable to popular sovereignty, just as much as the state is. Now we may have the freedom to quit our job, just as Mr. Fox had the freedom to starve rather than steal, but that's only freedom from a delusional point of view. You'll still need another job, which will look very much like the one you just quit. You still need the benefits a job provides. You need to work, and that means you need to work for someone. At the root there is a real problem about why we let so few own so much without any accountability. But until some fantastic Mr. Fox offers us our own little underground village, we'll continue to risk our encounters with the farmers and hope that we don't lose our tails.

11

WILLY WONKA AND THE IMPERIAL CHOCOLATE FACTORY

Ron Novy

Hershey pledges to end child slave labor in its cocoa production by 2020[1]

But I want an Oompa-Loompa![2]

Since its 1964 publication and into the present, Roald Dahl's *Charlie and the Chocolate Factory* has contained—and been part of—a secret history of race, slavery, colonialism, and consumerism. This history is present in the changing depictions of the Oompa-Loompa nation through two written versions, numerous illustrators, and two feature films: from 1964's abused, half-naked African pygmies to 1971's ominous, singing orange dwarves, to 1973's long-haired, little, white hippies and 2005's industrial army of indistinguishable nonwhite workers. In their story we encounter race and colonialism, slavery and delicate chocolates. The contrast of Wonka's "benevolent enslavement" of happy and grateful Oompa-Loompas against the thousands of workers he let go one afternoon with no severance and no pension also speaks to our ambivalent attitudes toward capitalism.

Through a survey of past iterations of *Charlie and the Chocolate Factory*, both book and film versions, it is possible to garner an appreciation for our changing sensibilities regarding race, class, and our colonial past. What we notice is that underlying a seemingly innocent and whimsical children's tale are assumptions about race and Western privilege, assumptions that have historically lead to the decimation of indigenous populations and that we swallow unthinkingly, because even racism and colonialism go down easy with a little help from the Candyman.

Spoiler alert: Willy Wonka, Charlie Bucket, and possibly Roald Dahl himself are not very nice guys. In 1973, children's writer and literary critic Eleanor Cameron already had declared *Charlie and the Chocolate Factory* to be "one of the most tasteless books ever written for children."[3] And, by the way, that bitter aftertaste accompanying your Kit Kat bar is the taste of slave labor.

SLAVERY: COVER IT IN CHOCOLATE AND ADD AN OOMPA-LOOMPA OR TWO

In the original 1964 version of *Charlie and the Chocolate Factory*, Roald Dahl presents the three thousand Oompa-Loompas as African pygmies whom Willy Wonka lured from their ancestral homeland to work in his factory. As Wonka describes them, "Pygmies they are! Imported direct from Africa! They belong to a tribe of tiny miniature pygmies known as the Oompa-Loompas. I discovered them myself.[4] I brought them over from Africa myself—the whole tribe of them, three thousand in all. I found them in the very deepest and darkest part of the African jungle where no white man has ever been before."[5]

When Wonka's guests first spot the Oompa-Loompas watching from the far side of the chocolate waterfall, Charlie exclaims, "Their skin is almost black! . . . You know what I think, Grandpa? I think Mr. Wonka has made them himself—out of chocolate! . . . Are they *really* made of chocolate, Mr. Wonka?"[6] And in the illustrations created by Joseph Schindelman, Oompa-Loompas were drawn to resemble minstrel show versions of Farina and Buckwheat from the *Our Gang* serials.

The first major adjustments to Dahl's novel came with the Paramount Pictures 1971 film *Willy Wonka and the Chocolate Factory*, starring Gene Wilder in the title role. Here the film's creators—likely motivated by some combination of racial sensitivity and an anticipated negative effect on ticket sales—found it necessary to *not* portray Oompa-Loompas as described in Dahl's book. They were no longer African pygmies, but rather little orange people with white eyebrows and green hair from the unspecified Loompaland.

In 1973, Dahl revised *Charlie and the Chocolate Factory* to remove and rewrite the racially problematic Oompa-Loompa material. Their description and visual representation (again by Schindelman) was of slightly unkempt long-haired white hippies, now officially hailing from Loompaland. As Dahl explains, "I created a group of little fantasy creatures. . . . I saw them as charming creatures, whereas the white kids in the books were . . . most unpleasant. It didn't occur to me that my depiction of the Oompa-Loompas was racist, but it did occur to the NAACP and others. . . . After listening to the criticisms, I found myself sympathizing with them, which is why I revised the book."[7] New Oompa-Loompas required that Charlie's reaction to their first encounter be retconned[8] as well: "Look at their funny long hair! . . . But they can't be *real* people."[9]

If you are looking at a copy of *Charlie and the Chocolate Factory* published since 1998, it is likely you found one illustrated by Quentin Blake. Blake starting with Dahl's new Oompa-Loompas imagines them as somewhat whimsical and visually dynamic, an effect gained by using a limited number of strong lines in contrast to Schindelman's style of repeatedly applied thin irregular scratches. With Blake's work, the book now has a long-lasting visual brand it previously lacked.[10]

The most recent iteration of Oompa-Loompas is found in the 2005 Warner Brothers film starring Johnny Depp as Wonka. There is much worth discussing in director Tim Burton's return to much of the original novel. Burton makes explicit the story's colonial undertones and encourages the audience to consider the alienation of the modern industrial worker. Burton's Oompa-Loompas share a single brown face,[11] capturing both the interchangeability of workers and the suppression of individual identity demanded by efficient production.

When Oompa-Loompas ceased to be African pygmies and become long-haired, tiny Caucasians from Loompaland, this presumably erased the original story's implication that a person of Northern European descent had enslaved a whole nation of people of African descent and that these dark-skinned people happily embraced their newfound enslavement. But, new artwork aside, it isn't all that farfetched to conclude nonetheless that the Oompa-Loompas are Africans. They remain a 'tribe" rescued from "a terrible country [of] thick jungles infested by the most dangerous beasts in the entire world—hornswogglers and snozzwanglers and those terrible wicked whangdoodles."[12]

There is no subtlety to the racial dynamics of Dahl's unrevised story. There is a white messiah to lead the miserable, hungry savages out of the terrible fate from which they cannot or will not free themselves. Someone so generous as

> To wait in heavy harness
> On fluttered folk and wild—
> Your new-caught sullen peoples,
> Half devil and half child. [13]

Wonka was willing to transport a whole African nation from its dark jungle of deadly animals and endless meals of foul-tasting caterpillars in order to make a fresh start—working and living in his lovely factory. A magical place where every Oompa-Loompa can have her wages paid in delicious cacao beans, and where predators are kept away by high walls and locked gates. Quite a deal indeed!

Even if the shift from 1964 to 1973 was an effort to make race invisible, it left the colonial ideology intact. Wonka's workers receive room, board, and cacao—the desire for which is described more like a drug addiction than merely an Oompa-Loompan cultural or aesthetic preference. Workers, by the way, who had been crated and shipped to the factory illegally and who by simply leaving the factory will die (at least in the winter months) or face kidnapping and extended interrogation by WonkaCorp©'s more cut-throat confectionary competitors.

And let's not forget the description of Oompa-Loompas that Wonka offers his guests: "They are wonderful workers. They all speak English now. They love dancing and music. They are always making up songs. I expect you will hear a great deal of singing today from time to time. I must warn you, though, that they are rather mischievous. They like jokes. They still wear the same kind of clothes they wore in the jungle. They insist on that." [14]

This description raises a number of questions. Foremost, why is it noteworthy that the Oompa-Loompas now speak Wonka's native language? After all, we know Wonka spoke with the tribe's chief in Oompa-Loompan when he "discovered" them as he traipsed through the jungle. Given their isolation and the fact that Wonka is supposed to be the first white man they had ever seen, it is unlikely anyone in the tribe spoke English. So this situation required Wonka to speak in the language of the three thousand—that is, all three thousand and one were able to communicate in one language. (Just how Wonka came to speak Oompa-Loompan will be left a mystery.)

While Wonka was thinking up this whole Golden Ticket advertising campaign, it was still the case that all three thousand and one people in the factory were able to communicate with one another in a single language. Now that shared language is English, and the three thousand have come to use the language of the one. I have little doubt that continuing adult education among the Oompa-Loompas is surely of some value; nonetheless, the tribe turning to English was in practical terms a waste of time and energy—they remain in the factory, never interacting with the townsfolk outside. To be made to attend to such a difficult, unnecessary, and unreasonable task is to be reminded that another has power over you and can exercise it any time.

Yet, not to get too hung up on depictions of race alone in *Charlie and the Chocolate Factory* and its various film incarnations, one must also consider the economic system underlying these depictions, colonial capitalism, and its effect on the whole community. Consider the Buckets.

SECRET (CHEAP, ILLEGAL, MIGRANT) WORKERS

Charlie's family is an interesting one, and one that might be unfamiliar to people living in an era in which older adults are warehoused in long-term "care" facilities and ignored. His mother, father, and biological grandparents all live together, and in the book his father is the sole breadwinner working at the local toothpaste factory. When he loses his job, things get hard. Really hard.

In the most recent film version, part of the backstory is that Grandpa Joe used to work for the chocolate factory, until Willy Wonka closed it. In the books, this wasn't part of the story, but the factory closure and subsequent unemployment do bear discussing. Here we have a narrative in which the factory, a major employer in the community, is closed. No matter which narrative you are going on, and regardless of whether Grandpa Joe was personally affected, people suffered as a result, seeking work desperately wherever they could. Wonka, after closing his factory and laying off hundreds, maybe even thousands, of local employees, a move that would surely throw a local community into economic turmoil and facilitate a depression, imports slave labor. No one thinks this is odd?

Isn't it curious that the Oompa-Loompas are a topic of fascination and curiosity as opposed to, well, misplaced anger?

It's odd to me that Dahl could so clearly pinpoint what happens when factories close and people struggle for work while making the architect of that closure the hero, instead of the villain. Oh, sure, he tries to villainize the other chocolate manufacturers who spied on Willy Wonka, but ultimately Wonka is the one who made the choice to close his factory. To deny jobs to the community. To import laborers from somewhere else and keep them as slaves.

Recall the scene in which Dahl describes the factory reopening and everyone rushing back for their jobs only to find the gates closed. He writes matter-of-factly about how people look up and see the Oompa-Loompas silhouetted in the windows, but he doesn't even suggest that the workers have any right to be upset. It's something that we see playing out a lot now, with class tensions between different groups of workers in the midst of factory closures and deprivation, with employers acting like bringing in outside labor because it's cheaper just "needs" to happen. It's worth noting how Dahl's indictment of class issues fell so woefully short here. How instead of challenging narratives about "outsiders" or questioning the use of slave labor, he used them as an innocuous backdrop to a children's story.

Now I know what some of you are saying: "It's just a children's story, it's harmless fun." Or perhaps you recognize the issues but want to retort, "But those were different times; people didn't think about things like that." The same trope people use to excuse President Andrew Jackson's forced relocation and subsequent decimation (that is, genocide) of American Indians. But don't tell me it was "just the times." *Charlie and the Chocolate Factory* was published in 1964. The civil rights movement was a thing. Anticolonialism was a thing. The depiction of Oompa-Loompas as ignorant, helpless Africans who need and are thankful to receive salvation from the white man is simply racism. There were great books being written about racial issues in 1964 (and even before!). There was great thinking on race. There was criticism of issues like slavery and human trafficking.

In the book we also encounter Veruca Salt, the pampered rich girl, referring to Oompa-Loompas as collectible objects or pets. "*But I want an Oompa-Loompa!*" screamed Veruca. "All *right*, Veruca, all *right*. But I can't get it for you this second. Please be patient. I'll see you have one before the day is out."[15] Here, Veruca is exercising her white privilege, her ability to demand everything, even ownership over another human being, and to expect that demand to be met. Veruca, like Wonka, makes the Other (in this case Africans) into objects of trade. From the abused, half-naked African pygmy slaves of the original book to their current incarnations, these people are commodities to be traded in. But evidently people think that the Oompa-Loompas are so integral to the story exactly as they are that it's okay to keep repeating the trope.

Dahl's portrait of the Oompa-Loompas includes the centuries-old Western notion of indigenous populations as exotic, simple, and miserable. They are portrayed as unable to survive without the white Western world's helping hand. Willy Wonka lulls his audience into quietly accepting this familiar idea. In the process, Wonka becomes exalted as a white messiah to be revered and worshiped by the (literally) lesser brown people for having led them out of darkness and into enlightenment and happiness. Throughout history, this false sense of altruism has closely accompanied racism.

In 2005, Warner Brothers released another version of the feature film, this time directed by Tim Burton and starring Johnny Depp. The new adaptation brings back the racism and colonialism that the 1971 film and the 1973 revised book attempted to downplay. In this most recent incarnation, we follow Willy Wonka, sporting the classic attire of the colonial explorer, complete with safari helmet, as he travels on screen to a distant tropical jungle called "Loompaland." He is, we are told, in search of "exotic" flavors for a new line of sweets. While depicted as silly and adventurous, the right of the Western entrepreneur to take whatever "flavor," plant or animal, he desires from developing countries is never questioned. It is just the kind of theft Western pharmaceuticals and agro-corporations have been engaged in throughout the developing world for centuries. The film does not mention whether Wonka claims intellectual property rights over the "flavors" he finds there, as is the case with his modern contemporaries.

During this colonial montage, Wonka encounters a jungle village built in the trees that the Oompa-Loompas inhabit. This time, however, they are portrayed as a primitive, miniature, brown-colored, indigenous people of nonspecific ethnic origin. They sport feather headdresses, tribal-style jewelry, and grass skirts while dining on visibly "disgusting" green caterpillars and worshiping the rare cacao bean. They are depicted as simple, whimsical, and of course miserable in their native home. Wonka "generously" rescues the Oompa-Loompas by offering them the opportunity to work and live in his Western factory. Later they are shown "happily" imprisoned inside Wonka's factory, which they conveniently cannot leave because they will be subject to chilly weather and die. The Oompa-Loompas also "willingly" allow themselves to be experimented on, much like laboratory animals, by Wonka as he tests his new, and sometimes dangerous, candy concoctions. Clearly, Wonka has not taken the time to explain the ins and outs of unionizing or worker health compensation to his imprisoned work force.

The Oompa-Loompas have no spoken language of their own and must resort to mime and gesture to communicate. However, they have learned to sing in English while they dance for the entertainment of Wonka and his all-white and full-sized guests. This happens in the 1971 film version, although in the 2005 version the songs are accompanied by the laughable sexual gyrations of Oompa-Loompas, encouraging the audience to laugh along at the supposed sexuality of the mini-male of color. This unfortunately follows a long and sad historical tradition of emasculating men of color for the enjoyment of white audiences.

Moreover, the Oompa-Loompas all look exactly alike, as they are played by one actor using composite visual effects. This is a new invention by the current film's creators. The visual effect is ironic, as it displays the problems at the very core of global labor issues: white populations perceive individuals of nonwhite populations as identical, lacking individual dignity. In this view, factory and sweatshop workers are ascribed no individual worth outside of the product they produce at low pay and in poor working conditions, unable to organize, form unions, and improve conditions.

Many will no doubt respond to this critique disparagingly. They will say that the movie is just that, a movie. They will state that it has no social connection to or cultural implications about the present Western mindset. However, it is important to consider that Roald Dahl himself eventually made revisions to his story to meet the concerns that accompanied the changing social ethics in 1973. The fact that, in 2005, Tim Burton chose to revert to the original description of the Oompa-Loompas as primitive "pygmies" is troubling. Burton has said in interviews that one of the things that attracts him to Dahl's work is the "politically incorrect" subject matter. Audiences all over the country seem to feel the same attraction.

ENSLAVED AND IMPRISONED

In *Charlie and the Great Glass Elevator* (1973), there is an illustration of Wonka and the Bucket clan preparing to step out of the elevator and into Loompaland, the ancestral home of his factory's laborers. There are Oompa-Loompas there to enthusiastically greet their arrival. Willy's earlier claim that he had brought all three thousand members of the tribe to his factory[16] was a rainbow-sparkled, Candyman lie, or maybe Wonka is attempting to repopulate Loompaland with obedient workers willing to despoil that place in order to build a WonkaCorp© plantation to provide cacao to his factory at cost.

In this picture, the Oompa-Loompas—arms raised in greeting—capture the bind in which colonized peoples find themselves living. While the colony's economy and environment has been converted to the production of export items (be they West African cacao beans or cheaply manufactured Bangladeshi apparel), the colony's native population is effectively enslaved in this process; yet they are nonetheless happy to see and are loyal to Willy Wonka. After all, it is WonkaCorp© that has supplied the Oompa-Loompas with whatever it is that they now have. The Oompa-Loompas understand the brutal logic of private ownership. Be it land or a Whipple-Scrumptious Fudgemallow Delight, ownership is the right to refuse use of a thing to another.[17]

While varying in the particulars, the relation of the colonizer to the colonized—that is, of the metropole to periphery—traditionally had been characterized by a near-total, one-way flow of command and control from the center to its distinct and separate territories. These territories in turn provide resources to the colonial power, an arrangement born of and continuing in the threat of violence from the metropole.[18] In their 1953 article "The Imperialism of Free Trade," authors John Gallagher and Robert Robinson argue that imperial expansion since the 1880s has taken a less formal arrangement via free trade principles that favor the developed metropole.[19]

Consider the Oompa-Loompas. These workers, crated up in their homeland and deposited in an alien culture, with no interaction with the world beyond the factory, remain imprisoned inside Wonka's workhouse, the value of their work being exploited by WonkaCorp© to turn out more and more delicious chocolates for the global consumer marketplace.

Cartelization of the candy-making industry and advancing industrial technology will force all countries to modernize in order to keep pace with market saturation. The land of the Oompa-Loompas has to switch from a preindustrial economy to a modern factory system in order to remain viable in today's marketplace. Such restructuring will lead to the wholesale seizure of inefficiently used land, which will make all of the "predatory species" like hornswogglers, snozzwanglers, and wicked whangdoodles prime fodder for extinction.

You may say, "Well, Wonka's not in charge anymore. He gave the factory to Charlie. Charlie is a sweet boy; he'll be better." No, Charlie won't be good to the Oompa-Loompas, because the capitalist bureaucracy already in place runs of its own accord. The problem is systemic. Regardless of who's in charge or how benevolent they might be, the harsh reality is that the global marketplace requires more exacting efficiency and product saturation than ever before. By now Charlie's probably got a website up and has downsized half the labor force. Now more and more Oompa-Loompas will join the Surplus Army of the Unemployed unless they can find jobs in another line of work, like dwarf tossing. I mean, what kind of work can undocumented, low-skilled, miniature laborers find in a depressed economy? And is that the fate you wish to consign them to? Dwarf tossing?

Dahl might have changed the color of the Oompa-Loompas' skin, but the explicit colonial ideas and discourse embedded in his expression is quite shocking. Dahl took a real nation of people and degraded them to "creatures." Even more interesting, to Dahl these creatures are "fantasy"; they don't operate in a real, civilized society. They don't work for money, but for food, in the same way an animal will perform for its favorite treat. Dahl instantly creates the binary opposition of "them" and "white." For him, "they" are so far removed from his white world that he can "create" them to be whatever he wants.

Even if Dahl meant the story to be a fantasy fairy tale free from the restrictions of plausibility and real life, he could not escape the ideologies embedded in his ideas. Wonka uses people from a distant land to work and build his Candyland empire, people thankful for his generosity in giving them a warm and safe place to live free from the deadly predators in their miserable jungle. Interestingly, and also serving to reinforce this notion, to his white counterparts Wonka is viewed as a hero, a pioneer in the field of candy making.

WHITE PRIVILEGE AND COLONIALISM

Recall Gene Wilder in the 1971 film serenading the children and their guardians as they enter the factory with the syrupy "Pure Imagination":

> If you want to view paradise,
> Simply look around and view it,
> Anything you want to, do it,
> Want to change the world, there's nothing to it.

The guests, from all appearances, are from Northern European stock, and—excepting Charlie and his grandfather—seem to be either middle-class or quite well-off. The song about the glorious possibilities awaiting them in the factory is also a reminder that anything you may ever want is there for the having: no asking and no being denied. White privilege goes still further—it is a birthright not merely that any door can be opened, any lunch counter sat at, and any desire might be fulfilled but also that one can be justifiably outraged if fulfillment is denied.

Wonka belongs to an imperial world, defined by capitalism. The Oompa-Loompas serve the research interests of their owner/handler, becoming happily expendable at any time for the greater good of all. Interestingly Wilder's Wonka asks, "Who can I trust to run the factory when I leave and take care of the Oompa-Loompas for me?" The factory only successfully operates because of the work of the Oompa-Loompas, but of course they can't be trusted to run it themselves. They are not educated enough; they need a white colonizer to organize them and reap the benefits.

We ought not be surprised that a discussion of the exploitation of a fictional tribe in a fictional chocolate factory by a fictional multinational corporation quickly turns to one of racism, colonialism, and slavery in the world reflected within this classic of children's literature. After all, no matter how fantastical or idiosyncratic the story, all writers, readers, film-makers, and viewers are of this world: a world in which we sometimes share one another's pain, joy, and bewilderment. There are times when an explicit or hidden horror in those very stories draws us into events we believe cannot exist in *our* world. Yet Hershey—ever aware of its bottom line—would not have made the commitment noted at the beginning of this chapter unless there existed a genuine problem. Nestlé, M&M/Mars, Cadbury, and Nutella maker Ferrero also have (or already had) pledged that by 2020 100 percent of cacao beans used will be certified by independent auditors to have come from "slave-free" sources. Such auditors, like Fairtrade International, would also make sure that cherry cordial is produced under internationally recognized standards for labor, environmental protection, and better farming practices. In 2001, the major global chocolate manufacturers and cocoa producers signed the "Harkin-Engel Protocol,"[20] a voluntary accord designed to combat the "worst forms of child labor." These industry standards and schedule were to have eliminated production of "blood chocolate" by 2005. UNICEF estimates that nearly a half million children work on farms across Côte d'Ivoire, which, with neighboring Ghana, produces roughly 70 percent of the world's supply of cacao on millions of small farms. The agency says hundreds of thousands of children, many of them trafficked across borders, are engaged in the worst forms of child labor.

Charlie and the Chocolate Factory is a fun story. It's full of lively, humorous characters and set in a child's paradise, an imaginative candy factory run by an eccentric. But behind the story are assumptions about how the world is or perhaps should be. These assumptions create, or rather reproduce, a world of white Western privilege in which a "savage," diminutive race of people is exploited by a business owner for his own profit. But it's excusable because they seem to be happy. Although some may think critiquing Dahl's classic on these grounds is taking the book too seriously for a piece of children's literature, our acceptance of this scenario, or our inability to see it for what it is, speaks to the need to have this discussion. The invisibility of the racism and the colonial assumptions in this story speaks to how readily we accept the idea of Western white exceptionalism and are dismissive of the needs and the value of native people. That's a problem. Our world, like Dahl's story, is built on assumptions, and some of these have real consequences, like slave labor, child labor, and exploitation. These need to be laid bare and questioned. Perhaps doing so while thinking about Willy Wonka will make it a little bit easier.

12

GEORGE'S MARVELOUS MEDICINE, OR, WHAT SHOULD WE DO ABOUT GLOBAL HUNGER?

Janelle Pötzsch

Political debates usually revolve around blaming and self-praise, whereas philosophical discussions are marked by complexity and hair-splitting. Troubles start when you mix the two, splitting hairs about who's to blame and applying complex formula to guarantee we get appropriate praise. The good thing is: it barely ever happens. The bad thing is: it barely ever happens. Sure, all of us like simple answers that are easy to implement. But, sadly, simple answers don't fit well in our complicated world. In that respect, philosophy has always functioned as a means to question established views and beliefs in order to widen our perspective. But since no one likes to relinquish long-cherished ideas, one can imagine that philosophers aren't always met with open arms. Perhaps this is why Socrates (469–399 BCE) called himself a gadfly: the philosopher as an annoying insect rousing people from their intellectual slumber.

Certainly, it can be nice and convenient to remain in such a reposing state of mind, and to question one's life all the time seems like the first step toward neurosis or depression. Still, there are issues in which sticking to one's point of view can become problematic or even dangerous. When it comes to our social and political order, expanding our viewpoint is important to accommodate the (sometimes divergent) needs of as many people as possible. This can't be achieved without reconsidering traditions or thinking things through. In that respect, literature can function as a bridge between philosophy and politics, for it encourages us to adopt new points of view and confronts us with unusual situations. Such is the case with good children's literature.

In *George's Marvelous Medicine*, we encounter a boy who brews a potion that enlarges animals as well as people. People? Well, he actually just wanted to teach his awful grandmother a lesson by making her a "magic medicine"—one that would make her nicer. Although George's medicine didn't better the "miserable old grouch" of a grandmother, it has the potential to improve the world, as his father is eager to point out: "Don't you understand what this tremendous invention of yours is going to do to the world! Nobody will ever go hungry again!"[1] Although that's a nice idea, someone less compassionate or perhaps more cynical than Mr. Kranky might ask: Why bother? That's when philosophers put pen to paper.

COSMOPOLITAN: SO MUCH MORE THAN A DRINK

The question of why we should care about people we've never met (and most likely never will) is nearly as old as philosophy itself. One prominent philosophical school of thought dealing with this matter is cosmopolitanism. Literally, the name translates as "world citizenry." Cosmopolitans hold that we shouldn't just bother about our own nationality or ethnic group. Instead, we should consider all human beings in our actions and decisions simply because all of us belong to the same human species and live on the same planet. It's like being nice to a grandma who's nothing more than a pain in the neck simply because she's related to you.

In 1988, philosopher Robert E. Goodin provocatively asked, "What's so special about our fellow countrymen?"[2] A concise answer to this question would be "not much." Goodin claims that the common ideas that we ought to treat our compatriots particularly well and that the needs of outsiders are negligible are unfounded. Instead, it is the other way round. Although we do have special obligations toward our own group, these obligations don't imply that we ought to treat them particularly well. To illustrate this point, Goodin refers to the way a single state treats its citizens. Now and then, members of a nation are treated worse than non-members. Only members are taxed or called to join the armed forces. The usual explanation for why a state is allowed to treat its members like this is that the arrangement is mutually beneficial. For instance, you pay taxes so that the state can build roads and schools and provide health care. In short, imposing harms is permissible when something positive comes of it.[3] Families display a similar mechanism. We tend to treat people we are well acquainted with less obligingly than we treat strangers. (And maybe even George's grandmother would be more polite to a child she's not related to. Of course, in her case that's not likely. She's a selfish grumpy old woman with a mouth like a dog's bottom.)

So, we try to get an idea about why we ascribe different duties to members and nonmembers by viewing nationalities as groups based on mutual benefit. Members have so-called positive rights. To have a positive right means that other people are obligated to actually do something for you. Grandma has a positive right to her medicine, which is why George (or any other family member) is obliged to provide her with it. In fact, her right to her medicine and decent treatment is probably the only thing motivating George and the rest of the family to treat her well. George truly hates that "horrid old witchy" grouch of a woman. In contrast to this, it is commonly thought that nonmembers have only negative rights. This means we ought to refrain from doing something that might harm them. Nonmembers have no further claim because they aren't usually asked to fulfil social tasks for a group they don't belong to.

Goodin, however, doubts this model of mutual benefit: after all, we consider people who don't contribute to overall social welfare (like children or old people) to be members of our nations (or families) as well. The Krankys don't evict Grandma even though she "spent all day and every day sitting in her chair by the window" ordering George about or giving him instructive advice like "stop growing."[4] So the idea that nations (or families) are built on mutual benefit doesn't seem to work. Goodin proposes another viewpoint, believing that we should characterize nations by applying an *assigned-responsibility model*.[5] According to this model, a nation is like an organizational unit that has been ascribed certain tasks—in this case, to take care of a certain group of people. Drawing a national border is like saying, "*You* keep an eye on *this*." Basically, it's like appointing a life guard on the beach. By hiring someone specific to do this job, you avoid two things: either that people will turn a blind eye to a drowning person or that they will impede each other because *everyone* rushes to help. It's the same when George's mother tells him to give Grandma her medicine: she doesn't have to worry that Grandma won't get her medicine at all, nor do all of the Krankys rush to give her a spoonful because they think no one has yet taken care of Grandma. So ascribing tasks to particular persons (or nations) ensures both that they will be carried out and that they will be performed efficiently.

Nations are hence nothing more (or less) than precise addressees of moral duties. This speaks to our question of why we should care about people who don't belong to our nation or ethnic group. On the one hand, borders are decisive because they facilitate fulfilling moral and social duties. On the other hand, they don't create any *special* duties toward those who live within them, as Goodin declares: "The duties that states . . . have vis-á-vis their own citizens are not in any deep sense special. At root, they are merely the general duties that everyone has toward everyone else worldwide."[6] Seen from that perspective, belonging to a state is like knowing who's responsible for your basic welfare.

But what if your state can't fulfil this duty (for instance, because it's too poor or it doesn't care)? In that case, other states have to step in. To refer back to the analogy between state and family, it's like sending the Youth Welfare Office to parents who can't take care of their children. Of course, it's easier if parents themselves looked after their children, but someone has to intercede if they fail to do so in order to ensure the children's well-being. Similarly, if a state isn't able or willing to provide for its citizens, others have to intervene on their behalf. For instance, if a state is too poor to provide for its citizens, other states should transfer resources to ameliorate this.

The just distribution of resources is meant to enable a state to fulfill its moral duties toward its people. However, it's not clear how such a transfer could be brought about. Poor states usually don't have a good bargaining position when it comes to the assertion of their interests. And rich countries are quite happy with their current situation. This is why philosopher Onora O'Neill declares, "Assigning obligations to secure justice beyond their borders to states may be no more sensible than assigning obligations to supervise hen houses to foxes."[7] We tend to witness things like this when it comes to trade negotiations between nations: all of them bargain for their own advantages or the advantages of their citizens. So far, nations neither act nor think as Goodin advises. For this reason, it might be more promising if individual people would try to address the current issue. But how and why should individual persons act when it comes to global hunger? Are there any other than commercial reasons why Mr. Kranky should breed gigantic animals? The Australian philosopher Peter Singer offers a controversial answer to this question.

DROWNING CHILDREN AND GROWING GRANNIES

Singer is disarmingly pragmatic when it comes to global hunger. In a very thought-provoking, even somewhat notorious comparison, Singer equates not helping the global poor with ignoring a child who is drowning right in front of us. He maintains, "If it is in our power to prevent something very bad from happening, without thereby sacrificing anything morally significant, we ought, morally, to do it."[8] The limitation "without sacrificing anything morally significant" means that we ought to prevent something bad only if doing so doesn't cause anything similarly bad to happen or if we aren't compelled to do something that is wrong in itself. For instance, if I can help a hungry person only by stealing bread from someone who is equally hungry, or if I have to kill someone to obtain some food, this isn't the way to go. Singer's qualification makes it clear that the end doesn't justify any or every means. The good has to outweigh the bad.

He also claims that his principle doesn't ask too much of people, because it "requires us only to prevent what is bad, and not to promote what is good."[9] In other words, Singer differentiates between positive and negative duties. A positive duty is a duty to actually do something, like "love thy grandmother." If, however, someone asks you to just refrain from doing something (like "thou shalt not enlarge thy grandmother, no matter how unpleasant she is"), that person is ascribing to you a negative duty. This distinction is important because it is usually more difficult to justify a positive duty than a negative one because positive duties are much more demanding. Yet Singer points out that the duty embodied in his principle would have far-reaching consequences. If acted upon, not only our personal lives but probably our whole world would undergo profound change.

First, Singer's moral principle doesn't distinguish between proximity and distance, which means that it applies regardless of the connection I may or may not have to the person who needs help: "It makes no moral difference whether the person I can help is a neighbor's child ten yards from me or a Bengali whose name I shall never know, ten thousand miles away."[10] The second, slightly burdensome point is that I am morally obliged to act upon Singer's principle even if there are other people around who could do the same. According to Singer, the idea that the presence of others discharges me of any moral duty is absurd: "Should I consider that I am less obliged to pull the drowning child out of the pond if on looking around I see other people, no further away than I am, who have also noticed the child but are doing nothing?"[11] George's father embodies this idea quite nicely, for he decides to tackle the issue of global hunger after he has heard about George's medicine. Although he does see the financial advantages of this venture ("We will become rich and you will become famous!"[12]), he takes the initiative himself and doesn't ponder how he'll make "barrels and barrels" of the medicine or how he'll distribute tons of it to "every farmer in the world."[13] Mr. Kranky sees the potential of George's medicine: "Don't you understand what this tremendous invention of yours is going to do to the world?" he asks George. "Nobody will ever go hungry again."[14] Killy Kranky is seriously concerned about the problem of global hunger and implores George not to waste time: "There isn't a minute to *wait*! We must get cracking at once!"[15]

But isn't Mr. Kranky just being charitable, and isn't charity about giving something *voluntarily*? So why does Singer claim that we are *obliged* to address the problem of global hunger? He maintains that the problem lies with the distinction between "charity" and "duty." Our current moral framework, according to which there's nothing wrong with *not* giving money to charity, is unfounded. Singer states that there aren't sufficient reasons for buying new clothes (or a book on philosophy) for oneself instead of giving that money to people who need it more urgently than you do. This is already implied in his qualification that we ought to do something if we aren't "thereby sacrificing anything morally significant." Since new clothes for rather affluent Westerners aren't more important than providing food for the hungry, Singer maintains, "When we buy new clothes not to keep ourselves warm but to look 'well-dressed' we are not providing for any important need. We would not be sacrificing anything significant if we were to continue to wear our old clothes, and give the money to famine relief. By doing so, we would be preventing another person from starving."[16] To do without the latest fashion is a small price to pay to save a human life. The same applies to "Helga's Hairset" or "Superfoam Shaving Soap"—since they're important ingredients of George's medicine, a medicine with the potential to end world hunger, it wouldn't be too much to ask his family, and others, to do without them.

So that's it? We have to help the global poor by giving as much of our money as possible to famine relief. No visits to the cinema, no new clothes, no books on philosophy. Admittedly, this idea makes Singer seem almost as curmudgeonly as George's grandmother: eat cabbage and earwigs instead of chocolate and give away all your money instead of spending it on something you like. Still, the reasons Singer gives for doing so are worth considering. Singer states that "moral attitudes are shaped by the needs of society, and no doubt society needs people who will observe the rules that make social existence tolerable."[17] Hence, the different importance (or moral weight) usually ascribed to charity and duty is based on social needs: to establish and maintain social order, it is more important that people act morally toward members of their own group rather than "outsiders." This was convenient and manageable hundreds, maybe even thousands, of years ago. But this was (and is) far from being ethical, especially now in our globally connected world: "From the moral point of view, the prevention of the starvation of millions of people outside our society must be considered at least as pressing as the upholding of property norms within our society."[18]

This may seem to be an outrageous standard at first, but Singer insists that the issue of global hunger is too urgent to be delayed or even hindered by reservations of spoiled Westerners: "The present way of drawing the distinction, which makes it an act of charity for a man living at the level of affluence which most people in the 'developed nations' enjoy to give money to save someone else from starvation, cannot be supported."[19] This is because such a distinction is rooted in custom, which is why we tend to reject Singer's proposal rather than embracing it. It is also easier to simply ignore the suffering of others, and enjoy our comfortable lives, instead of sacrificing, even a little bit of that comfort, for their needs. But just ask yourself whether you would like to hear others say about your demise, "Ah well, I suppose it's all for the best, really. She was a bit of a nuisance around the house, wasn't she?"[20] The suffering of those outside our in-group is very real, and turning a blind eye to it does not make it go away. If we would develop new moral standards that would make us consider outsiders as well as members of our own group, Singer's idea would no longer seem outlandish.

The need for new, more comprehensive moral duties is especially important in our globally connected world. Ignoring the global poor can become harmful for us; we might not get shrunk like Grandma because of our greed, but terrorism and mass migration do pose difficult issues. So apart from moral reasons, we should consider the need of the global poor for pragmatic reasons. But even if all of us followed Singer's demand and gave away as much money as possible, could we really succeed in saving more than a billion people from starvation? Given the size and scope of the problem, poor George would have to brew tons of his medicine. And given the amount of ingredients, including engine oil and various (animal) medicines, this would get extremely expensive and require a great many resources. Surely, the Krankys can't handle this problem on their own. A problem like global hunger can't be left to acts of philanthropy.

Wouldn't it be more effective if the British government instead of the Krankys took action? Singer doesn't deny that governments also ought to address the issue, especially because the private funding of individuals is not enough to abolish world hunger. Still, he points out that private funding could signal a government to take to action: if no one gives voluntarily, governmental bodies might assume that no one really cares about this issue and hence remain inactive. It is the role of governmental bodies with which German philosopher Thomas Pogge concerns himself. He suggests an entirely different method to end global hunger: rather than donating money or growing giant animals for slaughter, one should try to restructure society in such a way as to prevent hunger from arising in the first place. Pogge asks for institutional reform.

IT'S WHAT'S GOOD FOR YOU THAT COUNTS... SOMETIMES

Pogge raises a crucial point. The effectiveness of individual actions hugely depends on political and social background conditions. For instance, Mr. Kranky's endeavor to end world hunger would be pointless if, say, the British government prohibited the shipment of his giant animals to those who needed them. In his book *World Poverty and Human Rights* (2002), Pogge poses the question, "Does our new global economic order really not harm the poor?"[21] This query isn't as naïve as it may seem at first glance. Many aspects of our lives are influenced by powerful global institutions like the World Trade Organization, for instance—some of us benefit from them, while others don't. Why do some benefit while others suffer? According to Pogge, this is because of an asymmetry of power between richer and poorer nations, which the richer nations use to their own advantage. In other words, political representatives of rich nations are being partial to their own interests at the expense of the interests of poorer nations. But partiality is bound to take place when it comes to developing economic policy. We all seek our own advantage. Surely, George's father isn't being altruistic when it comes to George's medicine, as his excited "We will become rich and you will become famous!"[22] indicates. Mr. Kranky sees the potential for profit from George's medicine, and that may be a strong incentive for him to begin production of it on a mass scale. We would not begrudge him his ability to profit while simultaneously ending world hunger.

There's nothing wrong with profiting from helping others. But if in order to make George's medicine the Krankys had to decimate local populations, destroy local ecologies, or engage in sweatshop-style labor practices, then we might judge Mr. Kranky a bit more harshly. So what Pogge takes issue with is that wealthy nations currently profit from *harming* the poor. Like George's grandmother, we're simply a pain in the neck to developing countries because we don't consider the needs of their peoples. Speaking with Goodin, we still think that there's something special about our compatriots, or even ourselves.

Why does Pogge maintain that richer countries are taking advantage of developing nations? Are affluent citizens of Northern Europe or the United States acting immorally simply because we're rich while others go hungry? That would be an absurd claim. Pogge does concede that inequality as such is no proof of any violation of a moral duty. One is guilty of something only if one somehow contributes to it.[23] But in that respect, we shouldn't underestimate the role of shared global institutions. Pogge indicates that such institutions violate the moral duty not to harm if they meet three conditions:

1. There is a shared institutional order that is shaped by the better-off and imposed upon the worse-off.
2. This institutional order reproduces inequality insofar as there is a feasible alternative under which such inequality would cease to exist.

3. This inequality isn't rooted in any nonsocial factors like natural disasters or similar. [24]

Let's see whether the World Bank, [25] a highly influential economic institution Pogge criticizes, meets these criteria. To start with, a little more than 60 percent of all votes fall to industrial nations, even though they represent only 20 percent of the global population. This is because the shareholders' voting power depends on the amount of capital they've invested. One could put it in a less friendly way and say that money talks. For this reason, the United States currently holds 16 percent of all votes and has an absolute power of veto. All African countries combined possess roughly 6 percent of all votes. A "feasible institutional alternative" [26] that Pogge aims for would grant those who are most dependent on the World Bank's decisions a say in the matter.

But the World Bank is not the only global institution with a profound impact on millions of lives. According to Pogge, there are many culprits—the World Trade Organization (WTO), for instance, which regulates global trade. Pogge points out that the current trade agreements between countries are rather one-sided: "I do not complain that the WTO regime opens markets too much, but that it has opened *our* markets *too little*." [27] Due to this trade gap, developed nations are free to export their products to developing nations and at the same time shield their own markets from possible competition through import quotas or duties.

So we confront the problem Goodin pointed out: we still tend to cater more to the needs of our compatriots than those of outsiders. But in order to adequately deal with global problems, we ought to treat others more fairly. All it takes is to no longer apply different standards to the national and international orders. For instance, a prime minister who brings only his closest friends or even family members to his parliament would surely meet with little, if any, sympathy, respect, or trust. This attitude reflects our idea that a state should be organized in such a way that the human rights of all its members are recognized and respected and that no group or individual is being given undue preferential treatment.

Sadly, we don't judge the international community by this standard of fair and equal treatment. Instead, we expect our political representatives to use their bargaining power to strike advantageous deals for our sake, often at the expense of others. Pogge highlights that this is an inconsistent way of thinking: "How can we ask our officials to put their family's finances out of their minds when deliberating about the domestic economic order . . . and yet expect those same officials to have their own nation's finances uppermost in their minds when deliberating about the global economic order?"[28] One could argue against Pogge that the developed countries are somehow compelled to act like this; after all, if they didn't pursue their own interests with such zeal, other countries might take advantage of them in international negotiations. But according to Pogge, this could be prevented if all countries had roughly the same amount of bargaining power—which leads us back to the need for institutional reform.

Another possible objection to Pogge's idea that richer countries should try to make the international community more just would be to claim that doing so would be pointless unless those richer nations were already just themselves. The idea is that richer states should first try to abolish injustice within their own borders before trying to improve the political conditions elsewhere. Imagine Mr. Kranky trying to abolish world hunger but letting his own son go hungry! In short, charity begins at home. A state's foremost duty is to see to the well-being of its own citizens. The well-being of foreigners ought not to be of any concern for our government. Not only would Goodin strongly disagree with this, but Pogge also maintains that such a view applies only if the rights of foreigners were violated through no fault of the citizens or governments of the richer nations. But as we've seen, this condition isn't met when it comes to the global economic order. The global poor "are being harmed through a badly slanted global order in whose continuous shaping and coercive imposition we are materially involved."[29] In that respect, one could even say that George's mother is somewhat responsible for the bad treatment he experiences at the hands his grandmother. Although his grandmother only orders him around and emotionally abuses him when no one else is at home, his mother could ask George whether his grandmother treats him well. She is responsible for how she organizes her home, and that includes the relationship between George and his grandmother, as well as their well-being.

Our involvement with global hunger and poverty is similar. We may turn a blind eye to the misconduct of our state toward other nations. Still, such behavior does occur. This conduct may diminish our state's obligation to first establish justice at home. Before catering to the needs of its citizens, perhaps a nation should make amends for what it has done to

nonmembers. Like Singer, Pogge urges us to relinquish our limited
worldview according to which we see only single nations and single
national economies, without noticing that all of them act upon and influence each other. Within such a limited worldview, global hunger seems
like the result of bad domestic policy. It's like being reproached for
"growing the wrong way": if children had any influence over their physical development, puberty wouldn't be such a nightmare. Instead, all you
can do is wait and hope for the best. Similarly, developing nations have
simply arranged themselves with the institutional framework richer nations have designed. Therefore, we have to keep in mind that their domestic policies are shaped and influenced by global politics. World hunger
will remain a pressing problem as long as we ignore the interdependency
between nations and the role we play in the global economy.

It takes a certain kind of moral imagination before people are able and
willing to abandon long-held beliefs and perspectives. And such a moral
attitude and moral courage doesn't develop on its own. In that respect,
Dahl's children's literature constitutes a promising starting point. Characters like George and his father illustrate that what matters in social relations are empathy and kindness—and the will to change things for the
better. They simply do what they believe they owe to others, whether that
is to take care of a grandmother the family can barely tolerate or try to
raise enormous animals to feed the world's hungry. George's story demonstrates that there are both moral and pragmatic reasons to care about
others. So get cracking at once!

13

CRODSWOGGLE, FLUSHBUNKING, AND ALL THINGS FRIENDSHIP IN *THE BFG*

Chad Kleist

It is nearly impossible to imagine going through life without friends. When we face hardships, it is important to have friends see us through despair, and in good times, we love to share the moments with others. We use the term "friend" frequently, and my guess is that most of us can identify our friends with ease. However, it is not that simple to articulate what makes an individual a friend, or more specifically a "good friend," other than the fact that we enjoy spending time with her or him.

Aristotle (384–322 BCE), an ancient Greek philosopher, offers one of the most influential accounts of friendship. Friendship, according to Aristotle, requires that both parties (1) wish each other well for the other's sake (not merely for oneself), (2) reciprocate care for one another, (3) share similar interests and activities, and (4) be equal in social standing. Despite the plausibility of these central features of friendship, I believe the last two can be called into question.

Roald Dahl's story *The BFG* teaches us why it is not necessary for individuals to be of the same equal standing and have the same interests in order to be genuine friends. Sophie, an orphaned girl, and the Big Friendly Giant (BFG) have very little in common (at least on the surface) and would not be considered equal according to any standard. He is hundreds of years old and inhabits a faraway land, while Sophie is a young girl, yet wise beyond her years, who lives in a London orphanage. In light of these differences, they seem to develop a genuine friendship. I will use their relationship to challenge Aristotle.

Let's begin with a brief summary of *The BFG*. The story opens with a little orphan girl, Sophie, who is kidnapped from the orphanage by the Big Friendly Giant. He brings her back to Giant Country, land of ten giants, nine of which are ruthless and one friendly. The BFG is a good-hearted, well-intentioned, caring giant who lacks formal educational training, so his *langwitch* is not proper, but understandable. Sophie and he develop trust and ultimately a friendship. Upon learning from the BFG that the other giants gobble *human beans*, specifically children, from all around the world, Sophie develops a plan to end the madness. Because the BFG has the ability to mix dreams and plant them in those who are sleeping, Sophie suggests he give the Queen of England a dream of what actually happens that night in London, including the fact that Sophie will be waiting for her to wake on her windowsill. As the sun rises, the Queen is startled to learn that her dream was a reality, especially since the little girl is waiting at the window. Sophie's plan is a success, since the Queen sends her Air Force to capture the other giants, with the assistance of the BFG and Sophie, of course. Dahl provides his readers with many lessons through his imaginative tales, but the one I find most interesting, and will discuss at length here, is the lesson on friendship.

REACHING THE COMPLETE LIFE OF *RAZZTWIZZLER*

Aristotle claims that the ultimate goal of human activity is *eudaimonia*, often translated as "happiness" or "flourishing." The BFG also recognizes the greatness of this life, as he calls it a *razztwizzler*, or a *gloriumptious* experience.[1] It is the most complete of all ends—nothing could be added to make it any greater. The central feature to determine whether someone has flourished is by asking the question: Is this person virtuous? Simply put, a virtue is an excellence that contributes to flourishing. Something is "excellent" for Aristotle to the extent that it performs its function well. So human beings are able to become virtuous insofar as their actions avoid the extremes of deficiency and excess and instead manifest in the mean. For example, a person should strive for the virtue of courage (mean), while avoiding the extremes of rashness (excess) and cowardice (deficiency). Other virtues we should strive to acquire include wittiness (of which buffoonery and boorishness are the extremes) in social settings; truthfulness about one's accomplishments; and generosity toward others.

If one is able to realize these virtues, then we can properly label that person as virtuous with respect to that domain of his or her life. A virtue Aristotle discusses substantially in his most widely read ethical work, *Nicomachean Ethics*, is friendliness.

The virtue of friendliness lies between the extremes of flattery (excess) and unpleasantness (deficiency). On the one hand, the flatterer is someone who strives to be friends with everyone. He has not met someone whose company he didn't enjoy. Aristotle says we ought to avoid being this person because it would be nearly impossible to be a good friend to many people.[2] Being a good friend entails the responsibility of meeting the demands and needs of those we care for most deeply, and if one has too many friends, one runs the risk of being unable to support them in times of need.

On the other hand, the unpleasant individual is simply not enjoyable (for whatever reason) to be around. Unlike the flatterer, who has difficulty limiting the number of friends she has, the unpleasant person struggles to gain friends. For example, he might be a person who believes that whatever struggles another endures, he has it significantly worse. These people are often avoided as friends for fear that the friendship might be one-sided. However, the friendly person will have time to spend with her friends because she does not have too many, and she is pleasant to be around.

Most often, calling a person a friend is an all-or-nothing affair—that is, either the person is a friend or she is not. However, friendship for Aristotle is not all-or-nothing. Instead, he distinguishes between three types of friends—namely, friendships of utility (or benefit), pleasure, and character. A mutual object of affection binds each corresponding friendship. A friendship of utility is held together by the mutual object that serves as a benefit to each friend. A friendship of pleasure persists around the thing that brings pleasure to both friends. Finally, a friendship of character is formed by each person having an interest in the other's good character. Aristotle notes that friendships of utility and pleasure tend to be shorter than those of character since the former's mutual object of love is much more easily dissolvable.

Friendships of utility occur between people who each receive a benefit from one another. Despite not knowing each other very well, the BFG and the Queen's soldiers help one another to capture the flesh-eating giants. The BFG agrees to show them the location of Giant Country since it is off the atlas. In return, the soldiers provide the *bellypoppers* and nets to secure the giants and bring them back to London safely. To the extent that they are striving to apprehend the giants, both benefit from their relationship. The mutual objects in this case are the giants. It is likely that upon completion of the task at hand, their friendship will cease to exist in this capacity. It could be the case that the soldiers and the BFG also enjoyed spending time with one another, and in such an instance their friendship would continue existing, but in a different form—namely, that of pleasure.

Friendships of pleasure entail two people who share their mutual object of love around what is pleasant to both of them. For example, the bad giants enjoy eating human beans from around the world, including Greece, England, Japan, and Norway. Like those of utility, friendships of pleasure are not long-lasting, since people's preferences change with time. The BFG, however, doesn't enjoy eating human beans, which explains why he does not have a friendship of pleasure with the other giants. Furthermore, the malicious giants display their friendship of pleasure as they mutually bully the BFG. They toss him around as they stand in a circle approximately twenty yards from one another. Dahl explains, "The giants were playing ball with the BFG, vying with each other to see who could throw him the highest."[3] In either case, if one of the malicious giants decided he no longer enjoyed eating human beans or tossing the BFG, then he would lose the common object of interest that held together his friendship of pleasure with the others.

The final and most complete form of friendship is that of character. Here the parties come together not because of the benefits that result from their friendship, or simply the fact that each is pleasant to the other (even though both are likely to occur), but because of a mutual interest in the other person's character. Each person desires to see the other become more virtuous for her own sake. For example, the BFG points out Sophie's moral blind spots, such as letting her know that "Human beans is the only animals that is killing their own kind."[4] Furthermore, just as virtuous people enjoy performing virtuous actions, character friends likewise enjoy each other's company. Sophie and the BFG share many enjoyable experiences, including catching dreams in Dream Country and playing a prank on Fleshlumpeater. So, even though their friendship is not caused by something pleasant, they find pleasantry in one another. Ultimately, enjoying each other's company is a result of their respective good characters. Thus, just as Sophie and the BFG find one another pleasant, their friendship is also advantageous insofar as each friend can encourage the other to become the best person possible.

Aristotle believes character friendships are the most "complete" and "perfect" kind of friendship. The exemplar of a character friendship, according to Aristotle, is a "friendship of good men [in which] all the qualities we have named belong in virtue of the nature of the friends themselves."[5] However, as John Cooper argues, friendships of character do not necessarily require each party to be fully virtuous, but "only in *some*, in order for the friendship to exist."[6] It may be that each person is generous, displays humility, and of course is friendly, but perhaps lacks other virtues such as courage or wittiness. Cooper's point is that as long as both people are committed to the other's good character for the other's sake, despite not possessing all the virtues, a friendship of character exists. It is worth noting, though, that such friendships take time to develop since getting to know another's character does not happen overnight. Aristotle writes that "a wish for friendship may arise quickly, but friendship does not."[7] We see Sophie and the BFG's friendship develop immediately after he swoops her away from the orphanage and brings her back to his cave in Giant Country. Here, Sophie explains her fears and expectations, and the BFG reassures her that he will care for her. This is the development of a long-term friendship.

One may ask what is the connection between friendship and flourishing? To this, Aristotle begins with a discussion on external goods—that is, instrumental goods that contribute to human flourishing. Aristotle offers numerous examples of external goods, including beauty, good children, wealth, power, and moral luck. However, the "greatest of external goods" for him is friendship.[8] Even a person who has secured all other goods (e.g., rationality, honor, wisdom, temperance, and health) has not lived well if she has no friends, since it is important to share one's well-being with others.

THE *BABBLEMENT* OF FRIENDSHIP

The central features of Aristotle's conception of character friendship include caring and wishing the other well for their own sake, enjoying similar activities, and being equal in social standing. He is certainly not alone in identifying these features as central to a genuine friendship. Roald Dahl also seems to be sympathetic to most of these characteristics as they are shown in the relationship between the Big Friendly Giant and Sophie.

Friendship begins with each person having goodwill toward the other for the other's sake. By goodwill, I mean that one wishes the other well in all aspects of their life and does so not for one's own benefit (as in friendships of utility) but for the other's well-being. The BFG shows goodwill toward all children by catching *trogglehumpers*, as he calls them (meaning terribly scary nightmares). They are the worst of all dreams. In order to prevent children from having a *trogglehumper*, the BFG says, "I is never letting it go . . . If I do, then some poor little tottler will be having the most curdbloodlingly time! This one is a real kicksy bogthumper!"[9] Here he is showing goodwill toward all children, including Sophie, by ensuring their comfort while sleeping. He gains no benefit himself by catching *trogglehumpers*, and so their friendship is not based on utility (or even pleasure, for that matter).

Goodwill is not an asymmetrical relationship between the BFG and Sophie. Sophie displays just as much goodwill toward the giant as he does toward her. She provides encouragement and hope to the BFG to follow through on the plan to save children from being gobbled up by the other giants. Without her sincerest good wishes, it's not clear if the BFG would have had the confidence to follow through on the plan. This is significant because goodwill must be reciprocated by both parties in order to have a true friendship.

These examples reveal an important aspect of goodwill—namely, that goodwill per se is not enough to constitute a genuine friendship, since one may wish goodwill upon those who are not our friends or perhaps those we do not even know. Aristotle says that it is "not possible for people to be friends if they have not come to feel goodwill for each other, but those who feel goodwill are not for all that friends."[10] For example, the BFG wishes all children a comfortable night's sleep, despite the fact that he does not know all children in the world.

Since goodwill is a necessary but not a sufficient condition for friendship, Aristotle introduces another central tenet—reciprocated affection. Affection is not simply wishing another well. It is much more intimate. It requires a deeper level of understanding and intensity between the parties. Both Sophie and the BFG show a level of affection and care toward one another that extends well beyond mere well-wishing. After the BFG agrees to follow Sophie's plan to see the Queen, Dahl writes, "Sophie kissed him on the tip of his thumb [and said] 'I knew you'd do it! Come on! Let's hurry.'"[11] Even if it seems like a simple kiss on the thumb, a kiss is an intimate act. By kissing the BFG, Sophie demonstrates her affection and care for him. This moment reveals a bond that goes beyond goodwill.

An advantage of developing affection for one another is that it leads to a level of trust between one another that transcends goodwill. For example, the BFG teaches Sophie that a problem for "human beans . . . is that they is absolutely refusing to believe in anything unless they is actually seeing it right in front of their own schnozzles."[12] Sophie, previously denying the existence of that which she cannot see, becomes more open to a world previously unbeknown to her. This provides her with a greater skill in life—that is, recognizing that understanding the world may come from sources beyond her senses. More important, the BFG and Sophie begin to trust one another because now he feels comfortable sharing what he was doing in the village the night he took her away, which he had never shared before—namely, giving children lovely dreams.

The third aspect of friendship that Aristotle discusses is concord or agreement. For Aristotle, this is not simply sharing any belief, but agreement on "matters of consequences and in which it is possible for both or all parties to get what they want."[13] Mathematical questions, for instance, would not be a matter of concord. The answers to mathematical questions are fixed and cannot be disputed. Aristotle is most concerned with arriving at the same conclusion on practical matters, such as activities friends enjoy sharing with one another. Friendship requires both parties to find the same things pleasant, which explains why Aristotle says friends are "of one mind . . . and they wish for what is just and what is advantageous, and these are the objects of their common endeavour as well."[14]

It is important for friends to enjoy the same activities; otherwise, it would be difficult for them to spend time with one another. And, of course, if their time is hampered by their lack of harmony in preferences, they are unlikely to get to know one another on a deeper level, which will lead to a lack of trust. Thus, a friendship of character would be nearly impossible.

This concern is certainly not an issue for the main characters in Dahl's story. Sophie and the BFG enjoy their time together. Dahl describes an early interaction between them in which they laugh and joke around. Sophie, raised in a London orphanage, was taught to be prim and proper. The BFG wants to show her the importance of relaxing and having fun. So he drinks a bottle of *frobscottle*. Then, all of a sudden the "heavens opened and he let fly with a series of the loudest and rudest noises Sophie had ever heard in her life. . . . Now *that* is whizzpopping for you!"[15] The BFG explained that everyone—kings, queens, presidents, and movie stars—*whizzpoppers*. Sophie laughed with great jubilation, and at the request of the friendly giant she tried the *frobscottle*. The bubbles from the drink traveled down to her tummy, and then the "trumpets sounded and she too made the walls of the cavern ring with the sound of music and thunder."[16] There are other interactions that illustrate their enjoyment together, like the BFG blowing a *trogglehumper* of a nightmare in Fleshlumpeater's ear, which resulted in a fight among the other giants. The BFG and Sophie laughed at them from a distance.

The final feature of a character friendship, according to Aristotle, is equality. The parties in a friendship must be of equal standing with respect to one another. Aristotle advocates for equality in terms of a "common upbringing and similarity of age."[17] If people come from radically different backgrounds, it may be more difficult for them to relate to one another. We have all heard our parents and grandparents tell us, "One day you'll understand." There may be something to this insofar as with age comes experience and wisdom. If one person in a relationship has undergone significantly fewer life experiences by virtue of being younger, it will be likely that she will have a different worldview, which will make it difficult to maintain a character friendship with the older person. Yet Dean Cocking and Jeanette Kennett make the point that it is simply "common observation" that people who are "markedly dissimilar can be very good friends."[18]

Laurence Thomas explains that equality is not simply about identifying similarities between friends. He claims that if potential friends are "unequal with respect to their stations in life, the one with the higher station will be inclined to think that his utterances have more authority than the other's utterances."[19] Thomas is noting a problem that we ought to take seriously: the fear of a friend exploiting another simply in virtue of the former's higher social standing. This would explain why Aristotle claims friends ought to be similar in virtue, especially for character friendships. This will help avoid the person of lower virtue having a detrimental effect on the more virtuous individual.

Despite the fact that Sophie and the BFG enjoy their time together, and in some ways are of a like mind, they are very different people who never abandon their sense of self for the other. One reason the giant and orphan girl are able to maintain their differences is the fact that they are not equal in many respects; yet, contrary to Aristotle, it is ultimately their differences that create and maintain their character friendship. Through Sophie and the BFG, Dahl teaches us that people can inhabit different worlds and yet maintain a genuine friendship.

DAHL GOBBLEFUNKS ARISTOTLE

There are great differences between Sophie and the BFG, beginning with the most obvious, age. The BFG explains to Sophie that while she thinks she is eight years old, she truly is only four because she spends half her life sleeping. In stark contrast, he is an "old sage and onions who is hundreds of years more than [her]."[20] The BFG's experiences give him an understanding of the world that Sophie would have difficulty grasping. For example, Sophie expressed her disgust at the fact that giants ate human children. Of course, the BFG agrees that they should not do so. However, he helps Sophie see that humans also engage in ruthless behavior. He notes that "human beans is squishing *each other* all the time. . . . They is shootling guns and going up in aerioplanes to drop their bombs on each other's heads every week. Human beans is always killing other human beans."[21]

Sophie responds to the BFG by noting that at least human beings do not eat other humans, as the giants do. The BFG reminds Sophie that "the little piggy-wig is saying every day . . . I has never done harm to the human bean so why should he be eating me?"[22] These examples illustrate the lack of knowledge (and perhaps innocence) of a young child, although no one would reasonably expect her to understand the BFG's point prior to someone explaining it to her. The difference in age, however, does not hinder their chance of becoming friends, but rather fuels it, since it is an opportunity for the BFG to show Sophie the world from a different perspective.

Interestingly, their differences also help Sophie teach the BFG to be more confident. Because of the BFG's lack of education, his words do not always sound the way they were intended. Sophie defends the way in which the BFG articulated himself to the Queen and her Air Force. She is young and understands the difficulty of being taken seriously, and so she appreciates the value of allowing the BFG to express himself freely without being constantly corrected. For example, the BFG told the Air Force to bring their *bellypoppers*, but not use a *porteedo*, when trying to trap the other giants, to which the commander responded by asking whether he was being "rude." In both instances, Sophie did not correct the giant; instead, she used the proper terms of "helicopter" and "torpedo" as she responded to the commander. The little girl believes in the giant's potential, and at the end of the story, he asks Sophie to teach him how to speak properly and she happily agrees to do so.

Dahl shows us the importance difference plays in bettering the other person. In virtue of the BFG's experience and accumulated knowledge, he is able to be not only a friend but also a quasi-mentor to Sophie. Sophie, too, acknowledges this when Dahl writes that she "loved him as she would a father."[23] This shows that their relationship is built on caring for one another despite their differences. However, it is not merely caring for one another as in a parent-child relationship. There seems to be a genuine character friendship between the two of them, which is built on a relationship of navigating through their dissimilarities.

Aristotle tells us that in order to develop a character friendship, each person must be invested in the other's good character, and this creates the opportunity for individuals to flourish. The BFG and Sophie appear to be at different levels of virtue since, in part, we would tend to consider Sophie's social conduct to be much more appropriate than the BFG's. But, nonetheless, they are both committed to making each other better people. Consider the BFG's lack of etiquette. The goal of conversation is wittiness, but the BFG appears to be in excess. In social circumstances he comes off as a buffoon. He often jokes when he should be serious. For instance, the BFG is a bit too relaxed in front of the Queen, which is demonstrated by his free use of *whizzpoppers*. However, Sophie, while certainly not boorish (i.e., lacking self-expression), tends to be a bit on the timid side. I believe these differences bring them closer together. The friendly giant encourages the orphan girl to ignore the etiquette of being proper for a moment and have a *whizzpopping* good time, and Sophie helps the BFG learn to speak and write properly.

Aristotle is adamant that character friendships should be between people of similar virtue; otherwise what each finds pleasant will be very different, and then it will be difficult to maintain their friendship. In contrast, Dahl draws on inequities to reveal the good character of both Sophie and the BFG, including their ability to make each other better. For example, the BFG is virtuous when he displays courage by waiting in the dark to tell the Queen that the other giants are eating children, but he also performs nonvirtuous actions (albeit humorous) like planting a nightmare in Fleshlumpeater's dream. He, like Sophie, is far from being fully virtuous, and yet both strive through one another to become better.

One may argue that what marks their friendship as genuine is the fact that they are equal to the extent that neither is fully virtuous. However, I have my doubts that they are truly equal. In some domains, Sophie dominates the discussion because she is most familiar with the surroundings—for example, talking with the Queen. Meanwhile, the BFG dealt with matters in Giant Country because he is much more welcome, despite being bullied, than Sophie or any other human bean.

I am more sympathetic to Dahl's conception of friendship than Aristotle's because the former is better able to maintain the primacy of character friendships while still preserving individuality. Aristotle is overly concerned with friends being similar in the hopes that similar partners will push each other to be more virtuous. I fear that such friends will either remain stagnant or become the same person. This is problematic because people inhabit different social worlds and they need their own identity in order to face their unique moral dilemmas. Dahl offers us hope for developing and maintaining real friendships despite the fact that we may differ from our friends in considerable ways.

In sum, through Dahl we see that character friendships can form and develop through differences. Aristotle notes the common phrase of his day, "two of an age take to each other."[24] However, it is often said that "opposites attract," and it is with this saying that I am encouraged that character friendships are possible between those who are unequal and who may be dissimilar in terms of age, background, or interests. I am not claiming, following Dahl, that the BFG and Sophie are completely unlike one another; there are similarities. For example, both are orphans of a kind—Sophie lacks a biological family, and the BFG has been ostracized from the other giants. Furthermore, both are small, relative to their own species—the BFG is half the size of the other giants and Sophie is a child. But even with such similarities, there are marked differences. Sophie is human, which makes her giant food, and the BFG is a giant. They inhabit different worlds. Yet they wish each other well, care for one another deeply, encourage one another to become excellent persons, and thus have a friendship most of us would cherish.

FOLLOWING DAHL

Dahl offers his readers a vision of genuine friendships between dissimilar persons in other works as well. *Matilda*, for example, illustrates the way in which a teacher and student develop a close friendship. They are certainly not alike in all respects (although both are kind-hearted and have a passion for learning), but they differ in terms of equality—that is, a teacher is in a position of power over her students. Nonetheless, Dahl shows how Matilda and her teacher, Miss Honey, develop a bond that seems unbreakable. Despite their obvious differences, they complete one another.

I would encourage anyone who is interested in finding and developing a genuine friendship to follow Dahl—to look for someone who shows affection and wishes one well in all aspects of one's life. This person doesn't have to be similar to oneself. As we learn from the BFG and Sophie, a potential friend may be much older, inhabit a radically different world, and have different interests than ourselves; yet she will also be there when we need her and help us develop a good character. Sophie calls the friendly giant her "best friend," and he in turn calls Sophie his "little friend."[25] They teach us the importance of staying true to who we are, while still recognizing our limitations and being open to change.

14

CHARLIE AND THE NIGHTMARE FACTORY

The Art of Children's Horror Fiction

Greg Littmann

A boy swims desperately against the current, but is not strong enough; he is sucked under the surface and into the pipes, swept along toward the mechanical knives. Meanwhile, a wild animal breaks free in the city, killing and devouring two young parents, leaving their orphaned son to be abused by his two demented aunts. In space, the Vermicious Knids amass, leathery and terrible, ready to exterminate the humans as they have exterminated so many races before. All across the world, monstrous giants invade to butcher and consume human children in the night, while at a luxury hotel in Bournemouth, hideous child-hating witches plot the death of every child in England. Am I describing events from horror novels? Yes. They're from Roald Dahl's children's fiction.

Roald Dahl is perhaps the greatest writer of children's horror fiction who has ever lived. Of course, you won't find his work for children in the horror section of a bookstore or listed under "horror" on Amazon. Obviously, there are good, practical reasons for such businesses to clearly distinguish books suitable for adults from books suitable for children in this way. Yet to deny that Dahl's children's books constitute horror fiction, at least some of the time, is to fail to appreciate the way that he makes horror a primary tool for engaging the reader.

Charlie and the Chocolate Factory, one of the finest works in children's literature, is a surreal nightmare in which a group of children are picked off one by one in ways that suggest agonizing death or permanent disfigurement. All it needs to fit snugly in the horror section are fewer lucky escapes—Augustus Gloop is carved to pieces in the fudge machine as "a hundred knives go slice, slice, slice," and Veruca Salt tumbles screaming into the fires of the rubbish incinerator.

But if Dahl's children's books are horror fiction, what the devil are we doing giving them to children? Granted, Dahl's works are *children's* horror fiction, more restrained in many ways than adult horror. All the same, we might well wonder whether any works that focus so much on evil, fear, and the prospect of grizzly death are appropriate for impressionable kids.

As it happens, I badly want children to read Roald Dahl. Far from wanting to keep his work from their hands, I would like to see every kid have the opportunity to thrill at the mysterious Willy Wonka's chocolate factory, to laugh at the rude giant centipede from *James and the Giant Peach*, and yes, to get a little bit scared by those cruel witches from *The Witches*, the ones who hide among us, waiting to . . . *phwisst!* . . . "disappear" children. I'm so eager to pass on these stories that I'm even willing to "do the voices" when reading aloud, although I'm pretty bad at it—except for my evil giants.

Here you'll find a defense of the value of Roald Dahl's children's literature, in all its gruesome, violent, and disturbing glory. But before I go on to defend it, let's first establish beyond any doubt that Roald Dahl's children's literature really is horror for kids.

ROALD DAHL: THE MASTER OF CHILDREN'S HORROR

Most fiction features danger of one sort or another. However, fiction edges toward the horror genre in accordance with the potential degree of harm, especially bodily harm, suffered by characters, the amount of detail lavished on the potential for harm, and the apparent likelihood that characters, especially main characters, will actually be harmed. That's not a definition of "horror art," but these are three good rules of thumb that will usually distinguish horror art from other genres. And by all three standards, Dahl's work leans to the horrific.

In Dahl's stories, children face potential death all the time. Willy Wonka's factory is filled with ways for naughty children to die. Augustus

Gloop, once he has tumbled into the lake of chocolate, is first in danger of drowning, then of being cut up and made into fudge. Veruca Salt is in danger of being burned to death, Violet Beauregarde of being squeezed to death, and Mike Teavee of suffering perhaps the most gruesome death possible—partial materialization. Good children are not much safer. Every wild ride Charlie takes in Wonka's hurtling glass elevator is a gamble with his life, all the more so when carnivorous Knids or infectious Gnoolies await his arrival. Likewise, James Henry Trotter of *James and the Giant Peach* lives in danger of being drowned, eaten by sharks, murdered by the monstrous Cloud-Men, and falling hundreds of feet to his death in a spray of peach juice on the streets of New York. In *The BFG* it is revealed that hideous giants regularly raid our cities under the cover of night to eat "human beans," especially children, while the unnamed child protagonist of *The Witches* faces the possible extermination of every child in England.

The detail Dahl lavishes on the threats in his stories is striking, especially for children's literature. The threats in *Charlie and the Chocolate Factory* may mostly be conveyed by suggestion, but the Oompa-Loompas never let an opportunity pass to ghoulishly elaborate in song about what each vanished child may be suffering: the predicted slicing, boiling, and transformation into fudge of Augustus Gloop, the possible death of Violet Beauregarde from being squeezed in the juicing room, the disgusting filth into which Veruca Salt is plunged as she hurtles into the rubbish furnace, and the possibility that Mike Teavee will remain inches tall for the rest of his life. The Oompa-Loompas may sometimes be lying (as may Wonka when he casually remarks on the likelihood of one of the children dying in some horrible way), but for all the reader can tell, they are speaking the truth. Their songs provide particularly dark little horror stories within the main narrative. If you took the Oompa-Loompas' song about Augustus Gloop out of the novel and included it instead in *Revolting Rhymes* as an independent poem, it would become a straightforward story of a human being getting cut up and turned into food.

Likewise, in *James and the Giant Peach*, Dahl delights in giving frightening descriptions of encounters with alien life. When James first enters the peach, we're told, "Every one of these 'creatures' was at least as big as James himself, and in the strange greenish light that shone down from somewhere in the ceiling, they were absolutely terrifying to behold. 'I'm hungry!' the Spider announced suddenly, staring hard at James."[1]

And upon first seeing the Cloud-Men, "it became obvious that these 'things' were actually living creatures—tall, wispy, wraithlike, shadowy, white creatures who looked as though they were made out of a mixture of cotton-wool and candyfloss and thin white hairs."[2] On further inspection, "James Henry Trotter, glancing up quickly, saw the faces of a thousand furious Cloud-Men peering down at him over the edge of the cloud. The faces had almost no shape at all because of the long white hairs that covered them. There were no noses, no mouths, no ears, no chins—only the eyes were visible in each face, two small black eyes glinting malevolently through the hairs."[3]

Similarly horrible descriptions are given of Vermicious Knids and the intangible Gnoolies in *Charlie and the Great Glass Elevator*; evil human-eating giants like the Bloodbottler, Childchewer, and Fleshlumpeater in *The BFG*; and the haggish witches in *The Witches*. Dahl relates in loving detail the rashy pimpliness of the witches' bald, scabby heads, their clawed hands and square, toeless feet, and the pale blue spittle clinging to their pointed teeth, set in gums that are "like raw meat."[4]

Perhaps most powerfully, Dahl makes the danger in his tales seem real because the worlds he portrays are worlds in which terrible things happen to people. We already know that Charlie Bucket is vulnerable long before he steps into the chocolate factory, because of just how hard a life the author has already given him. Charlie is not just our eyes and ears in the novel but also our mouths and tummies, and we have been feeling him starve. Giving credibility to the danger of Wonka's factory, it is made clear that Oompa-Loompas can and do suffer awful industrial accidents, being turned into blueberries, tumbling down the fudge mountain, or even floating away forever because they drank experimental "fizzy lifting drink" but failed to "do a great big long rude burp." The Oompa-Loompas know how dangerous conditions are in Wonka's factory: "Watching them, Charlie experienced a queer sense of danger. There was something dangerous about this whole business, and the Oompa-Loompas knew it. There was no chattering or singing among them here, and they moved about over the huge black camera slowly and carefully in their scarlet space suits."[5] Things only grow worse for them in *Charlie and the Great Glass Elevator*, in which Wonka's reckless experiments turn 131 Oompa-Loompas into minuses, to face the prospect of painful subtraction and long division in Minusland. They were probably safer back in the jungles of Loompaland, hiding in trees to escape the wangdoodles.

It is knowing that terrible things happen to people in Charlie's universe that gives the danger an edge. The reader can believe that Augustus really might be slaughtered by the knives of the fudge machine and boiled into "Augustus-flavoured chocolate-coated Gloop," that Veruca Salt really might be burned alive in the bowels of the rubbish furnace, that Mike Teavee really might stumble forth as half a person after being sent by television, spraying gore in all directions from his ruined body. In *The Great Glass Elevator*, Charlie listens as the Knids devour the passengers of a commuter shuttle in space: "The screams continued. They were so loud the President had to put his fingers in his ears. Every house in the world that had a television or radio receiver heard those awful screams. There were other noises, too. Loud grunts and snortings and crunching sounds. Then there was silence."[6]

In *James and the Giant Peach*, the horrible and meaningless death of innocent people is a recurring theme. James's parents are snatched away from him when "Both of them suddenly got eaten up (in full daylight, mind you, and on a crowded street) by an enormous angry rhinoceros which had escaped from the London Zoo."[7] The fact that rhinos don't eat meat just underlines the arbitrariness of their deaths. For no good reason and without warning, James's parents are suddenly lost forever: "They were dead and gone in thirty-five seconds flat." Twice on the journey of the flying peach, Miss Spider breaks the narrative to tell a story of her own about the horrible death of a beloved relation, each a sentient spider like herself, at the hands of Aunt Sponge. Her father drowned when Sponge flushed him down the plughole of the bathtub, while her grandmother survived for six months stuck in paint upside down on the ceiling until she was crushed by Sponge's mop.

In *The BFG*, the BFG assures Sophie, "Giants is all cannybully and murderful! And they *does* gobble up human beans! . . . Bonecrunching Giant crunches up two wopsey whiffling human beans for supper every night! Noise is earbursting! Noise of crunching bones goes cracketycrack for miles around!"[8] Children are particularly likely to be eaten. The Queen notes regarding one massacre, "Eighteen girls vanish mysteriously from their beds at Roedean school! Fourteen boys disappear from Eton! Bones are found underneath dormitory windows!"[9]

Even when reading the book of poetry *Dirty Beasts*, we soon realize that a child introduced at the start of a poem is very likely to be dead by the end of it, often through no fault of their own. In *The Witches*, the child protagonist, by being transformed into a mouse, is cursed to die within nine years. The book ends with the curse unlifted and with the implication that it is unliftable. In Dahl's worlds, sometimes even heroic children die.

Of course, death isn't the only horrible thing that can happen to a child in Dahl's children's fiction. In *Matilda*, we know that the evil headmistress, Miss Trunchbull, might break Matilda's arm because she broke Miss Honey's arm when she was a little girl. In *Charlie and the Chocolate Factory*, Charlie's poverty and the way that he suffers because of it turn his search for the Golden Ticket into something desperate. Every time it fails to turn up in a Whipple-Scrumptious Fudgemallow Delight or a Nutty Crunch Surprise, it is an assurance that the universe does not automatically help children to prevent them from starving. The way that James from *James and the Giant Peach* is abused by his Aunts Spiker and Sponge is so vicious that it is unfilmable. In particular, capturing the violence visually requires making it too concrete to be appropriate for children. In the 1996 Disney film of *James and the Giant Peach*, the two aunts, for all their unkindness, are never shown physically *hurting* James. The difference between children's horror like Dahl's and adult horror is likewise often not a matter of the events depicted but of the detail given. In a poem in *Dirty Beasts*, Chocky-Wock the Crocodile eats multiple children at every meal. If this were depicted in visceral detail on the page or the screen, the result would be too horrible for a kid.

CHOCOLATE, SEX, AND OTHER SINFUL INDULGENCES

Many of the specific themes employed by Dahl are familiar from adult horror fiction, literary and cinematic alike. The plot of *Charlie and the Chocolate Factory*, in which a group of people are invited to a wonderful event by a mysterious figure, only to be punished one by one for their sins in frightening ways, is one of the most familiar set-ups in horror films. For example, Vincent Price as millionaire Fredrick Loren in the horror classic *House on Haunted Hill* (1959) throws a party in a haunted house, promising $10,000 to anyone who stays the night, but what he really has in mind is settling grudges with his guests. The idea was old even then, and the theme of an invitation to what turns out to be revenge or punishment has been used by countless cinematic crazies since.

And make no mistake, the whole chocolate factory adventure *is* a setup to punish the wicked. Wonka decides that Charlie is the one to inherit the factory by a process of elimination. His plan, it appears, is to conduct a tour through his factory until enough of the children take themselves out of the running by being incapacitated in some terrible way. The Oompa-Loompas are more explicit about their role in setting traps for naughty children and bad parents. Describing how they chose to deal with Augustus Gloop's gluttony, they sing "'Come on!' we cried. 'The time is ripe / To send him shooting up the pipe!'"[10] They boast that when Augustus fell into the lake of chocolate, it was all according to their plan. Likewise, they describe the way they will deal with Violet Beauregarde in the Juicing Room, not as a cure for being a blueberry but as a cure for chewing gum, apparently their intention all along. After Veruca Salt and her parents are thrown down the rubbish chute by squirrels, the Oompa-Loompas sing of having polished the three of them off, as though they were masterminding the whole thing. Of course, that's exactly what they've been doing.

Another favorite theme of Dahl's that he shares with much adult horror fiction is the frightening punishment of overindulgence. In *Charlie and the Chocolate Factory*, overindulgence of some form or other is the crime for which each of the four "bad" children are punished. Augustus Gloop eats too much, Veruca Salt gets too many material goods, Violet Beauregarde chews too much gum, and Mike Teavee watches too much television. Of course, they are also selfish, rude, and disobedient, but the crime that Wonka and his Oompa-Loompa workers focus on is always that they get too much of something, not that they hurt other people. No child's identifying sin is that they are a bully, a thief, or a vandal, for instance. (Ironically, the two characters in the novel most guilty of putting others in harm's way are Wonka himself and Grandpa Joe, one for endangering the lives of children and the other for encouragingly shouting "yippee!" while he does it.)

The frightening punishment of overindulgence is common in adult horror. Whereas in Dahl's children's fiction, the iconic overindulgence is food, the most familiar overindulgence in popular adult horror is sex. In the seminal slasher film *Friday the 13th* (1980), the shenanigans of hot-blooded teenage campers prevent them from noticing the machete-wielding maniac until it is too late. In *Nightmare on Elm Street* (1984), the heroine, Nancy, marks herself out as a survivor by declining intercourse with her boyfriend, while her friend Tina, the Augustus Gloop of sex, heads upstairs with *her* boyfriend. All it takes is a few quick slashes from Freddie Krueger's glove and virginity is vindicated. In *Hellraiser* (1987), Frank is sent to hell for the crime of opening a magic box that is supposed to be full of pleasure, in the hopes that there is some hot sex in there.

These examples are all modern, but the theme of punishing overindulgence is an old staple in horror. In Mary Shelly's *Frankenstein* (1818), Victor Frankenstein overindulges his love of science, taking his experiments too far by giving life to dead flesh. In Robert Louis Stevenson's *The Strange Case of Dr Jekyll and Mr Hyde* (1886), Hyde's degeneracy is marked by his succumbing to his animal appetites, of which the thrill of violence is only one. As for Count Dracula of Bram Stoker's *Dracula* (1897), he is the Veruca Salt of the undead who wants more of *everything*: more power, more wealth, and, above all, more life.

So Dahl's work is horror fiction, part of a long and ongoing tradition of art designed to inspire fear and other negative emotions. This forces us to face the question of how horror fiction can be appropriate for children. Even if you don't agree with me that his work should be classified as "horror" (and if not, kindly boil your head), you will at least agree that dark themes abound in his fiction for children, forcing us to decide whether such dark literature is all right for kids. A good first step in understanding the importance of dark art for children is to understand the importance of dark art for *adults*. For the roots of *that* debate in Western thought, we need to turn to ancient Greece.

ARISTOTLE KICKS VERUCA SALT DOWN
THE RUBBISH CHUTE

Figure 14.1.

The bearded old man in figure 14.1 is Aristotle (384–322 BCE). How d'you do? And how d'you do? And how d'you do again? He is not pleased to meet you. In fact, he's disgusted! Nobody alive today is culturally "Greek" by a standard he would recognize, and to his mind, if you aren't Greek, you are a barbarian best suited to slavery. So there! Why am I introducing you to this nasty old man who doesn't like you? Because, for all his human failings, he's brilliant! Possibly the single most influential intellectual figure in Western thought, he wrote groundbreaking works on politics, morality, logic, metaphysics, the natural world, and art. Perhaps if you'd done all that, you'd be snooty too.

What makes Aristotle particularly interesting to us here is that he was the first to offer reasoned arguments for including dark themes in art. His direct concern was with Greek tragic theater, an art form every bit as bleak as it sounds. However, the arguments he offers for the value of dark themes in tragedy seem to apply to any dark themes in art, including dark themes in children's literature like Roald Dahl's.

Aristotle believed that enjoying dark art allows us to purge ourselves of negative emotions like pity and fear by feeling them on behalf of fictional others. For example, by feeling pity for Charlie Bucket in his poverty, a child works through their own fear of the uncertainties of life, leaving them less afraid for having confronted these feelings. Likewise, by feeling fear on behalf of Augustus Gloop as he is sucked up the chocolate pipe, the child is allowed to face their fear of death and injury and purge it. In *James and the Giant Peach*, James is shown facing death with full acceptance as the peach plunges down toward New York City. "'James!' cried the Earthworm. 'Do something, James! Quickly, do something!' 'I can't!' cried James. 'I'm sorry! Good-by! Shut your eyes everybody! It won't be long now!'"[11] Below them, a great metropolis also prepares to die, in the belief that it is under nuclear attack: "A few women screamed. Others knelt down on the sidewalks and began praying aloud. Strong men turned to one another and said things like, 'I guess this is it, Joe,' and 'Good-by, everybody, good-by.'"[12] Similarly, fear of the death of parents is faced in *James and the Giant Peach*, fear of school in *Matilda*, and fear of monsters in *Charlie and the Great Glass Elevator*, *The BFG*, and *The Witches*. Aristotle called this process of purging negative emotions *katharsis*, a Greek word referring to any kind of purging, including throwing up (Dahl would surely approve). This became our English word "catharsis."

Another function of literary and dramatic art, according to Aristotle, is that it allows us to explore human nature and thus to learn more about humanity. Aristotle claims in his *Poetics* that the difference between history and poetry is that "the one describes the thing that has been, and the other a kind of thing that might be. Hence poetry is something more philosophical and of graver import than history."[13] By considering people in hypothetical situations, such as by wondering how a group of children might behave if let loose in a chocolate lover's paradise, we reflect on human nature. Aristotle recognizes that the scope of our reflections will be severely limited if we restrict ourselves to thinking about cases in which people behave as they ought to and in which nothing bad ever happens. We don't understand people at all if we don't understand human weakness and wickedness, and we don't understand life at all if we don't understand that life can be tragic.

Applying Aristotle's view to children's horror literature, the inclusion of bad behavior and awful misfortune helps children to think about morality, psychology, politics, and the various harsh realities of existence. To shield them from thoughts about negative things is to stop them from thinking about the most important issues they will face, as children and adults. Do other children in the world really starve like Charlie Bucket? Why? Is there something wrong with spending your life passively being entertained like Mike Teavee? Why? Do I ever act like Veruca Salt, and, if so, what's so bad about that? These are just a few of the issues that a child is invited to reflect on by *Charlie and the Chocolate Factory*, in a way that would be difficult to do without depicting vice and the suffering of innocents. Likewise, *The Witches* invites the child to consider how far strangers should be trusted, *James and the Giant Peach* to face the mortality of parents, and *The BFG* to face the mortality of children.

Of course, it is possible to depict bad behavior and undeserved misfortune in children's literature without penning tales of horror as Roald Dahl did. Even if we allow that exploring extreme misfortune tends naturally to horror, exploring moral choice doesn't. Augustus Gloop could gorge on chocolate without facing the prospect of the hundred knives of the fudge machine, and Veruca Salt could act like a spoiled brat without being thrown into a furnace. However, books only do any good when they are read, and Dahl's mastery of horror is one of the elements that have kept children glued to the page since the 1960s. Horror remains an invaluable tool for getting children to read and to think.

Obviously, we don't just give Roald Dahl to children to help teach them to read and think. For most of us, we want to pass Dahl's books on because they gave us such pleasure when we were children. We want other kids to know the delight of taking a tour through Willy Wonka's incredible factory and soaring over the ocean in a peach borne by seagulls. Aristotle understands that pleasure obtained through art can itself be a good thing, even if it just relieves us of some of the stresses of life. He writes in his *Politics*, regarding the use of music for recreation, that "the end is not desirable for the sake of any future good, nor do the pleasures which we have described exist for the sake of any future good but of the past, that is to say, they are the alleviation of past toils and pains. And we may infer this to be the reason why men seek happiness from these pleasures."[14] In other words, art can have value without training us to better face the future. Art can have value just because it is enjoyable.

Then again, perhaps the very fact that children enjoy horror stories like Dahl's is a reason to be concerned. Perhaps there are some sorts of stories that we don't *want* kids to enjoy. Isn't there something *sadistic* about taking delight in the imagined suffering of others? If a child gets a thrill of pleasurable excitement at the prospect of Augustus Gloop being pushed irresistibly into the slicing knives of the fudge machine, isn't there something *vicious* about that?

Dahl's children's works have often been targeted for criticism because of their gruesome content, just as adult horror has often been targeted for criticism for reveling in violence and cruelty. However, the puzzle inherent in enjoying the depiction of terrible things has been around for much longer than there have been recognizable genres of "horror" and "children's fiction" for people to get their knickers in a twist about.

Just as the first defenses of dark fiction were defenses of tragedy, so the first philosophical inquiries into why decent people enjoy fictional suffering were directed at tragedy. In tragedies, terrible things happen to people. In *Oedipus the King* by the Greek playwright Sophocles (496–406 BCE), Oedipus accidentally murders his father and marries his mother, leading him to tear out his own eyes and go mad with grief. In *King Lear* by William Shakespeare (1564–1616), Lear is betrayed by his own daughters and also goes mad with grief, and when his loyal friend the Earl of Gloucester tries to help him, one of Lear's daughters has Gloucester's eyes torn out. (Not to be outdone, Dahl has the Oompa-Loompas sing "Last week in someone's place we saw / A dozen eyeballs on the floor."[15]) Even philosophers who firmly believed that tragedy is a valuable form of art wondered how it could be that depictions of suffering could be a source of enjoyment.

WHY DAVID HUME LIKES IT WHEN A RHINOCEROS EATS SOMEONE'S PARENTS

Figure 14.2.

The fat Scotsman in a wig in figure 14.2 is David Hume (1711–1776). How d'you do? He is pleased to meet you. After two hundred years of being dead, he's pleased to meet anybody. Another brilliant philosopher, he made invaluable contributions to the philosophy of morality, metaphysics, religion, and art. Of particular interest to us here is his essay *Of Tragedy* about how the depiction of suffering in tragedy can become a source of enjoyment for an audience. He wrote, "It seems an unaccountable pleasure which the spectators of a well-written tragedy receive from sorrow, terror, anxiety, and other passions, that are in themselves disagreeable and uneasy."[16]

Hume begins his search for a solution by considering the explanation offered by the French historian and literary critic Jean-Baptiste Dubos (1670–1742). Dubos suggested that people hate boredom so much that they will welcome any strong emotion that relieves it, even a negative emotion. We might be reminded of the way that Mike Teavee uses violence on television to work himself up into a frenzy of excitement: "Teavee himself had no less than eighteen toy pistols of various sizes hanging from belts around his body, and every now and again he would leap up into the air and fire off half a dozen rounds from one or another of these weapons."[17] It seems that Mike likes to relieve his boredom by getting all worked up.

However, Hume recognizes that Dubos's solution doesn't work. It simply isn't true that any strong emotion delights us. In particular, "It is certain that the same object of distress which pleases in a tragedy, were it really set before us, would give the most unfeigned uneasiness, though it be then the most effectual cure to languor and indolence."[18] In other words, we might enjoy a performance of *Oedipus* or *King Lear*, but if we saw some fellow actually getting his eyes ripped out in the street, we wouldn't enjoy it at all, even though it would completely cure our boredom. Likewise, as enjoyable as it is to read *Charlie and the Chocolate Factory*, if you really saw a child being sucked into a drain, you wouldn't enjoy the sight at all (unless you are Spiker or Sponge or someone else who needs to be squashed by a peach).

Next, Hume considers the proposed solution of author and philosopher Bernard Le Bovier de Fontenelle (1657–1757). Fontenelle suggests that the difference between pleasure and suffering is a matter of degree. He notes that tickling in moderation can be a pleasure, but that too much tickling becomes unpleasant. (His choice of example is charming, suggesting as it does that Monsieur Fontenelle liked to be tickled, but Madame Fontenelle had occasionally gone too far.) In Fontenelle's view, just as tickling is pleasant up to a point, even sorrow is pleasant up to a point. We can enjoy tragedy because our sorrow is sufficiently weakened by the knowledge that the people we feel sorry for aren't real. For instance, we may feel sorry for the plight of poor, cold, and hungry Charlie Bucket, but the reader is prevented from feeling *too* sorry for him because they know there is no such person. We feel sorry enough to enjoy his sad story, but not so sorry that reading the novel stops being fun.

Hume thinks that Fontenelle is on the right track but hasn't yet found the answer. What about the literary depiction of real horrible events? Don't people enjoy literature of this sort too? Consider Dahl's first biographical work, *Boy: Tales of Childhood*. Some of the book is heartwarming, while other parts, such as the descriptions of how Dahl was beaten at school as a child, are sickening. In particular, it is difficult to read the tale of Dahl's headmaster beating four small children at the behest of a vicious old lady who hates little boys: "boys is 'idious and 'orrible!"[19] she declares. She watches the beating with sadistic glee, urging him to hit the children harder: "''Arder!' shrieked Mrs Pratchett. 'Stitch 'im up! Make it sting! Tickle 'im up good and proper!'"[20] But if the narrative is so revolting, why would we want to read it? It can't be because fiction gives us emotional distance, because it all really happened.

Hume's solution is that it is our delight in art itself, executed well, that turns sorrow into something pleasant. It isn't the strength of sorrow per se that makes a difference, as is demonstrated by the fact that there are sorrows that could be weakened without ever growing pleasant. You will feel more sorrow over losing ten dollars than five dollars, but losing a penny will never bring you pleasure. However, we can take pleasure in reading *Boy* because it is so well written, and even adults can take delight in Dahl's children's fiction for exactly the same reason.

Obviously, a work could be well written without depicting tragedy or scenes of horror. Literary giants like Jane Austen, Charles Dickens, and Mark Twain may not have forsworn tragedy, but they all proved themselves capable of producing beautifully written work while using the lightest touch. However, according to Hume, well-written work dealing with dark themes is able to take the very strength of our negative reaction to suffering and convert it into pleasure. As long as the suffering we feel is not too great to be converted, this can give works dealing in dark themes an advantage over works that don't in providing enjoyment. Because the idea of safety and contentment does not provoke the same emotional response in us as the idea of danger and suffering, there is less emotion for the artist's skill to convert into pleasure, and consequently there may be less enjoyment.

Dahl could, in theory, have written *Charlie and the Chocolate Factory* just as skillfully as a tale of a happy boy from a prosperous family who is one of five good little children who visit Wonka's marvelous factory, see wonderful things, and all get cut in for a piece of the old man's fortune. But such a story, however well written, is almost certainly not going to engage us, and is especially unlikely to engage a child. Without the pity we feel for Charlie and the danger faced by the children and adults alike, the reader would lose emotional investment in the story. Hume compared the way that the suffering from a tragic play is converted into pleasure with the way that the discomfort of a mystery can be converted into pleasure. Almost immediately, the reader of *Charlie and the Chocolate Factory* is hit by mysteries that they want the answers to. What is going on in Wonka's legendary factory? How is it running when nobody ever comes out and nobody ever goes in? Yet if we want the answers to these mysteries, why wouldn't it be more pleasurable for us if Dahl answered them all immediately, instead of playing the information out bit by bit? The Humean answer would be that through his skill as a writer, Dahl takes our hunger for answers and converts it into pleasure as he slowly satisfies it. Thanks to his talents, we enjoy stepping inside Wonka's incredible world all the more for having had to wait for admittance.

Hume's account demonstrates that enjoying dark themes in fiction doesn't require a callous or sadistic attitude toward others. Enjoying horror like Roald Dahl's children's literature doesn't require the reader to suspend their sympathy for other people. Rather, it invites them to engage their sympathy. To feel the horror, they have to put themselves in the victim's place, as they are sucked beneath the whirling chocolate or overwhelmed by squirrels and thrown down the chute to the incinerator. Hume's account won't provide a general defense of horror fiction, adult or children's, since not all horror fiction is produced with artistic skill. Similarly, it doesn't provide a general defense for including horrible events in children's literature, since plenty of children's literature is horrible and has little artistic value. But it does provide a defense of giving Roald Dahl's works to children. What turns the child's horror into delight when reading Roald Dahl is the skill with which Dahl weaves the story. What the children are discovering is not the joy of cruelty but the joy of *literature*.

A HORRIBLE GIFT FOR CHILDREN

Children's horror fiction, like that produced by Roald Dahl, has received too little respect as a legitimate literary genre and an important form of art. We are right to be concerned about exposing kids to ideas that will disturb them and right also to be concerned that children don't form harmful views of what sorts of behavior are safe and appropriate. However, as Aristotle reminds us, fiction is an important tool for thinking about the world. Our protectiveness toward children becomes harmful if we do not allow them to think about negative emotions, about awful things happening and about people behaving very badly. To never think of dark things is to never think about the real world at all, and to never think about terrible actions is to never think about morality. Tragedy and wickedness are an integral part of the world in which children live and which they will inherit as adults. Children *must* learn to think about them.

Many parents fear dark children's literature under the impression that to enjoy imagining terrible things is to learn to enjoy terrible things. They fear, for instance, that a child who enjoys reading about Augustus Gloop being sucked up the chocolate pipe is learning to enjoy the suffering of others. However, as Hume shows us, the enjoyment offered by the artistic depiction of terrible things need not be sadistic. Instead, the strength of the reader's negative reaction can be converted into pleasure by means of the artist's skill. Because Roald Dahl tells stories of terror, violence, and death with such consummate skill, their very gruesomeness brings us pleasure. In fact, Roald Dahl's ability to enrapture children through his horror fiction makes him too important a cultural force not to be made widely available to children. After all, the most important lesson that every human being needs to learn about literature is how to *love* it. In that spirit, let the fudge machine slice and the rhinoceroses tear parents apart; let the giants fart and the murderous child-hunting begin. Who knows? We might survive! The Oompa-Loompas only light the incinerator every other day.

15

BRIMFUL OF BUZZBURGERS

A Human Bean's Wild Possibilities

Miranda Nell

Making sense of creativity is not something that has always been given close attention by philosophers, which means that those who grew up reading Roald Dahl will not be satisfied with the story of the imagination that is generally found in the Western canon. Due to a focus on the power of logic and reason in the philosophical tradition, the power of imagination has commonly been overlooked. It has not been completely ignored: rather more dismissively, it has usually been considered a component of the mind subordinate to more important elements. Instead of being seen as a source of humanity's greatest ideas, it has been understood as a basic capacity shared with animals.

In essence, imagination was described as comparable to memory, except that the imagination has the further power to move memories around and predict what might happen next. This concept of the imagination goes well with the ancient notion of art as *techne*, the root of our *technique* and *technical*—essentially, craft. If we think of skill and precision instead of expression and experimentation as the important aspects of art, then the imagination would be better understood as a tool that provides access to simple ideas rather than as the origin of anything itself.

But the worlds of Roald Dahl reveal a different landscape of the mind. Dahl exhibits a playfulness and a sense of spontaneity and, perhaps as important, sometimes lacks a certain skill or care. He has been accused of allowing characters too cruel or distasteful into his stories, or of not wrapping up the tales properly, but in truth these are reasons that children love him. What he puts on the page is freedom. The anarchy of the imagination is available to explore—there are certain familiar themes we come across, but nonetheless any direction is open.

In this chapter, I will show that the classical idea of the imagination is insufficient for explaining human thought and how what is commonly seen as merely aesthetic philosophy is really the center of consciousness. Dahl's work is purposively nonsensical, as well as specifically contradictory in three ways: through humor, through his particular form of magic, and through his use of the taboo. These methods of crossing lines and expanding potential worlds show why the productive imagination that Kant explored should be understood, as Sartre later said, as "the whole of consciousness as it realizes its freedom."[1]

REPRODUCTIVE IMAGINATION: LET'S STAND ON OUR HEADS

The simple, logical notion of imagination that is standard in the philosophy of mind is something like an "image-maker": It is that part of the mind that can hold an image of something after the real item is no longer in front of one's eyes. Imagination becomes defined as the ability to reproduce what has been experienced once the sensory reality is no longer available. This concept dates back to Plato (427–347 BCE), who provides a famous introduction to this breakdown of the mind in *The Republic*. In the traditional interpretation of Plato, he is held to maintain that there are four hierarchical components of the human mind. At the very bottom of the ladder is imagination, or the ability to capture images. Still rudimentary but a little more advanced than imagination is belief. These two parts of the mind are considered sensory and so are considered to live in the dark. It is only once the mind sees the light of reason and graduates to rational thought that the higher parts of the mind—thought and understanding—are engaged.

While many people have since reinterpreted Plato, there is no doubt that this classical understanding of the arrangement of the mind set philosophy on a particular path, in which logic and rational thought reigned—a world Roald Dahl liked to poke fun at:

All the furniture . . . was stuck upside down to the ceiling. . . . And [the floor] had been painted white to look like the ceiling.

"Look!" screamed Mrs. Twit. "That's the floor! . . . "

"We're UPSIDE DOWN" gasped Mr. Twit. "We must be upside down . . ."

"Oh help!" screamed Mrs. Twit. "Help help help! I'm beginning to feel giddy! . . ."

"I've got it!" cried Mr. Twit . . . *"We'll stand on our heads, then anyway we'll be the right way up!"* [2]

The Twits may very well be employing sound logic, but clearly, well, they are still twits. Yet even thinkers like John Locke (1632–1704) and David Hume (1711–1776), esteemed for having their feet firmly planted on the ground instead of getting lost in abstract arguments, understood imagination primarily as a compiler of information rather than a creative force. Locke makes the case by pointing out that a blind man could never imagine color; without the sense impression of light in the eye, the idea of color is simply outside the perceptive, and therefore imaginative, realm of someone blind. [3] According to Locke, the imagination can only reproduce. David Hume allows for at least a question of flexibility when he suggests the problem of the "missing shade of blue": Could a person imagine a medium shade of blue between a lighter and a darker blue that they have seen, when they have never actually seen the missing shade? [4] He ultimately leaves the question unanswered, and the tradition of philosophy does not give it much attention. Instead, the primary concern remains how we organize the sense-based information we take in.

By this understanding, sense impressions provide access to the basis of knowledge in the most direct way. The job of the imagination is only to allow for comparisons—to bring forth remembered impressions so they can be set up against current ones and ultimately lead to the formation of the higher capacities of understanding and reason. In this way, the imagination serves as a kind of bridge between immediate sensation and abstract rational thought. Of course, if you think about it, the Twits were also relying on empirical evidence—their problem was expectations.

PRODUCTIVE IMAGINATION: PEACHES AND DREAMS

Immanuel Kant (1724–1804) gave a new perspective to these issues in the eighteenth century. By examining the role of the imaginative and artistic with philosophical rigor, Kant made it possible to reconsider the entrenched viewpoints. He determined that art had to be distinguished from nature, from science, and, most important for our concerns, from craft:

> *Art* is likewise distinguished from *craft*. The first is also called *free art*, the second could also be called *mercenary art*. We regard free art as an art that could only turn out purposive (i.e., succeed) if it is play, in other words, an occupation that is agreeable on its own account; mercenary art we regard as labor, i.e., as an occupation that on its own account is disagreeable (burdensome) and that attracts us only through its effect (e.g., pay) so that people can be coerced into it. [5]

This notion of playfulness as necessary to art is the key to the reconsideration of imagination. Rather than merely reproducing what is sensed, there is room for the notion that some other part of the mind has productive power. This connection between play and production is a central component of imagination, and one place they come together is in humor.

Dahl is known for being funny, and much of this humor is achieved by a characteristic approach, the creation of bizarre or novel details about what might otherwise seem a fairly ordinary situation. Many of his stories are filled with the random and ridiculous. These unexpected descriptions can arouse a sense of wonder or delight in the reader. If James had traveled in a boat or a hot air balloon, his trip might still have been an interesting tale, but it wouldn't have been fantastic. Given that his mode of transport was a giant floating peach powered by seagulls, there is a sense that anything is possible. Ungluing the reader from the rules of everyday life and releasing the reader's consciousness to explore what has not yet been considered makes Dahl's work compelling.

Another way play and production come together is in magic. Magic is not unfamiliar in children's writing, but we can distinguish between two types of it. One is when it represents power, as in a magical authority like a wizard or fairy. The ability to make something happen that otherwise or normally could not be done can provide that character with special status and allow him or her to achieve things at will. But another kind of magic is simple contradiction. This kind of magic challenges the reader's preconceptions. The rules were always that things worked a particular way, but in a magical account, they simply do not have to. The form of magic associated with power is the sort that fulfills wishes—a fantasy of one's desires or needs being met without compromise. But the kind of magic that represents imagination is less structured than that.

The playfulness of impossibility is clear in the way we enjoy tricks and jokes. No one gets pleasure watching a magician pull a rabbit from a hat because now they foresee a limitless supply of rabbits. It is not a wish fulfillment or a source of power—it is the illusion of something that cannot be done that we like. When faced with something unlike what is expected, the mind is pushed beyond the boundaries previously accepted.

When Kant speaks of productive imagination, he refers to the ability of poetry or other works of genius to expand the cognitive powers of the mind. He states, "A poet ventures to give sensible expression . . . in a way that goes beyond the limit of experience, namely, with a completeness for which no example can be found in nature."[6] The poet's task to say the unsayable calls for the use of the imagination, and it results in the production of *aesthetic ideas* that in turn impact the capacity of the rational mind:

> Now if a concept is provided with a presentation of the imagination such that . . . it prompts so much thought as can never be comprehended within a determinate concept and thereby the presentation aesthetically expands the concept itself in an unlimited way, then the imagination is creative in all of this and sets the power of intellectual ideas in motion: it makes reason think more, when prompted by a presentation, than what can be apprehended and made distinct.[7]

For a mature mind, it is the poet who stretches the limits. For the young, things are slightly more concrete: fairy tales and magical stories fulfill the same purpose. At one time, fairy tales mixed magic with the everyday quite well—but the everyday of most fairy tales is medieval Europe. The worlds Roald Dahl created are a little bit magical, though not in a particularly reliable way. This means seemingly impossible things might happen, but that does not guarantee anyone around has super powers or control of the situation. Magic is not the answer to problems and will not simply fulfill expectations. It is only another layer of possibility that makes the potential of the world slightly more exciting.

In fact, Dahl often involves nonmagical solutions or endings even when the initial situations are paranormal. In *The BFG*, it is the heads of state and their armies who ultimately manage to contend with the unfriendly giants, while in *James and the Giant Peach* the magical adventure ends not in a fairyland of some sort, but in New York City, when the peach is spiked by the Empire State Building. The earthly components of the stories are just as important because they keep the flights of fancy connected to the ordinary, humble, and even unpleasant.

What matters about this is that the magical element is not separated or explained away. It is possible to interpret many children's books as having temporary magic—when we get to the end of the story, Alice might have been dreaming, and the same could be true of Dorothy. C. S. Lewis even has a section in one of the later books of his Narnia series in which the older Susan is said to scoff at her fellow travelers for believing that what they experienced was real. But even if the magic is real, or you decide to "believe," it is still usually designated as belonging in a special domain the protagonist discovers. For Roald Dahl, the impossible or unreal parts of life mix freely with the everyday.

GENIUS: THOSE WHO DON'T BELIEVE IN IMAGINATION WILL NEVER FIND IT

The everyday, or familiar, in this context can be thought of as representing the conceptual or the known. Kant explains that genius is not just imagination alone, but also the connection of imagination with the understanding:

> An aesthetic idea is a presentation of the imagination which is conjoined with a given concept and is connected, when we use imagination in its freedom, with such a multiplicity of partial presentations that no expression that stands for a determinate concept can be found for it. Hence it is a presentation that makes us add to a concept the thoughts of much that is ineffable, but the feeling of which quickens our cognitive powers and connects language, which otherwise would be mere letters, with spirit. [8]

Poetry connects intellectual concepts with aesthetic ideas and, through this, expands the power of thought. But before such an abstract level of thinking has emerged, a more immediate version of the same relationship exists for the young in the imaginative writing of Dahl. Rather than concepts, we begin with examples—characters, houses, schools, stories—and imagination presents not the ineffable but the impossible. Certain familiar archetypes or tropes show up in stories, the way the known concepts are present in poetic writing. But in order to expand the dimensions of thought instead of just confirming the already known, imagination reveals an original vantage point through a nonrational route. Dahl refers to witches, giants, orphans, and evil aunts, but his versions are solidly associated with the modern world. Perhaps the clearest examples Dahl provides for his love of classic tropes are his retellings of old nursery rhymes and fairy tales. Dahl's version of Little Red Riding Hood includes access to some contemporary technology, for instance:

> "That's wrong!" cried Wolf. "Have you forgot
> To tell me what BIG TEETH I've got? . . ."
> The small girl smiles. One eyelid flickers.
> She whips a pistol from her knickers.

In his version of Cinderella, marrying the prince is not so important after all:

> Within a minute, Cinderella
> was married to a lovely feller
> A simple jam-maker by trade,
> Who sold good home-made marmalade. [9]

In poetry, logical ideas are broadened through the use of nonlogical or poetic ideas. In Dahl, typical characters or stories are broadened through the use of atypical or unexpected ideas.

This current of familiarity in the work of Roald Dahl is important. We recognize certain archetypes, especially in the moral realm. Often, as in classic fairy tales, grown-ups or grumpy people or physically scary people are best avoided, while children on their own make good decisions, and people who trust children are generally okay. Of course, there are sometimes children who have forgotten how to be children—the bullies and spoiled ones—and just like adults, their problem is having lost touch with their inner nature. This division of characters is found throughout classic stories. As Kant makes clear, in order for the poetic to be universally compelling, the initial concept must be sharable across humanity; however, in order to teach us something new, the offering of the artist has to go beyond any concept we know. To apply this to children's literature is to look back to the beginning of that same process. In order to nudge the imagination in its early stages rather than enforce already conceptualized thoughts and diminish creativity, a story needs both a sense of familiarity and a sense of freedom. The brave protagonist fighting dark forces, overcoming trials, and using ingenuity to save the day sounds familiar, but the dark forces in Dahl might be square-toed witches, and saving the day could involve the marriage of a ladybug to the head of the NYFD.

Dahl rarely tells a story with what might be called a sitcom plot, in which the primary situation is exactly the same at the end of the adventure as it was at the beginning. While classic fairy tales commonly involve characters whose lives are changed by the actions they take, many modern classics prefer the dream or perhaps the road trip: Alice wakes up from Wonderland, Dorothy finds her way home to Kansas, and even the children of Narnia—who rule the kingdom for years—get back to England in time for supper, thanks to some lucky time shifts. For Dahl, though, usually something significant has taken place, and the decisions made have borne consequences—not just in a fantasy world but also in the life of the protagonist. An enemy is defeated, a bad situation escaped, and the child or the good adult has found a new way forward. This is the universal element of the story, which provides the conceptual component of the aesthetic.

But there is an imaginative angle, and in Dahl it is most evident in examples like *The Witches* in which the outcomes are especially unusual. In this story, while the evil foes are vanquished and our hero survives, he is also turned into a mouse and expected to grow old and die in mouse-years (which is to say, not very many). It is worth it, since he defeated the witches and since his closest companion is his elderly grandmother (who won't last forever either), but it is not a standard form of "happily ever after." But it is just this openness to unexpected options that makes Dahl's stories enticing. It is never assured that everything will work out the way you might have hoped. But, then, perhaps the way you hoped was not the most interesting anyway.

An ending like the one in *The Witches* deepens the story in two ways. One is that it forces us to reconsider what a happy ending is. Wish fulfillment leads to spoiled children, after all, and things can work out in truly remarkable ways that are just not what you had in mind at the start. In *The Witches*, the details of the narrator living as a mouse make his new life actually sound quite fascinating—there are gadgets and slides for getting around to human-size stuff, and the fun of seeing everything from this new vantage point is revealed in description. By the end of the book it seems like he is not condemned to this fate, but rather given an exciting opportunity, and he takes it on happily. [10] It is not the ending one started out hoping for; yet it becomes an ending one is able to enjoy and love. This shows that it is not the intellectual or conceptual ending, but an imaginative and aesthetic one.

The other aspect of Dahl's work that deepens his stories is that he emphasizes that actions and decisions have consequences. When faced with a difficulty, there may be things one can do to solve the problem, but the protagonist probably will not just wake up and discover it was all in their mind or in a magical land no one else can see. For Dahl, the magical is very much entwined with the real, and real life involves change and adaptation. This gives a sense of meaning and responsibility to the story. Even if things do end up well, this emphasizes that happiness involves going through changes and that these changes are significant; they are not merely a game being played for an afternoon, but rather constitute a new path in life. In this sense, Dahl takes seriously the mortality of his characters. Imagination is not a side project that allows for a secondary life, to avoid the knowledge of one's own finitude. Instead, it is the power to create the best life possible out of what you find yourself with here and now.

TABOO AND TRANSGRESSION: HE'S DOTTY, HE'S BARMY, HE'S BATTY!

Central to the power of imagination is the pushing of boundaries. To allow the mind to explore beyond what it knows means to graduate to a nonconceptual state. In poetic works, the use of metaphor and creative descriptions is common, but for a children's author fear and humor are more immediate. Scary, creepy, funny, or otherwise weird situations and characters express the extending of the mind beyond the concepts that are already fully stabilized.

A key ingredient to Dahl's work is his signature mischievous style. All throughout his writing, he dances around descriptions of evil and suffering and manages to make them funny. There are plenty of characters in Roald Dahl's novels who are quite hilariously nasty, like George's grandmother in *George's Marvelous Medicine* or Matilda's headmistress, Miss Trunchbull. Ultimately, the awful characters end up seeming pitiful instead of powerful, but there is a sense of glee in their introductions. These inventions are so vile as to be ridiculous, and each new detail manages to combine the terrible, terrifying, and terrific. The conversation in *The Witches* in which Grandmamma explains what witches are like is a good example, since it provides the reaction as well as the descriptions. Our narrator responds to every piece of information with shock, trusting his loving grandmother, yet scarcely able to believe that these outrageous creatures—who wear wigs and gloves and pointy shoes so they look like women, but who are actually bald with claws and square feet, with blue spit and big nostrils to smell children who bathe too often—truly exist. The suggestion that a smart child probably wouldn't want to bathe more than once a month, since a good layer of dirt masks that child-smell witches can pick up, is just the sort of impish humor Dahl likes to sprinkle throughout his stories. It's not something a sensible mom or dad would advise; instead, it's an in-joke between the reader and the author.

This kind of voice opens up a sense of freedom and imagination. Dahl shows through such nods and winks that he is not concerned with following rules, explaining facts, and teaching right answers. He is having fun, and the young reader understands that there are no limits—exploring ideas means discovering what thoughts are out there, not intending a particular conclusion. This feeling of anarchy is exciting, encouraging, and a little bit frightening at the same time. Perhaps most important is that it gives the smart reader the power to read actively, to enjoy the book both on its straightforward level and as a conversation between the reader and author.

By exaggerating the nastiness of the malevolent beings in his tales, Dahl makes them scary but allows them to become ultimately symbols of evil rather than actual individuals we might feel worried about. When Willy Wonka is understood as a strange chocolatier who punishes children, his persona seems funny or even disconcerting, but when the story is read as a modern morality tale, he is destroying archetypal vices that all of us face—gluttony, as embodied by Augustus Gloop, or pride as Violet

Beauregarde represents it, for instance. We are dealing not with other people but with tendencies in ourselves, when we face such clearly awful demons; their destruction is the removal of cruelty from the world.

Dahl is also comfortable crossing this border in his descriptions of good characters, the well-intentioned odd ones out, who may be grumpy or ugly or just strange in some way—the BFG with his giant ears, Grandmamma in *The Witches* who smokes cigars, frenetic Willy Wonka. These characters are not the cause of the world's pain, but they are aware of it. Unlike more innocent characters who are baffled by unfair behavior and unsure how to respond except by running away or reacting emotionally, these figures have often been around the block and are ready to take action instead of turning the other cheek. Dahl's *Little Red Riding Hood* conclusion is a punchy summation of this, as she says, "Hello, and do please note / my lovely furry WOLFSKIN COAT."[11] This may seem shocking to someone expecting a Disney finale, but understood as a challenge and metaphor, it brings a smile to one's face.

THE CREATIVE MIND

What is intriguing to the philosopher about this kind of thinking is the combination of spontaneity and nonrationality. Philosophy has traditionally presumed that the capacity to be an original source of mental activity is tied to the rational will. In other words, a person has to choose to have an idea. But in experience that is not how it generally works. As Roald Dahl himself puts it, after comparing ideas to dreams that disappear as you awaken, "A story idea is liable to come flitting into the mind at any moment of the day and if I don't make a note of it at once, right then and there, it will be gone forever. So I must find a pencil, a pen, a crayon, a lipstick, anything that will write, and scribble a few words that will later on remind me of the idea."[12]

One way to explain this is to consider it as associative. This is a common approach when the attempt is made to boil down the process of thought to a logical structure. The claim is that random thoughts or memories get combined or associated, and the resulting combination seems novel enough to be considered a new idea. A sailor sees a fish while thinking of a woman and then imagines a mermaid. Or Roald Dahl has a

peach for breakfast while thinking about telling the story of a boy traveling to New York.

But this doesn't really answer the question. Plenty of people have
eaten peaches without writing stories about traveling on them, and quite
often associations that seem to be the root of ideas are very weak—just
because a person is aware of two things is hardly reason to expect those
two particular things to end up together, or especially to end up together
in precisely the way they do in someone's original idea. A new idea is
less like math, in which two and two will always be four, and more like
chemistry, in which carbon can be coal or diamond—or any living thing.

It is central to philosophy whether imagination is merely a supportive
aspect of the mind that allows for the development of more important
capacities like concept formation or actually the fundamental self-guided
nature of consciousness. Rather than seeing the mind as a tool based in
reproduction, it must be reconceptualized as an active and inventive capacity. Imagination is not just the collecting of images to build concepts
but also a creative and experimental way of existing. As Roald Dahl
shows, the human mind can keep track of multiple levels at one time. In
the world, it would be paradoxical for a thing to both be and not be the
case. But in stories, in words and images, contradictions are just ways to
push boundaries.

If we understand the mind as creative rather than merely reproductive,
the reflective nature of consciousness is not a result of atomic structure
but a temporally extended state of intentionality. The imagination is not
simply a weak tool that connects memories, but rather a central power of
human freedom. Instead of thinking of the process of imagining as secondary, the mind can be understood as a united power that includes its
creative element. There is never a formation of memory or thought that is
perfectly reproductive; even in our best attempts at simply retaining an
experience we infuse variation and distinction into the mental product.

By being reflective, we add doubt, wonder, and imagination to any
conscious state. The important thing about imagination is that it is addi-
tive. The world begins for us as the experience of certain information, but
due to this quality of self-motivated creative thought, new possibilities
come into existence that are distinct from the material past.

Philosophers cannot ignore that our minds are active, creative, and
productive. Roald Dahl mixes classic and futuristic qualities naturally, so
that his worlds land somewhere between magic and science fiction. The

imagination of humankind continuously results in the machinery and technology that surround us, and we should remember Arthur C. Clarke's famous notion that any sufficiently advanced technology is indistinguishable from magic. [13] All too often this is thought to reduce magic to "mere" technology. Instead, it should be remembered that imagination itself is a magical quality, the capacity to create. In Roald Dahl, we see this creative element in its wild, active form, as impossible magic, unlikely technology, and unseemly outcomes. The challenging energy of his stories allows for the expansion of the productive imagination and shows humanity as creatures rooted in pure freedom, pure imagination.

16

DEWEY'S MARVELOUS MEDICINE

Negative Capability and the Wonder of Roald Dahl

Tanya Jeffcoat

"How fascinating this all is!" cried James. "And to think that up until now I had never even *wondered* how a grasshopper made his sounds." "My dear young fellow," the Old-Green-Grasshopper said gently, "there are a whole lot of things in this world of ours that you haven't started wondering about yet."[1]

It doesn't take long to discover, when reading Roald Dahl, that the children in his stories learn early on that life is dangerous and can be terribly painful. Young Charlie faces starvation, and both James and the little boy in *The Witches* lose their parents in horrible accidents. When faced with such hard lives, many people lose hope; in fact, for a while James himself decides that "all hope of a happier life had gone completely" when he is forced to live with his abusive aunts. No matter how hopeless their situations at first seem, the children in Dahl's books all discover that the world remains a wonderful, mysterious place full of possibilities, and this discovery allows them to transform themselves and the circumstances surrounding them for the better. It is this process of discovery and transformation that fuels much of John Dewey's philosophy, and it is this avenue that we will explore here.

John Dewey (1859–1952) was an American pragmatist and is probably best known for his philosophy of education. But he was also a public intellectual in the first part of the twentieth century. Like the children in

Dahl's books, Dewey learned at an early age that life is hard. He was named after his older brother, who died before Dewey was born, and he was a small boy during the US Civil War—a war bloodier than the two world wars that he also witnessed. Dewey saw both his local and national communities struggle with racism, economic injustice, and religious intolerance. But he also saw the science that gave humans the ability to soar above the clouds and to talk to loved ones thousands of miles away. His philosophy grew from these experiences.

LIFE IS HARD: CAR WRECKS, BULLIES, AND AN ANGRY RHINOCEROS

Over and over again, Roald Dahl repeats the same lesson: life is hard. Sometimes this lesson appears as the loss of a loved one: Danny's mother dies when he is only four months old, James's parents are eaten by an angry rhinoceros, and the parents in *The Witches* die in an automobile accident. Others discover that the people who are supposed to love and care for them don't: Matilda's parents do nothing to help her develop, and Miss Honey's aunt cheats her out of her inheritance. The little boy from *The Witches* learns that normal-looking people can be dangerous and predatory, and Danny learns that wealth can be used callously and inhumanely. Several of the youngsters in Dahl's books learn the extent to which those in power will go to maintain their status: the Trunchbull physically and mentally abuses the children and bullies the teachers in order to maintain her absolute control over her school, the farmers in *Fantastic Mr. Fox* destroy an entire hillside in their attempts to kill the fox that they know is accessing their hoards, and Victor Hazell posts keepers to shoot or trap anyone poaching the birds he raises for the sole purpose of proving his social status. In each of these examples, those in power act in ways that show that they believe that their status is more important than the welfare of the people around them. While many children's authors might be reluctant to expose their readers to these painful lessons, Dahl does not hesitate in showing the harsher realities of life.

Although Dewey's writings focus upon human possibilities, he also writes about human hardships. In *Experience and Nature*, he emphasizes the dynamic nature of existence—an existence that is often precarious:

> Man finds himself living in an aleatory world; his existence involves,
> to put it baldly, a gamble. The world is a scene of risk; it is uncertain,
> unstable, uncannily unstable. Its dangers are irregular, inconstant, not
> to be counted upon as to their times and seasons. . . . Plague, famine,
> failure of crops, disease, death, defeat in battle, are always just around
> the corner, and so are abundance, strength, victory, festival, and song.
> Luck is proverbially both good and bad in its distributions. The sacred
> and the accursed are potentialities of the same situation; and there is no
> category of things which has not embodied the sacred and accursed:
> persons, words, places, times, directions in space, stones, winds, ani-
> mals, stars.[2]

The dangers are both in nature and in our institutions. No matter how
hard we work to make sure that our homes are secure, one tornado can
take everything from us. Likewise, there is little that a single person can
do to avoid the large-scale problems that happen when our political and
social institutions falter. When the Great Depression began, many citizens
who had worked diligently to protect themselves financially discovered
that their investments were not as secure as they had previously believed.
And the consequences of these dangers can be overwhelming: people die
in tornadoes and can lose everything during an economic downturn. Since
we live in a world that is dangerous and live lives that—according to
Dewey—are gambles, what can we do to "hedge our bets"?

TRYING TO RECOGNIZE WITCHES: SCARY SITUATIONS AND THE QUEST FOR CERTAINTY

Dewey recognizes that when people face hard times, especially those that
appear to be dangerous, people become fearful and want security. The
little boy in *The Witches*, for example, hopes that his grandmother can
give him a sure means of detecting witches but finds that every single
method has been counteracted by the clever demons. For him, the world,
once so seemingly secure, has now become a place of danger. For Dewey,
the danger and our desire to counteract it often leads us to develop philosophies and religions that promise us security and certainty. The Platonic
realm of forms, absolute truth, and the heaven promised by various religious traditions offer solace against the pains and tribulations of a frightening and precarious world: "The quest for certainty is a quest for a peace

which is assured, an object which is unqualified by risk and the shadow of fear which action casts. For it is not uncertainty *per se* which men dislike, but the fact that uncertainty involves us in peril of evils. . . . Quest for complete certainty can be fulfilled in pure knowing alone. Such is the verdict of our most enduring philosophic tradition."[3]

Dewey worries that in developing such philosophies and religious traditions, we often orient ourselves away from the world surrounding us and lose sight of the transformational possibilities this world contains. Philosophies such as those above too often have "diverted thought from inquiring into the purposes which experience of actual conditions suggest and from concrete means of their actualization. It translated into a rational form the doctrine of escape from the vicissitudes of existence by means of measures which do not demand an active coping with conditions."[4] This escape might manifest in an acceptance of social injustice, either in the belief that the truly real transcends the world of mere appearance and physicality or in the hope of justice and reward after death. In both cases, the escapist philosophy does not in itself require confronting or addressing the unjust situation.

Dewey's own philosophy (even his religious philosophy) orients itself away from a search for absolute truth and certainty and instead turns toward the world and the possibilities that he believes are an ever-present feature of human existence. For instance, Dewey continually emphasizes the importance of experience in his philosophy. People's philosophies reflect and arise from their lived experiences, and hopefully philosophy will turn back to lived experience in order to prepare them for transforming the situation at hand. Philosophy's role, for Dewey, is "to search out and disclose the obstructions; to criticize the habits of mind which stand in the way; to focus reflection upon needs congruous to present life; to interpret the conclusions of science with respect to their consequences for our beliefs about purposes and values in all phases of life."[5]

But even when we start with lived experience, it is all too easy to get so caught up in theory that we lose sight of the reason we started in the first place. For instance, when the giant insects land in New York in *James and the Giant Peach*, they are initially feared and then welcomed. However, when they decide to remain, a number of important questions will ultimately arise, all of which are vital to the lived experiences of the insects. Thanks to their magical transformation, these insects are no longer garden variety. They are capable of rational discourse, and presumably they will want to secure the rights associated with citizenship. While many might readily agree that of course such fascinating and wonderful creatures should become full citizens, others might hesitate and argue that doing so might open the door to allowing all insects access to citizenship. A Deweyan approach would find no problem in discussing the nature of citizenship, personhood, and community with regard to this new development. However, if the debate became fixated upon finding precise and unchanging definitions for the vocabulary terms being used, or if the giant insects' situation were "solved" merely verbally (a *de jure* or legal solution that left the *de facto* or real-world situation unresolved), then something that might have started out as an authentic philosophical inquiry with hope for solution would have turned into another type of quest for certainty. Dewey wants to remind us that our philosophy should mean more to our lives than we have allowed it to. Striving to tie philosophy to experience helps ensure philosophy's relevance to our lives.

So Dewey thinks that we should hedge our bets in an aleatory—that is, risky—world first of all by rejecting the quest for certainty. But he also looks to the importance of human relationships—especially community relationships—for achieving relative security in a precarious world. Dahl seems to agree, for time and again he shows people working together to achieve their goals. When James enters the center of the peach, the Ladybug greets him by saying, "You are one of *us* now, didn't you know that? You are one of the crew. We're all in the same boat." These insects and the small boy who has become one of the crew must learn to work together to survive their "frantic and terrible trip."[6] Not one of these intrepid travelers could have managed the ordeal alone; yet together they took a precarious situation and created new lives for themselves. Likewise, Matilda and Miss Honey form a bond that allows them both to transform their situations into something that allows each of them to flourish. The bonds of human companionship, paired with a philosophical commitment to the lived experiences of the people in our communities, promote relative security in a world that is often dangerous.

THE IMPORTANCE OF WONDER:
NEGATIVE CAPABILITY IN DEWEY AND DAHL

Perhaps because they recognize that life is often difficult and security is fleeting, both Dewey and Dahl emphasize the importance of wonder in their works. For instance, Dahl presents a number of characters who have lost their sense of wonder but are transformed when it is restored. Unfortunately, there are also characters, such as Matilda's parents, who seem incapable of recognizing the wondrous even when it stands right before them. When James loses the magical green crocodile tongues, he loses all hope of escape from his awful aunts; for him, "All hope of a happier life had gone completely now. Today and tomorrow and the next day and all the other days as well would be nothing but punishment and pain, unhappiness and despair."[7] Likewise, Charlie's four grandparents, who slept in the same bed and were "so tired, they never got out of it,"[8] seem to have given up all hope of better days. However, within moments of losing the crocodile tongues, James realizes that the magic hasn't been lost and that *"something peculiar is about to happen,"*[9] a something that opens new possibilities and allows his escape. Upon learning that Charlie has purchased the candy bar containing the final Golden Ticket, Charlie's Grandpa Joe, "in one fantastic leap, this old fellow of ninety-six and a half, who hadn't been out of bed these last twenty years, jumped on to the floor and started doing a dance of victory in his pajamas."[10] In each case, life moves from being anesthetic to being imbued with possibility and wonder.

It is no surprise that Dewey takes up wonder in his texts on aesthetics, for he thinks that most of human existence has become similar to the way that Charlie's grandparents live, which is to say, a life that is anesthetic or without beauty. In such a life, "Things happen, but they are neither definitely included nor decisively excluded; we drift. We yield according to external pressure, or evade and compromise. There are beginnings and cessations, but no genuine initiations and concludings. One thing replaces another, but does not absorb it and carry it on. There is experience, but so slack and discursive that it is not *an* experience. Needless to say, such experiences are anesthetic."[11] Life too easily becomes humdrum; yet we are surrounded by aesthetic possibilities that encourage a "heightened vitality" and an "active and alert commerce with the world."[12] We see this heightened vitality in Grandpa Joe after Charlie discovers the final ticket, for in that moment the world becomes alive with possibilities for himself and his grandson.

So often, when we are trying to figure out the world, we lose sight of exactly how complicated and wondrous it actually is. We become accustomed to our immediate environment, and we become so used to our surroundings that we allow our habits to carry us through the day instead of engaging life. It is all too easy to sleepwalk, and even sleep-drive, through life. To understand the power of habit, but also its numbing, anesthetic quality, we only have to remember our first experience driving a car. In all probability, we were like Danny, who says of his first experience on the road, "My heart was thumping away so fiercely I could hear it in my throat."[13] That first time, the roads were far too narrow and the operations far too complex for proficient driving, and the car seemed so responsive that it might leap into the next lane or roar down the road at the slightest pressure on the gas pedal. Driving required a vigilance that was almost exhausting, but it was invigorating because it required such attention to so many things. (As Danny reminds us, "Most of the really exciting things we do in our lives scare us to death. They wouldn't be exciting if they didn't."[14]) Soon, however, habits formed and the process was more natural. Before long, the process becomes so habitual that people speak of arriving at work without remembering the drive at all, at which time the experience has become anesthetic. Only when something extraordinary happens does the driver come to life—a near collision or a complicated route snaps the driver's attention back to the situation at hand, if only for a moment. Moments like these remind us, Dewey says, that we do not have to be "cold spectators" to life.[15] We can engage life and create new possibilities from the situations of which we are a part.

Our mental habits, including our philosophies, can undermine our active engagement with the world, as surely as can our physical habits. When we get our news from the same source each day or assume that our beliefs are shared by all those who matter, we limit ourselves by closing off other possibilities. For Dewey, Western philosophy, in emphasizing reason as the sole source of reliable philosophical truth, has given a false sense of how the world works and how we actually arrive at truth. For Dewey, too many philosophical systems forget that the world is messier than our systems acknowledge. While our systems may be logical and streamlined, "Man lives in a world of surmise, of mystery, of uncertainties."[16] Dewey emphasizes the role of imagination and personal preference in philosophical inquiry by noting that "no reasoning as reasoning, that is, as excluding imagination and sense, can reach the truth. Even 'the greatest philosopher' exercises an animal-like preference to guide his thinking to its conclusion. He selects and puts aside as his imaginative sentiments move."[17]

Is this to say that reason isn't important? Of course not. Analysis and cleverness are vital, as exhibited by the fantastic Mr. Fox, who is able to outwit the farmers, feed his family, and build a community thanks to his ability to analyze a dangerous situation and respond in an unexpected way. When the farmers surrounded the opening to the foxes' den, they thought that they could simply wait until the foxes either came out for food or starved. Mr. Fox, however, analyzed his circumstances and realized that his family was not limited to a single avenue of escape. They were diggers and—although boxed in by Boggis, Bunce, Bean, and their helpers—they could dig outside the box by going underneath the men who were trying to destroy them. George, however, lucked out with his marvelous medicine when he threw things willy-nilly into a giant pot.[18] Most of the time, chucking hair remover, flea powder, floor polish, and a variety of other household chemicals in a bowl will result in sickness or death, not something marvelous. Analysis serves as an element of reliable inquiry, but at times we forget that underneath our inquiry remains that wonderful mystery of why things are exactly what they are.[19] Analysis, no matter how rigorous, starts at a certain point, presupposes a vast amount of information (including personal and social biases that might mislead us), and works toward a particular goal we have established. All of these are present in inquiry, and yet all encourage us to discard or overlook elements that distract us from our particular goal. To Dewey's mind, supposing that reason can be pure is short-sighted, and to demand logical certainty sabotages inquiry since the dynamic world of lived experience continually outpaces our formulations of it. For Dewey, analysis and cleverness are certainly vital, but they are not necessarily the most important or the whole story when it comes to philosophy.

In particular, Dewey emphasizes the importance of wonder and imagination in philosophy, and he draws heavily upon John Keats's concept of negative capability. For Keats, a person of negative capability is one "capable of being in uncertainties, mysteries, doubts, without any irritable reaching after fact and reason."[20] While some thinkers might discard an idea if it doesn't fit previous views or if it isn't clear, the person of negative capability is able to move forward with partial knowledge in order to see where the idea might lead. For instance, James has no idea whether his plan for using seagulls to lift the peach will work, but despite his own doubts and the ridicule he initially receives, he convinces his friends to try his idea, and they are able to escape the sharks who are trying to devour the peach. While analysis initially causes James to doubt the seagull solution, his willingness to go beyond his partial knowledge opens up a life-saving solution.[21] For Dewey, this is the spirit of the scientific method on one hand and of art on the other. Both require the individual to move forward in the spirit of discovery, searching for answers and insights and circling back to rework as new skills and information come to light. Dewey contrasts philosophy that maintains its quest for certainty with his own more open philosophy by employing one of his rare dichotomies: "Ultimately there are but two philosophies. One of them accepts life and experience in all its uncertainty, mystery, doubt, and half-knowledge and turns that experience upon itself to deepen and intensify its own qualities—to imagination and art."[22] The other philosophy is one that is bound to the quest for certainty and will sacrifice poetic wisdom in the name of academic rigor. Negative capability also appears in experimental science, for in science half-knowledge serves as the basis for hypotheses that lead to further knowledge and new questions. In art, philosophy, and science, negative capability is a willingness to move forward with partial data in order to see what possibilities will appear in the process of exploration.

Willy Wonka, in all his madness, seems to have negative capability to spare, for he is continually expressing an exuberant delight in discovery. The Inventing Room, "the room he loved best of all,"[23] is the most important part of the factory because it is the place of exploration and discovery. Here the children find everlasting gobstoppers, hair toffee, and the chewing-gum meal, all of which, in different ways, are absurd inventions. Yet the process of discovery often produces absurdities that, in time and through further work, become commonplaces. While Wonka certainly should cultivate a spirit of prudence alongside his sense of wonder, he uses his knowledge to discover new possibilities and open up new worlds with his inventions. Some of his experiments work and others don't, just as it is in our own lives. Wonka, for all his craziness, reminds us that we, too, can live lives of wonder and exploration, continually open to the aesthetic possibilities surrounding us. A world in which human flight and

space exploration were once but are no longer absurd still contains sur-
prises for those who allow their imaginations to push against the boundaries of the certain. We don't need to wait until we receive tickets to a
magical place usually barred to us, for we already live in a world of
marvelous possibility.

Therefore, negative capability isn't a negative at all. It is an ability to
recognize that no matter how much we know, there is far more that we
don't. This realization should encourage humility in our intellectual pursuits, but it should also serve as a call to find out more, all the while
realizing that even as our knowledge grows, so should our appreciation of
the larger mysteries of existence.

A WORLD OF THINGS TO WONDER ABOUT:
BEING SPARKY WHEN OTHERS ARE STODGY

No one wants to live a life that is anesthetic and practically devoid of
wonder. Yet time and time again, people fall into just such a situation.
Even the Earthworm, a creature who should be continually reminded of
wondrous possibilities, continually falls into fatalistic and anesthetic
thinking, going so far as despairing that "the problem is that there is no
problem!"[24] There is security in old habits, even those that we know
undermine our current and future happiness, and societies are made up of
social habits or expectations, some of which are limiting. Even if the
habit doesn't fit people's needs, many people will do what they are supposed to rather than reject the status quo and create something new.

Dahl, however, encourages parents to be "sparky" instead of "stodgy,"
even if it means going outside social norms.[25] Danny's father steps outside traditional social habits in a number of ways and thus provides a
model for his son to do the same. For instance, he takes on many roles
historically associated with women when he rears his son on his own, and
he blurs the adult/child dichotomy by playing with Danny and including
him in his work at the filling station. He rejects a number of other social
conventions by encouraging minor illegalities such as poaching. But his
decisions do not seem to be arbitrary. He and others (including the local
policeman) poach the pheasants of Victor Hazell, a man who takes every
opportunity to flaunt his wealth and power and who tries to hurt anyone
who stands up to him. The father's poaching undermines Hazell's status

and calls into question an economic system that allows men such as Hazell to use their wealth inhumanely. The lesson that Danny seems to learn is not that rules don't matter, but that people matter more than rules.

Each of Dahl's protagonists must make a similar discovery: things as they are are not what they have to be. Matilda transforms her situation and that of Miss Honey. The young boy turned mouse in *The Witches* accepts his shortened life span with no regrets, knowing that he will live his life with new purpose and with someone he loves. Mr. Fox and his family transform the underground community, and James creates a home where all are welcome. In each case, their willingness to leap into an uncertain future with insufficient knowledge of how things might end allows them to become creators of a new future.

It is this spirit that Dewey encourages in his writings on both aesthetics and democracy. Changing social situations require us to step outside of social norms and engage the world in a new way, a way that can be aesthetic. Most often, when people discuss the nature of philosophy, they emphasize rigorous analysis and the search for absolute, certain truth. However, John Dewey points to another option: a rejection of the "quest for certainty" in favor of negative capability. Both he and Roald Dahl continually remind us of those aspects of our world (and ourselves) that are mysterious, uncertain, and fallible. The children in Dahl's books learn that even though the world is dangerous, they can overcome hardships and create a better future for themselves. Dewey's philosophy likewise orients us toward the messy world of everyday experience in the hope that we will see new possibilities for continually transforming ourselves and our world into something better than it was before.

NOTES

INTRODUCTION

1. The title of this chapter alludes to Albert Camus, "The Myth of Sisyphus," in *Basic Writings of Existentialism*, ed. and intro. Gordon Marino (New York: Modern Library, 2004), 476.

2. Camus, "The Myth of Sisyphus," 441.

3. Roald Dahl, *James and the Giant Peach* (New York: Puffin Books, 1996), 1.

4. Camus, "The Myth of Sisyphus," 460.

5. Camus, "The Myth of Sisyphus," 470.

6. Camus, "The Myth of Sisyphus," 470.

7. Camus, "The Myth of Sisyphus," 479.

8. Roald Dahl, *The Witches* (New York: Puffin Books, 1983), 207.

9. Dahl, *The Witches*, 207.

10. Arnold Lobel is one of my favorites. From the Frog and Toad collections and *Owl at Home* to *Grasshopper on the Road* and his book of fables, his books are wonderful.

1. EPICURUS AND THE CHOCOLATE FACTORY

1. Epicurus, "Letter to Menoeceus," in *Hellenistic Philosophy: Introductory Readings*, 2nd ed., ed. Brad Inwood and L. P. Gerson (Indianapolis: Hackett, 1997), 30. All citations and quotations from Epicurus are from Inwood and Gerson's collection.

2. This argument appears in Cicero, *On Goals* 1.30, in Inwood and Gerson, *Hellenistic Philosophy*, 57–58.

3. Epicurus, "Letter to Menoeceus," 30–31; see also Epicurus, *Principle Doctrines* III, XVIII, XXI, in Inwood and Gerson, *Hellenistic Philosophy*, 32–34.

4. Roald Dahl, *Charlie and the Chocolate Factory* (New York: Knopf, 1964), 8.

5. Epicurus, *Vatican Saying* 25, in Inwood and Gerson, *Hellenistic Philosophy*, 37.

6. Epicurus, "Letter to Menoeceus," 30.

7. Dahl, *Charlie and the Chocolate Factory*, 6.

8. Epicurus, "Letter to Menoeceus," 29–30; *Principle Doctrines* XXIX–XXX, 34–35.

9. Epicurus, "Letter to Menoeceus," 30.

10. Epicurus, *Principle Doctrine* XXVI, 34; see also *Vatican Saying* 71, 39.

11. Epicurus, *Principle Doctrines* XV, XXI, 33–34. See also Epicurus, "Letter to Menoeceus," 30: "Everything natural is easy to obtain and whatever is groundless is hard to obtain. . . . Barley cakes and water provide the highest pleasure when someone in want takes them."

12. "Chance has a small impact on the wise man, while reasoning has arranged for, is arranging for, and will arrange for the greatest and most important matters throughout the whole of his life" (Epicurus, *Principle Doctrine* XVI, 33). To be fair to Epicurus, he is not saying that *everyone* has easy access to the essentials of life. Rather, he thinks a prudent man can arrange things to ensure a consistent supply.

13. Dahl, *Charlie and the Chocolate Factory*, 5.

14. Dahl, *Charlie and the Chocolate Factory*, 40.

15. Epicurus, *Principle Doctrine* XXVII, 34.

16. Epicurus, "Letter to Menoeceus," 30.

17. See Epicurus, *Vatican Saying* 21: "One must not force nature but persuade her. And we will persuade her by fulfilling the necessary desires, and the natural ones too if they do not harm [us], but sharply rejecting the harmful ones" (37). See also Epicurus, *Principle Doctrine* XXVI, 34.

18. A scholiast on *Principle Doctrine* XXIX reads, "Natural and not necessary are those [desires] which merely provide variations of pleasure but do not remove the feeling of pain, for example expensive foods" (34, footnote 20).

19. See Epicurus, *Principle Doctrine* XXX: "Among natural desires, those which do not lead to a feeling of pain if not fulfilled and about which there is an intense effort, these are produced by a groundless opinion and they fail to be dissolved not because of their own nature but because of the groundless opinions of mankind" (34–35).

20. Dahl, *Charlie and the Chocolate Factory*, 21–22.

21. Dahl, *Charlie and the Chocolate Factory*, 24–25.

22. Dahl, *Charlie and the Chocolate Factory*, 72–75.

23. Epicurus, *Vatican Saying* 68, 39.

24. Dahl, *Charlie and the Chocolate Factory*, 95–98.

25. Dahl, *Charlie and the Chocolate Factory*, 111–13.

26. Dahl, *Charlie and the Chocolate Factory*, 130–34.

27. Dahl, *Charlie and the Chocolate Factory*, 83.

28. Dahl, *Charlie and the Chocolate Factory*, 148–50.

29. Dahl, *Charlie and the Chocolate Factory*, 15–19.

30. Dahl, *Charlie and the Chocolate Factory*, 57–58.

31. For a discussion of this topic, see Jacob M. Held's "On Getting Our Just Desserts: Willy Wonka, Immanuel Kant, and the *Summum Bonum*" in this volume.

32. In some ways, of course, he's not a god at all—he's very old, but not immortal, and while he's calm in the face of unexpected setbacks, he's not entirely free from disturbing emotions like anger, jealousy, and anxiety. He brings the children into the factory because he needs someone to carry on his work after he's gone (Dahl, *Charlie and the Chocolate Factory*, 151). Perhaps it's more accurate to say that he's a very advanced Epicurean sage.

33. Epicurus writes, "What is blessed and indestructible has no troubles itself, nor does it give trouble to anyone else, so that it is not affected by feelings of anger or gratitude. For all such things are a sign of weakness" (*Principle Doctrine* I, 32).

34. Lucretius, *The Nature of Things*, trans. A. E. Stallings (New York: Penguin Classics, 2007), 102.

35. Lucretius, *The Nature of Things*, 103.

36. Dahl, *Charlie and the Chocolate Factory*, 150.

37. Epicurus, "Letter to Menoeceus," 31.

2. ON GETTING OUR JUST DESSERTS

1. This pun had to be made, so here it is. It won't happen again.

2. Some may disagree as to whether Charlie actually is an underdog. For a discussion of this issue, see Marc Napolitano's contribution to this volume, "'He Will Be Altered Quite a Bit': Discipline and Punishment in Willy Wonka's Factory."

3. This is an allusion to the Mother Goose poem.

4. Immanuel Kant, *Critique of Pure Reason*, trans. Norman Kemp Smith (New York: St. Martin's, 1965), 635 [A 805, B 833].

5. Immanuel Kant, *Critique of Pure Reason*, 636 [A 805, B 833].

6. See Immanuel Kant, *Groundwork of the Metaphysics of Morals*, trans. and ed. Mary Gregor (Cambridge: Cambridge University Press, 1998), First Section.

7. Kant, *Groundwork of the Metaphysics of Morals*, 38 [4:429].

8. Immanuel Kant, "Part Two: Critique of Teleological Judgement," in *The Critique of Judgement*, trans. James Creed Meredith (Oxford: Clarendon, 1952), 118.

9. Immanuel Kant, *Critique of Practical Reason*, trans. and ed. Mary Gregor (Cambridge: Cambridge University Press, 1997), 93 [5:110].

10. Immanuel Kant, *Lectures on Ethics*, ed. Peter Heath and J. B. Schnee-wind, trans. Peter Heath (Cambridge: Cambridge University Press, 1997), 227 [29:600].

11. Kant, *Critique of Practical Reason*, 108 [5:130].

12. Kant, *Critique of Practical Reason*, 99, 120 [5:119, 144].

13. Ha, a second pun. I knew I'd have to do it again.

14. Friedrich Nietzsche offers an interesting case for this point in his *On the Genealogy of Morals*, Second Essay.

15. Roald Dahl, *Charlie and the Chocolate Factory* (New York: Puffin Books, 1964), 21.

16. Dahl, *Charlie and the Chocolate Factory*, 22.

17. Dahl, *Charlie and the Chocolate Factory*, 72.

18. Dahl, *Charlie and the Chocolate Factory*, 78.

19. Dahl, *Charlie and the Chocolate Factory*, 80.

20. Dahl, *Charlie and the Chocolate Factory*, 99.

21. Dahl, *Charlie and the Chocolate Factory*, 98.

22. Dahl, *Charlie and the Chocolate Factory*, 139.

23. Dahl, *Charlie and the Chocolate Factory*, 8.

24. Dahl, *Charlie and the Chocolate Factory*, 40.

25. Dahl, *Charlie and the Chocolate Factory*, 40.

26. Dahl, *Charlie and the Chocolate Factory*, 6.

27. Dahl, *Charlie and the Chocolate Factory*, 27.

28. Dahl, *Charlie and the Chocolate Factory*, 27.

29. Dahl, *Charlie and the Chocolate Factory*, 151.

30. Terry Pratchett, *Hogfather* (New York: Harpertorch, 1996), 337.

3. MATILDA, EXISTENTIALIST SUPERHERO

1. Thomas Flynn, *Existentialism: A Short Introduction* (Oxford: Oxford University Press, 2006), x.

2. Flynn, *Existentialism*, x.

3. Roald Dahl, *Matilda* (London: Puffin Books, 2007), 26.

4. Dahl, *Matilda*, 10, 102, 231, 11.

5. Dahl, *Matilda*, 10, 23, 27, 30.

6. Dahl, *Matilda*, 12, 96–97, 22–24, 53.

7. Dahl, *Matilda*, 10, 9.

8. Dahl, *Matilda*, 11, 22, 55.

9. Dahl, *Matilda*, 38–39.

10. Dahl, *Matilda*, 41.

11. Friedrich Nietzsche, *The Gay Science*, in *Existentialism*, ed. Robert Solomon (Oxford: Oxford University Press, 2005), 74.

12. Søren Kierkegaard, *The Present Age*, in *Existentialism*, ed. Solomon, 4.

13. Kierkegaard, *Present Age*, 6.

14. Søren Kierkegaard, *Concluding Unscientific Postscript*, in *Existentialism*, ed. Solomon, 23.

15. Dahl, *Matilda*, 49.

16. Dahl, *Matilda*, 28–29.

17. Dahl, *Matilda*, 29.

18. For further reading, see Søren Kierkegaard's works: *Either/Or* (1843), *Stages on Life's Way* (1845), and *Concluding Unscientific Postscript* (1846).

19. For further discussion of this issue, specifically as it pertains to faith and *James and the Giant Peach*, see Matthew Bokma and Adam Barkman's "The Existential Journey of James Henry Trotter: Kierkegaard, Freedom, and Despair in *James and the Giant Peach*" in this volume.

20. Dahl, *Matilda*, 67, 82–83, 216.

21. For further reading, see Friedrich Nietzsche's works *Beyond Good and Evil* (1886) and *On the Genealogy of Morals* (1887).

22. Dahl, *Matilda*, 152.

23. Dahl, *Matilda*, 168, 171.

24. Dahl, *Matilda*, 177.

25. Dahl, *Matilda*, 230.

26. Flynn, *Existentialism*, 49. This slogan of Sartrean existentialism is a paraphrase of Jean-Paul Sartre's statement, "Man is nothing else but that which he makes of himself." See Sartre, "Existentialism Is a Humanism," in *Existentialism*, ed. Solomon, 207.

4. THE EXISTENTIAL JOURNEY OF JAMES HENRY TROTTER

1. In many of his works, Kierkegaard examines the nature of three existential "stages" or "spheres" of existence: the aesthetic, the ethical, and the relig-

ious. However, for our purposes, the terms "religious" and the "fantastic" will be used synonymously.

2. The following are examples of the philosophical discontinuity among the different pseudonyms: Anti-Climacus—the pseudonymous writer of Kierkegaard's *The Sickness Unto Death*—writes with Christian assumptions, whereas the pseudonymous author of *Concluding Unscientific Postscript* explicitly states that he is not a Christian. Furthermore, Kierkegaard's *Either/Or* consists of two volumes, each with different pseudonymous authors. The author of volume I remains anonymous and exemplifies aestheticism, whereas the author of volume II—Judge Williams—criticizes the aesthete's position and argues for the superiority of the ethical position.

3. C. Stephen Evans, *Kierkegaard: An Introduction* (New York: Cambridge University Press, 2009), 1–2.

4. *James and the Giant Peach*, directed by Henry Selick (1996; Burbank, CA: Warner Home Video, 2010), DVD.

5. Roald Dahl, *James and the Giant Peach* (New York: Puffin Books, 1995), 70.

6. Gene Wilder utters this line in *Willy Wonka and the Chocolate Factory*, directed by Mel Stuart, screenplay by Roald Dahl (1971; Burbank, CA: Warner Home Video, 2011).

7. Søren Kierkegaard, *The Sickness Unto Death*, ed. and trans. Alastair Hannay (New York: Penguin, 2008), 9.

8. Søren Kierkegaard, *The Concept of Anxiety*, ed. and trans. Howard V. Hong and Edna H. Hong (Princeton, NJ: Princeton University Press, 1980), 44.

9. Dahl, *James and the Giant Peach*, 1.

10. Kierkegaard, *The Sickness Unto Death*, 30.

11. Dahl, *James and the Giant Peach*, 12.

12. Kierkegaard, *The Sickness Unto Death*, 11.

13. Kierkegaard, *The Sickness Unto Death*, 9.

14. Dahl, *James and the Giant Peach*, 7.

15. Ecclesiastes 8:15 (King James Version).

16. Dahl, *James and the Giant Peach*, 7.

17. Dahl, *James and the Giant Peach*, 49.

18. Søren Kierkegaard, *Either/Or*, ed. and trans. Howard V. Hong and Edna H. Hong, 2 vols. (Princeton, NJ: Princeton University Press, 1987), 325.

19. Dahl, *James and the Giant Peach*, 63.

20. Kierkegaard, *Either/Or*, vol. I, 39.

21. Kierkegaard, *Either/Or*, vol. II, 68.

22. Kierkegaard, *Either/Or*, vol. II, 68.

23. Dahl, *James and the Giant Peach*, 87.

24. Ephesians 2:9 (King James Version).

25. Dahl, *James and the Giant Peach*, 5.

26. Evans, *Kierkegaard: An Introduction*, 1–2.

27. The first patriarch of the Israelite covenant with God recorded in the book of Genesis. In his book *Fear and Trembling*, Kierkegaard understands Abraham as a true man of faith, and despite the principles of formal (communicable) ethics, Abraham obeys God's seemingly absurd command to kill his dearly beloved son Isaac. Søren Kierkegaard, *Fear and Trembling*, ed. and trans. Howard V. Hong and Edna H. Hong (Princeton, NJ: Princeton University Press, 1983).

28. Dahl, *James and the Giant Peach*, 10

29. Kierkegaard, *The Concept of Anxiety*, 42.

30. Kierkegaard, *The Concept of Anxiety*, 15.

31. Dahl, *James and the Giant Peach*, 57.

32. Dahl, *James and the Giant Peach*, 12.

33. Dahl, *James and the Giant Peach*, 144.

5. OF MICE AND (POSTHU)MAN

1. Roald Dahl, *The Witches* (London: Puffin Books, 2007), 15.

2. This is not to claim that Dahl intended his book as feminist, or even that the misogynistic interpretation doesn't have merit. Dahl himself was an admitted and well-known philanderer and anti-Semite. Dahl's infamous quote regarding Jewish people was reprinted in a *New York Times* op-ed shortly after his death. Dahl had reported to *The New Statesmen*, "There is a trait in the Jewish character that does provoke animosity, maybe it's a kind of lack of generosity towards non-Jews. I mean there is always a reason why anti-anything crops up anywhere; even a stinker like Hitler didn't just pick on them for no reason." He was less explicitly vocal about his attitudes toward women, but women who worked with him famously called him a bully. See Abraham Foxman, "Roald Dahl Also Left a Legacy of Bigotry," letter to the editor, *New York Times*, December 7, 1990, http://www.nytimes.com/1990/12/07/opinion/l-roald-dahl-also-left-a-legacy-of-bigotry-880490.html.

3. Catherine Itzin, "Bewitching the Boys," *Times Educational Supplement*, December 27, 1985, 13.

4. Dahl, *Witches*, 53 (emphasis mine).

5. In a critical theoretical vein, Jennifer Mitchell argues that the boy's transformation goes beyond simply precluding his participation in adult human gender norms by actually transforming his gender. She contends that since the gender and sex of the "mouse-boy" is fundamentally distinct from human gender and sex, the *trans*formation of the boy into a mouse is a "trans" practice akin to a playful reimagining of transgenderism. See Jennifer Mitchell, "'A Sort of

Mouse-Person': Radicalizing Gender in *The Witches*," *The Free Library*, January 2012, 1, http://www.thefreelibrary.com/"A sort of mouse-person": radicalizing-gender in The Witches.-a0298173243.

6. Dahl, *Witches*, 16.

7. For a detailed discussion on this point, see Jacob M. Held's "On Getting Our Just Desserts: Willy Wonka, Immanuel Kant, and the *Summum Bonum*" in this volume.

8. Rosi Braidotti, *The Posthuman* (Cambridge: Polity, 2013), 65.

9. In his *Anthropology from a Pragmatic Point of View*, Kant even writes about how witches are to blame for the spread of irrationality. He does not believe that witches are truly supernatural, but he blames them as women who are "poor" and "ignorant," and he uses those terms as derogatory remarks. Immanuel Kant, *Anthropology from a Pragmatic Point of View*, trans. and ed. Robert B. Louden (Cambridge: Cambridge University Press, 2006), 42.

10. Braidotti, *Posthuman*, 26.

11. Braidotti, *Posthuman*, 89.

12. Donna Harraway, "A Cyborg Manifesto: Science, Technology, and So-cialist-Feminism in the Late Twentieth Century," in *Simians, Cyborgs, and Women: The Reinvention of Nature* (New York: Routledge, 1991), 163.

13. Dahl, *Witches*, 368.

14. Dahl, *Witches*, 12.

15. Harraway, "Cyborg Manifesto," 152.

16. Dahl, *Witches*, 92.

17. Dahl, *Witches*, 96.

18. Perhaps the best articulation of this understanding of human-animal relationships is Harraway's hopeful claim that "many people no longer feel the need for such a separation; indeed many branches of feminist culture affirm the pleasure of connection of human and other living creatures. Movements for animal rights are not irrational denials of human uniqueness; they are a clear-sighted recognition of connection across the discredited breach of nature and culture. Biology and evolutionary theory over the last two centuries have simultaneously produced modern organisms as objects of knowledge and reduced the line between humans and animals to a faint trace re-etched in ideological struggle or professional disputes between life and social science." Harraway, "Cyborg Manifesto," 152.

19. Braidotti, *Posthuman*, 65.

20. Dahl, *Witches*, 40.

21. Dahl, *Witches*, 208.

22. Karen Barad, "Posthumanist Performativity: Toward an Understanding of How Matter Comes to Matter," *Signs: Journal of Women in Culture and Society* 28, no. 3 (2003): 808.

23. Dahl, *Witches*, 368. I return to this line again to illustrate his adaptability. It is also worth noting that he uses the language "mouse-person" rather than "mouse-boy," leaving his cyborg identity open to crossing gender divisions as well.

24. Dahl, *Witches*, 13.

25. Dahl, *Witches*, 20.

26. In developing the contrast between autonomy as traditionally understood in humanism and natality as the primary focus of posthumanism, Drucilla Cornell writes, "There is a distinction, then, between this view of natality and a more traditional Kantian understanding of the role of autonomy. In Kant, the subject of reason, the transcendental subject, is the 'I', which commands the empirical subject of desire. Reason, in Kant, is pitted against desire, in part because desire itself is relegated to an empirical 'property' of the concrete 'me'. The concrete 'me' of empirical desire is a reality. One does not so much change that 'me' as control it. What I am suggesting is that Peirce's understanding of the self as 'habit' or, as I have interpreted it, as the natality that allows for innovation, means that there is no empirical 'me' that is simply there." Drucilla Cornell, *Transformations* (New York: Routledge, 1993), 42.

27. Cornell, *Transformations*, 44.

28. Braidotti, *Posthuman*, 196.

29. Dahl, *Witches*, 353.

30. Dahl, *Witches*, 18.

31. Braidotti, *Posthuman*, 75.

32. Dahl, *Witches*, 371.

33. Braidotti, *Posthuman*, 196–97.

34. Barad, "Posthumanist Performativity," 827.

35. Braidotti, *Posthuman*, 197.

36. Dahl, *Witches*, 375.

6. "WHO IS THIS CRAZY MAN?"

1. In developing this chapter I had the pleasure of conversing with a number of people who offered astute feedback and ongoing support, including Christopher J. Greig, Michelle McGinn, Michael K. Potter, and Jacob M. Held. Katie and Stella Cobb kept me focused on the perspective of the younger reader along the way.

2. Roald Dahl, *Charlie and the Chocolate Factory* (New York: Puffin Books, 2007), 85.

3. Dahl, *Charlie and the Chocolate Factory*, 20, 154.

4. Michel Foucault described the disciplinary powers of normalization in works such as *Discipline and Punish: The Birth of the Prison* and *Madness and Civilization: A History of Insanity in the Age of Reason.*

5. Michel Foucault. *Madness and Civilization: A History of Insanity in the Age of Reason*, trans. Richard Howard (New York: Vintage Books, 1988), 194.

6. Foucault, *Madness and Civilization*, 258.

7. Foucault, *Madness and Civilization*, 257–59.

8. Foucault, *Madness and Civilization*, 258.

9. Dahl, *Charlie and the Chocolate Factory*, 63.

10. Dahl, *Charlie and the Chocolate Factory*, 64.

11. Dahl, *Charlie and the Chocolate Factory*, 66.

12. Dahl, *Charlie and the Chocolate Factory*, 94.

13. Dahl, *Charlie and the Chocolate Factory*, 150.

14. Plato, *Phaedrus*, trans. Robin Waterfield (Oxford: Oxford University Press, 2009), 8.

15. Plato, *Phaedrus*, 54.

16. Foucault, *Madness and Civilization*, 210.

17. Dahl, *Charlie and the Chocolate Factory*, 20.

18. Dahl, *Charlie and the Chocolate Factory*, 152.

19. Dahl, *Charlie and the Chocolate Factory*, 57–58.

20. Dahl, *Charlie and the Chocolate Factory*, 62.

21. Dahl, *Charlie and the Chocolate Factory*, 58.

22. Dahl, *Charlie and the Chocolate Factory*, 64.

23. Dahl, *Charlie and the Chocolate Factory*, 85–86.

24. Dahl, *Charlie and the Chocolate Factory*, 76.

25. Dahl, *Charlie and the Chocolate Factory*, 98.

26. Dahl, *Charlie and the Chocolate Factory*, 113.

27. Dahl, *Charlie and the Chocolate Factory*, 132.

28. Dahl, *Charlie and the Chocolate Factory*, 77.

29. Francis Bacon, *The Essays* (New York: Penguin, 1985), 76.

30. Dahl, *Charlie and the Chocolate Factory*, 91.

31. Dahl, *Charlie and the Chocolate Factory*, 103.

32. Dahl, *Charlie and the Chocolate Factory*, 105.

33. Dahl, *Charlie and the Chocolate Factory*, 126.

34. Dahl, *Charlie and the Chocolate Factory*, 127.

35. Foucault, *Madness and Civilization*, 95.

36. It is important to note that Wonka's freedom also led him to exploit the Oompa-Loompas, his own contingent of migrant workers. See Clair Bradford, "Race, Ethnicity and Colonialism," in *The Routledge Companion to Children's Literature*, ed. David Rudd (New York: Routledge, 2010), 39–50.

37. Foucault, *Madness and Civilization*, 214, 279, 282.

38. Foucault, *Madness and Civilization*, 217.

39. According to Foucault, some who are seen as mad live in a state of constant judgment. See *Madness and Civilization*, 265–69.

7. "HE WILL BE ALTERED QUITE A BIT"

1. Roald Dahl, *Charlie and the Chocolate Factory* (New York: Knopf, 1964), 149.

2. Roald Dahl, *Boy* (New York: Farrar, Strauss, and Giroux, 1984), 47–49.

3. Roald Dahl, *Danny, the Champion of the World* (New York: Knopf, 1975), 108–9.

4. Donald Sturrock, *Storyteller: The Authorized Biography of Roald Dahl* (New York: Simon & Schuster, 2010), 72.

5. Sturrock, *Storyteller*, 72.

6. Michel Foucault, *Discipline and Punish: The Birth of the Prison*, trans. Alan Sheridan (New York: Pantheon, 1977), 14.

7. Foucault, *Discipline*, 8.

8. Foucault, *Discipline*, 15.

9. Foucault, *Discipline*, 109.

10. Foucault, *Discipline*, 55.

11. Dahl, *Charlie and the Chocolate Factory*, 38.

12. Dahl, *Charlie and the Chocolate Factory*, 31.

13. Foucault, *Discipline*, 9. Tim Burton humorously addresses this inevitability in his 2005 film adaptation, as several characters point out that Wonka and the Oompa-Loompas seemed to have prescient knowledge of Augustus's punishment. *Charlie and the Chocolate Factory*, directed by Tim Burton (2005; Burbank, CA: Warner Home Video, 2005), DVD.

14. Dahl, *Charlie and the Chocolate Factory*, 60.

15. Dahl, *Charlie and the Chocolate Factory*, 60.

16. Dahl, *Charlie and the Chocolate Factory*, 59.

17. Charlie is also identified by the crowd and subjected to several rude remarks based on his class status and appearance as opposed to his behavior; however, he is never censured or criticized. Dahl, *Charlie and the Chocolate Factory*, 60.

18. Foucault, *Discipline*, 94.

19. Foucault, *Discipline*, 94.

20. Foucault, *Discipline*, 95.

21. This is changed in the 1971 film *Willy Wonka and the Chocolate Factory*. In this adaptation, Wonka requires the children to sign a contract that establishes the rules of the factory. Ironically, in spite of this modern component of the

factory's penal system, the film's presentation of Willy Wonka is very similar to Foucault's old-fashioned "sovereign" due to his despotic behavior and his ability to selectively enforce the laws of the factory. Though Charlie and Grandpa Joe break the rules by stealing Fizzy Lifting Drink, Wonka chooses to "pardon" them and reward Charlie. *Willy Wonka and the Chocolate Factory*, directed by Mel Stuart (1971; Burbank, CA: Warner Home Video, 2001), DVD. This is a gross violation of Foucault's fourth rule, which states, "The monarch must renounce his right to pardon so that the force that is present in the idea of punishment is not attenuated by the hope of intervention." Foucault, *Discipline*, 96.

22. Dahl, *Charlie and the Chocolate Factory*, 93.

23. Dahl, *Charlie and the Chocolate Factory*, 92.

24. Dahl, *Charlie and the Chocolate Factory*, 97.

25. Foucault, *Discipline*, 93.

26. Foucault, *Discipline*, 98.

27. Dahl, *Charlie and the Chocolate Factory*, 155–56.

28. Foucault, *Discipline*, 98.

29. Dahl, *Charlie and the Chocolate Factory*, 125.

30. Dahl, *Charlie and the Chocolate Factory*, 125.

31. Foucault, *Discipline*, 99.

32. Dahl, *Charlie and the Chocolate Factory*, 109.

33. Foucault, *Discipline*, 94.

34. Foucault, *Discipline*, 95.

35. Dahl, *Charlie and the Chocolate Factory*, 109, 123, 155.

36. *OED* Online (Oxford University Press).

37. Foucault, *Discipline*, 200.

38. Dahl, *Charlie and the Chocolate Factory*, 126.

39. Foucault, *Discipline*, 203–4.

40. Foucault, *Discipline*, 184.

41. Dahl, *Charlie and the Chocolate Factory*, 157.

42. *Willy Wonka and the Chocolate Factory*, dir. Stuart, 1971 (emphases added).

43. Roald Dahl, *Charlie and the Great Glass Elevator* (New York: Knopf, 1972), 152.

44. Dahl, *Charlie and the Great Glass Elevator*, 4, 152.

45. Foucault, *Discipline*, 193.

46. For a detailed discussion of this point, see Jacob M. Held's "On Getting Our Just Desserts: Willy Wonka, Immanuel Kant, and the *Summum Bonum*" in this volume.

8. *MATILDA* AND THE PHILOSOPHY
OF EDUCATION

1. Roald Dahl, *Matilda* (New York: Puffin Books, 2013), 6.

2. Dahl, *Matilda*, 61.

3. Dahl, *Matilda*, 15.

4. Aristotle, *Politics*, trans. Benjamin Jowett (Oxford: Clarendon, 1966), 1337a11–12.

5. Aristotle, *Politics*, 1337a22–28.

6. Aristotle, *Politics*, 1339a32–35.

7. Dahl, *Matilda*, 60.

8. Dahl, *Matilda*, 63.

9. Dahl, *Matilda*, 82.

10. Dahl, *Matilda*, 98.

11. "William C. Bagley (1874–1946): Early Career, Teachers College," in *Education Encyclopedia—StateUniversity.com*, J. Wesley Null, n.d., http://education.stateuniversity.com/pages/1780/Bagley-William-C-1874–1946.html.

12. Kevin Ryan and James M. Cooper, *Those Who Can, Teach*, 12th ed. (Boston: Wadsworth/Cengage Learning, 2010), 316.

13. "William C. Bagley."

14. Ryan and Cooper, *Those Who Can, Teach*, 316.

15. Plato, *The Republic*, trans. Benjamin Jowett (New York: Vintage, 1991), 410a–412e.

16. Plato, *The Republic*, 377c–378c.

17. Plato, *The Republic*, 537a–540e.

18. Immanuel Kant, *On Education*, section 6, trans. Annette Churton, http://oll.libertyfund.org/?option=com_staticxt&staticfile=show.php%3Ftitle=356&Itemid=27.

19. Kant, *On Education*, section 25.

20. Kant, *On Education*, section 67.

21. Dahl, *Matilda*, 60.

22. Dahl, *Matilda*, 128.

23. Dahl, *Matilda*, 112.

24. Dahl, *Matilda*, 189.

25. Dahl, *Matilda*, 222.

26. Dahl, *Matilda*, 81.

27. Dahl, *Matilda*, 141.

28. Jean-Jacques Rousseau, *Émile*, trans. Barbara Foxley, www.gutenberg.org/ebooks/5427, 87.

29. Rousseau, *Émile*, 60.

30. Rousseau, *Émile*, 98.

31. Rousseau, *Émile*, 92.

32. Rousseau, *Émile*, 514.

33. Rousseau, *Émile*, 134.

34. Rousseau, *Émile*, 117.

35. Ryan and Cooper, *Those Who Can, Teach*, 316.

36. "FAQs," *A.S. Neill's Summerhill*, Summerhill School, n.d., www. summerhillschool.co.uk/QAs-2009.pdf.

37. Peter Wilby, "Summerhill School: These Days Surprisingly Strict," *The Guardian*, May 27, 2013, www.guardian.co.uk/education/2013/may/27/ summerhill-school-head-profile.

38. Sarah Cassidy, "Summerhill Alumni: 'What We Learnt at the School for Scandal,'" *The Independent*, October 20, 2011, www.independent.co.uk/news/ education/schools/summerhill-alumni-what-we-learnt-at-the-school-for-scandal-2373066.html.

39. Daniel Greenberg, Mimsy Sadofsky, and Jason Lempka, *The Pursuit of Happiness: The Lives of Sudbury Valley Alumni* (Framingham, MA: Sudbury Valley School Press, 2005), 109.

40. John C. Holt, *How Children Fail* (New York: Pitman, 1964), 157.

41. Holt, *How Children Fail*, xiii.

42. Dahl, *Matilda*, 130.

43. Dahl, *Matilda*, 103.

44. John T. Gatto, *The Underground History of American Education: A Schoolteacher's Intimate Investigation into the Problem of Modern Schooling* (New York: Oxford Village Press, 2001), xxix.

45. Gatto, *Underground History*, xxx.

46. Gatto, *Underground History*, 43.

47. Valerie Strauss, "A Decade of No Child Left Behind: Lessons from a Policy Failure," *Washington Post*, January 7, 2012, www.washingtonpost.com/ blogs/answer-sheet/post/a-decade-of-no-child-left-behind-lessons-from-a-policy-failure/2012/01/05/gIQAeb19gP_blog.html.

48. *Matilda*, directed by Danny DeVito (1996; TriStar Pictures, 2005).

49. Howard E. Gardner, *The Unschooled Mind: How Children Think and How Schools Should Teach* (New York: Basic Books, 2011), 259.

50. Ryan and Cooper, *Those Who Can, Teach*, 416.

51. "School Bullying Statistics," Bullying Statistics, n.d., www. bullyingstatistics.org/content/school-bullying-statistics.html.

52. Julia Lawrence, "Number of Homeschoolers Growing Nationwide," *Education News*, May 21, 2012, www.educationnews.org/parenting/number-of-homeschoolers-growing-nationwide.

53. Juju Chang, "Extreme Homeschooling: No Tests, No Books, No Classes, No Curriculums," *ABC News*, April 19, 2010, video, http://abcnews.go.com/GMA/Parenting/unschooling-homeschooling-book-tests-classes/story?id=10410867.

54. Kant, *On Education*, section 7.

55. Dahl, *Matilda*, 204.

9. SHATTERING THE GLASS ELEVATOR

1. Joseph Foy would like to express his sincere thanks to his wonderful children for being constant reminders of the vast potential of all humanity. You give me faith, and I am so proud to share these stories with you both. This is the most fun research a daddy could ever do.

2. Roald Dahl, *The Twits* (New York: Puffin Books, 1980), 9.

3. Roald Dahl, *James and the Giant Peach* (New York: Puffin Books, 1961), 2.

4. Dahl, *James and the Giant Peach*, 6.

5. Dahl, *James and the Giant Peach*, 6.

6. Dahl, *James and the Giant Peach*, 2.

7. Martin Heidegger, *Being and Time*, trans. John Maquarrie and Edward Robinson (Oxford: Blackwell, 1962), 205.

8. *Matilda*, directed by Danny DeVito (1996; TriStar Pictures, 2005).

9. Heidegger, *Being and Time*, 184.

10. Jean-Paul Sartre, *Being and Nothingness*, trans. Hazel E. Barnes (New York: Washington Square Press, 1993), 89.

11. Sartre, *Being and Nothingness*, 115.

12. *Matilda*, dir. DeVito.

13. Michel Foucault, *Discipline and Punish: The Birth of the Prison*, trans. Alan Sheridan (New York: Pantheon, 1977), 308.

14. For a detailed discussion of this point, see Marc Napolitano's "'He Will Be Altered Quite a Bit': Discipline and Punishment in Willy Wonka's Factory" in this volume.

15. Michel Foucault, *Madness and Civilization*, trans. Richard Howard (New York: Vintage, 1988), 60.

16. Aristotle, *Politics*, trans. C. D. C. Reeve (Indianapolis: Hackett, 1998), 1253a1–3.

17. John Rawls, *A Theory of Justice* (Cambridge, MA: Harvard University Press, 1971), 60.

18. Rawls, *A Theory of Justice*, 302.

19. For a detailed discussion of this point, see Jacob M. Held's "The Fantastically Just Mr. Fox: Property and Distributive Justice according to Foxes and Other Diggers" in this volume.

20. Amartya Sen, *Development as Freedom* (Oxford: Oxford University Press, 1999), 87.

21. Rawls, *A Theory of Justice*, 560.

22. Iris Marion Young, *Inclusion and Democracy* (Oxford: Oxford University Press, 2000), 119.

23. Roald Dahl, *Charlie and the Great Glass Elevator* (New York: Puffin Books, 2007), 88.

10. THE FANTASTICALLY JUST MR. FOX

1. Roald Dahl, *Fantastic Mr. Fox* (New York: Puffin Books, 2007), 2–4.

2. Dahl, *Fantastic Mr. Fox*, 5

3. John Locke, *Second Treatise of Government*, ed. with intro. C. B. Macpherson (Indianapolis: Hackett, 1980), 19.

4. Locke, *Second Treatise of Government*, 19.

5. Locke, *Second Treatise of Government*, 21.

6. Locke, *Second Treatise of Government*, 52.

7. Locke, *Second Treatise of Government*, 66.

8. Locke, *Second Treatise of Government*, 66.

9. See Thomas Hobbes, *Leviathan*, edited by Richard Tuck (Cambridge: Cambridge University Press, 1997), chapter XIII, "Of the Natural Condition of Mankind, as concerning their Felicity, and Misery."

10. Locke, *Second Treatise of Government*, 20.

11. Locke, *Second Treatise of Government*, 21. Money does change the relationship somewhat, since one's goods can now be turned into a nonperishable good (currency) and land can be cultivated by laborers, but the moral limit to ownership still stands. Property is necessary for individual survival and is a right we all possess naturally, so the ability to own must be respected.

12. Dahl, *Fantastic Mr. Fox*, 58–59.

13. Dahl, *Fantastic Mr. Fox*, 60.

14. John Rawls, *A Theory of Justice*, rev. ed. (Cambridge, MA: Belknap Press of Harvard University Press, 1999), 123–25.

15. John Rawls, *Political Liberalism* (New York: Columbia University Press, 1996), 23.

16. Rawls, *Political Liberalism*, 24.

17. Jeffrey Reiman, *As Free and as Just as Possible: A Theory of Marxian Liberalism* (Malden, MA: Wiley-Blackwell, 2012), 24.

18. Reiman, *As Free and as Just as Possible*, 121.
19. Dahl, *Fantastic Mr. Fox*, 59–60.
20. Reiman, *As Free and as Just as Possible*, 100.

11. WILLY WONKA AND THE IMPERIAL CHOCOLATE FACTORY

1. Headline, *New York Daily News*, October 5, 2012.
2. Veruca Salt, in Roald Dahl, *Charlie and the Chocolate Factory* (New York: Knopf, 1964).
3. Eleanor Cameron, "A Reply to Roald Dahl," *The Horn Book Magazine*, April 1973.
4. While forgotten by those a few years beyond a social studies class, "discovered" here has much the same problem as the claim that "Columbus discovered America"—the land is not merely already inhabited, but the inhabitants themselves also seem to know just where they are!
5. Dahl, *Charlie and the Chocolate Factory*, 73.
6. Dahl, *Charlie and the Chocolate Factory*, 72–73.
7. Mark I. West, "Trust Your Children: Voices against Censorship in Children's Literature," *Children's Literature Review* 41 (1996): 4.
8. "Retcon" is short for "retroactive continuity," the practice of altering the backstory of a character or characters to generate or explain new storylines regardless of consistency with what had been established to that point. For a vigorous discussion on the benefits and harms of retconning (complete with multiple examples), spend an afternoon hanging out at your local comics shop.
9. Roald Dahl, *Charlie and the Chocolate Factory* [revised Oompa-Loompa edition] (New York: Random House, 1973), 68.
10. There were two additional *Charlie and the Chocolate Factory* illustrators before Blake: Faith Jaques, who illustrated the first UK edition, and Michael Foreman, who illustrated a 1985 edition.
11. That of Kenyan-born Indian actor Deep Roy.
12. Roald Dahl, *Charlie and the Chocolate Factory* [revised 1998 edition] (New York: Puffin Books, 1998), 69.
13. From Rudyard Kipling's poem "The White Man's Burden," published in *McClure's Magazine* in February 1899. Subtitled "An Address to the United States," the poem calls for the United States to take its place among imperial power and fulfill its "moral duty" to civilize the uncivilized lands and peoples acquired with the recent end to the Spanish-American War.
14. Dahl, *Charlie and the Chocolate Factory* (1964), 76; (1973), 71.
15. Dahl, *Charlie and the Chocolate Factory* (1964), 76–77.
16. Dahl, *Charlie and the Chocolate Factory* (1964), 73.

17. For a detailed discussion of private property, see Jacob M. Held's "The Fantastically Just Mr. Fox: Property and Distributive Justice according to Foxes and Other Diggers" in this volume.

18. For a more complete discussion of the metropole-periphery relation of the British colonial period, see Anthony Webster, *The Debate on the Rise of the British Empire* (Manchester: Manchester University Press, 2006).

19. John Gallagher and Ronald Robinson, "The Imperialism of Free Trade," *Economic History Review* 6, no. 1 (August 1953): 1–15.

20. Named for Representative Tom Engel and Senator Tom Harkin, who in their respective houses of Congress sponsored and shepherded the measure to end child slavery among West African cacao producers—particularly in Côte d'Ivoire.

12. *GEORGE'S MARVELOUS MEDICINE,* OR, WHAT SHOULD WE DO ABOUT GLOBAL HUNGER?

1. Roald Dahl, *George's Marvelous Medicine* (London: Puffin Books, 2013), 74.

2. Robert E. Goodin, "What Is So Special about Our Fellow Countrymen?" *Ethics* 98 (1988): 663–86.

3. Goodin, "What Is So Special," 675.

4. Dahl, *George's Marvelous Medicine*, 2.

5. Goodin, "What Is So Special," 675.

6. Goodin, "What Is So Special," 681.

7. Onora O'Neill, "Global Justice: Whose Obligations?" in *The Ethics of Assistance: Morality and the Distant Needy*, ed. Deen K. Chatterjee (Cambridge: Cambridge University Press, 2004), 242– 59, 243.

8. Peter Singer, "Famine, Affluence, and Morality," *Philosophy & Public Affairs* 1, no. 3 (1972): 229–43, 231.

9. Singer, "Famine," 231.

10. Singer, "Famine," 231f.

11. Singer, "Famine," 233.

12. Dahl, *George's Marvelous Medicine*, 63.

13. Dahl, *George's Marvelous Medicine*, 63.

14. Dahl, *George's Marvelous Medicine*, 63.

15. Dahl, *George's Marvelous Medicine*, 75.

16. Singer, "Famine," 235.

17. Singer, "Famine," 236.

18. Singer, "Famine," 237.

19. Singer, "Famine," 235.

20. Dahl, *George's Marvelous Medicine*, 89.

21. Thomas Pogge, *World Poverty and Human Rights* (Cambridge: Polity Press, 2002), 18.

22. Dahl, *George's Marvelous Medicine*, 73.

23. Pogge, *World Poverty*, 204.

24. Pogge, *World Poverty*, 205.

25. The World Bank provides poorer countries with credits to facilitate their economic development (which is thought to be a decisive factor for ending global hunger). The interested reader can find more thorough (albeit very critical) analyses in Bruce Rich, *Mortgaging the Earth: World Bank, Environmental Impoverishment and the Crisis of Development* (London: Earthscan, 1994), and Catherine Caufield, *Masters of Illusion: The World Bank and the Poverty of Nations* (London: Pan Books, 1996).

26. Pogge, *World Poverty*, 205.

27. Pogge, *World Poverty*, 18.

28. Pogge, *World Poverty*, 130.

29. Pogge, *World Poverty*, 139.

13. CRODSWOGGLE, FLUSHBUNKING, AND ALL THINGS FRIENDSHIP IN *THE BFG*

1. Roald Dahl, *The BFG* (New York: Puffin Books, 1982), 70.

2. Aristotle, *Nicomachean Ethics*, 1171a10. All citations and quotations from Aristotle are from *The Complete Works of Aristotle*, revised Oxford translation, ed. Jonathan Barnes (Princeton, NJ: Princeton University Press, 1984).

3. Dahl, *The BFG*, 74.

4. Dahl, *The BFG*, 78.

5. Aristotle, *Nicomachean Ethics*, 1156b22.

6. John M. Cooper, "Aristotle on the Forms of Friendship," *Review of Metaphysics* 30, no. 4 (June 1977): 627.

7. Aristotle, *Nicomachean Ethics*, 1156a30–32.

8. Aristotle, *Nicomachean Ethics*, 1169b9.

9. Dahl, *The BFG*, 84.

10. Aristotle, *Nicomachean Ethics*, 1167a7.

11. Dahl, *The BFG*, 124.

12. Dahl, *The BFG*, 99.

13. Aristotle, *Nicomachean Ethics*, 1167a30.

14. Aristotle, *Nicomachean Ethics*, 1167b6–9.

15. Dahl, *The BFG*, 68.

16. Dahl, *The BFG*, 69.

17. Aristotle, *Nicomachean Ethics*, 1161b34.

18. Dean Cocking and Jeanette Kennett, "Friendship and the Self," *Ethics* 108, no. 3 (April 1998): 507.

19. Laurence Thomas, "Friendship," *Synthese* 72, no. 2 (August 1987): 222.

20. Dahl, *The BFG*, 80.

21. Dahl, *The BFG*, 78–79.

22. Dahl, *The BFG*, 79.

23. Dahl, *The BFG*, 207.

24. Aristotle, *Nicomachean Ethics*, 1161b33.

25. Dahl, *The BFG*, 76, 79.

14. CHARLIE AND THE NIGHTMARE FACTORY

1. Roald Dahl, *James and the Giant Peach* (London: Puffin Books, 1996), 27.

2. Dahl, *James and the Giant Peach*, 87.

3. Dahl, *James and the Giant Peach*, 96.

4. Roald Dahl, *The Witches* (New York: Puffin Books, 2007), 35.

5. Roald Dahl, *Charlie and the Chocolate Factory* (New York: Penguin Classics, 2011), 198.

6. Roald Dahl, *Charlie and the Great Glass Elevator* (London: Puffin Books, 2009), 67.

7. Dahl, *James and the Giant Peach*, 7.

8. Roald Dahl, *The BFG* (London: Puffin Books, 2007), 17.

9. Dahl, *The BFG*, 142.

10. Dahl, *Charlie and the Chocolate Factory*, 104.

11. Dahl, *James and the Giant Peach*, 110.

12. Dahl, *James and the Giant Peach*, 111.

13. Aristotle, *Poetics*, in *The Complete Works of Aristotle*, ed. J. Barnes (Princeton, NJ: Princeton University Press, 1984), 2323.

14. Aristotle, *Politics*, in *The Complete Works of Aristotle*, ed. Barnes, Book VIII, 2125.

15. Dahl, *Charlie and the Chocolate Factory*, 150.

16. David Hume, "Of Tragedy," in *Essential Works of David Hume* (New York: Bantam Books, 1965), 441.

17. Dahl, *Charlie and the Chocolate Factory*, 41.

18. Hume, "Of Tragedy," 442.

19. Roald Dahl, *Boy: Tales of Childhood* (New York: Penguin Classics, 2009), 44.

20. Dahl, *Boy: Tales of Childhood*, 47.

15. BRIMFUL OF BUZZBURGERS

1. Jean-Paul Sartre, *The Imaginary: A Phenomenological Psychology of the Imagination*, trans. Jonathan Webber (London: Routledge, 2004), 186.

2. Roald Dahl, *The Twits* (New York: Scholastic, 1980), 70–71.

3. John Locke, *An Essay Concerning Human Understanding*, edited with a foreword by Peter H. Nidditch (Oxford: Clarendon Press, 1979), 97.

4. David Hume, *A Treatise of Human Nature*, ed. David Fate Norton and Mary J. Norton (Oxford: Clarendon Press, 2007), 5.

5. Immanuel Kant, *Critique of Judgment*, trans. Werner S. Pluhar (Indianapolis: Hackett, 1987), 171.

6. Kant, *Critique of Judgment*, 183.

7. Kant, *Critique of Judgment*, 183.

8. Kant, *Critique of Judgment*, 185.

9. Roald Dahl, *Revolting Rhymes* (New York: Random House, 1982), 54, 16.

10. For further discussion on this idea, see Taine Duncan's "Of Mice and (Posthu)Man: Roald Dahl's *The Witches* and Ethics beyond Humanism" in this volume.

11. Dahl, *Revolting Rhymes*, 54.

12. Roald Dahl, "Ideas to Help Aspiring Writers," *The Roald Dahl Treasury* (New York: Viking, 1997), 409.

13. See Arthur C. Clarke, "Hazards of Prophecy: The Failure of Imagination," in *Profiles of the Future: An Inquiry into the Limits of the Possible* (New York: Harper & Row, 1962).

16. DEWEY'S MARVELOUS MEDICINE

1. Roald Dahl, *James and the Giant Peach* (New York: Puffin Books, 1996), 78.

2. John Dewey, *Experience and Nature: The Collected Works of John Dewey, 1882–1953*, vol. 1, ed. Jo Ann Boydston (Carbondale: Southern Illinois University Press, 1984), 43.

3. John Dewey, *The Quest for Certainty*, vol. 4 in *The Collected Works of John Dewey, 1882–1953*, ed. Jo Ann Boydston (Carbondale: Southern Illinois University Press, 1984), 7.

4. Dewey, *The Quest for Certainty*, 14.

5. Dewey, *The Quest for Certainty*, 250.

6. Dahl, *James and the Giant Peach*, 30.

7. Dahl, *James and the Giant Peach*, 14.

8. Roald Dahl, *Charlie and the Chocolate Factory* (New York: Puffin Books, 2007), 4.

9. Dahl, *James and the Giant Peach*, 15.

10. Dahl, *Charlie and the Chocolate Factory*, 49.

11. John Dewey, *Art as Experience*, vol. 10 in *The Collected Works of John Dewey, 1882–1953*, ed. Jo Ann Boydston (Carbondale: Southern Illinois University Press, 1987), 47.

12. Dewey, *Art as Experience*, 25.

13. Roald Dahl, *Danny, the Champion of the World* (New York: Puffin, 2007), 53.

14. Dahl, *Danny, the Champion of the World*, 55.

15. Dewey, *Art as Experience*, 11.

16. Dewey, *Art as Experience*, 41.

17. Dewey, *Art as Experience*, 40.

18. Roald Dahl, *George's Marvelous Medicine* (New York: Puffin Books, 2007).

19. See John Dewey, "Time and Individuality," in *Human Nature and Conduct*, vol. 14 of *The Collected Works of John Dewey, 1882–1953*, ed. Jo Ann Boydston (Carbondale: Southern Illinois University Press, 1988), 112.

20. Dewey, *Art as Experience*, 39.

21. Dahl, *James and the Giant Peach*, 62–69.

22. Dewey, *Art as Experience*, 41.

23. Dahl, *Charlie and the Chocolate Factory*, 88.

24. Dahl, *James and the Giant Peach*, 54.

25. Dahl, *Danny, the Champion of the World*, 206.

INDEX

happiness, 2, 5, 8–9, 13, 14, 16, 17, 21,
    24–25, 29, 30, 52, 135, 143, 162, 199,
    214
Harraway, Donna, 65–66, 68–69, 224n18
Hazell, Victor, 206, 214
hedonism, 52, 53
Heidegger, Martin, 109
Hobbes, Thomas, 127
Holt, John C., 102
homeschooling, 104–105
Honey, Jennifer, 38, 40–41, 43, 44, 45, 93,
    95, 97, 98–99, 100, 102, 103, 104, 106,
    112, 172, 178, 206, 209, 215
hope, 2, 20, 21, 25, 32, 51, 62, 69, 205
hubris, 74, 75–76, 80
Hume, David, 185–188, 189, 193

Icarus, 76
imagination, 21, 25, 48, 49, 57, 79, 107,
    119, 191–202, 211–212, 214
injustice, 5, 20–21, 108, 129, 159, 206, 208
integrity, 6
Itzin, Catherine, 60

James. *See* Trotter, James Henry
James and the Giant Peach, 2, 47–57, 85,
    174, 175–176, 177, 178, 182, 183, 196,
    208
Judge Williams, 54, 222n2
justice, 6, 16, 19–20, 21, 26, 30, 32, 107,
    114–117, 118, 121, 122, 124, 129–135,
    208

Kant, Immanuel, 21–25, 63, 65, 96–97,
    106, 192, 194, 195, 196, 197–198,
    224n9, 225n26
katharsis, 182
Kierkegaard, Søren, 33–34, 37–38, 40, 41,
    42, 43, 44, 47, 48, 49–50, 51–52,
    53–54, 55–56, 221n1–222n2, 223n27
Kranky, George, 1, 2–3, 113, 150, 151,
    154, 156, 157, 160, 212
Kranky, Mr (Killy), 150, 153, 154, 156,
    157, 159

labor, 123, 124–125, 127, 128, 130, 137,
    138, 141, 142, 144, 148, 194
libertarian, 129–130, 133, 135

liberty, 64, 80, 115, 123, 126, 127, 128,
    130, 131, 132, 133, 134–135. *See also*
    freedom
Lobel, Arnold, 217n10
Locke, John, 123–124, 125–126, 127, 130,
    131, 134, 135, 193
love, 11–12, 17, 33, 54, 69, 76
Lucretius, 16, 17

madness, 73–80, 91, 213
magic, 2, 3–4, 70, 110, 194–195, 196, 199,
    210
Matilda. *See* Wormwood, Matilda
Matilda, 5, 33–45, 85, 93–106, 172, 178,
    182
mediocrity, 33–34, 37, 38, 42, 45
Mike. *See* Teavee, Mike
Mitchell, Jennifer, 223n5
monism, 65
morality, 23, 24, 25, 31, 37, 39–40, 41, 42,
    43, 45, 63, 74, 113, 114–115, 118, 122,
    129, 156, 160, 164, 189

natality, 69
Nicomachean Ethics (Aristotle), 163
Nietzsche, Friedrich, 33–34, 37, 42–43, 44
normalcy/normalization, 63, 73–74, 80, 91,
    92, 113

O'Neill, Onora, 152
Oompa-Loompas, 16, 27, 78, 84, 88, 89,
    137–147, 175, 176, 179, 184, 189
original position, 131, 132, 135

pain, 3, 5, 6, 8, 10–11, 147, 201
Panopticon, 90–91
Phaedrus (Plato), 76
Plato, 7, 76, 96, 192
pleasure, 7–9, 10, 28, 40, 52–49, 54, 183,
    184, 185, 186, 187, 188, 189
Poetics (Aristotle), 182
Pogge, Thomas, 156–160
Politics (Aristotle), 94, 183–184
posthuman(ism/ist), 64–65, 66–69, 70, 71
poverty, 9, 11, 19, 23, 29, 116, 119, 128,
    132–133, 135, 159
pragmatist, 205
Principal Trunchbull. *See* the Trunchbull

TWITS, WITCHES, AND DIRTY BEASTS: AUTHOR BIOGRAPHIES

Adam Barkman (PhD, Free University of Amsterdam) is associate professor of philosophy at Redeemer University College (Canada). He is the author and coeditor of more than half a dozen books, most recently *Imitating the Saints* (2013), *The Culture and Philosophy of Ridley Scott* (2013), and *The Philosophy of Ang Lee* (2013). He is grateful to Roald Dahl and his parental figure villains for making him, a so-so father, look like a hero to his four awesome children: Heather, Tristan, Kaitlyn, and Baby L.

Matthew Bokma is an independent scholar with interests in existentialism, phenomenology, and peaches.

Elizabeth Butterfield is associate professor of philosophy at Georgia Southern University, where she regularly teaches courses in existentialism, philosophy of religion, and ethics. She is the author of *Sartre and Posthumanist Humanism* (2012), as well as several articles addressing topics such as Sartre, Beauvoir, Marcuse, motherhood, and James Bond. She herself is mother to a Matilda and a Charlie, and she doesn't mind that people constantly say "like in the movie!" as long as they think of her less as a Wormwood and more as Miss Honey.

Cam Cobb is assistant professor at the University of Windsor. He focuses on differentiated learning and social justice in his research and teaching. While he has ventured on numerous field trips over the years, he has never actually taken a class to a chocolate factory.

Timothy M. Dale is assistant professor of political science at the University of Wisconsin–La Crosse. He teaches in the area of political philosophy, and his research interests include democratic theory, political messaging in popular culture, and the scholarship of teaching and learning. He is coeditor of the collections *Homer Simpson Ponders Politics: Popular Culture as Political Theory* (2013) and *Homer Simpson Marches on Washington: Dissent in American Popular Culture* (2010); he is also a coauthor of *Political Thinking, Political Theory, and Civil Society* (2009).

Taine Duncan is assistant professor of philosophy and director of the gender studies program at the University of Central Arkansas. She works in critical theories of all kinds, from Rosi Braidotti to Jürgen Habermas to George Yancy. Her recent research is on solidarity and how to conceptualize emancipation beyond difference. When she was a small and bookish girl, she could make pencils fly with her mind, but now she needs a computer to write.

Joseph J. Foy is associate campus dean and professor of political science at the University of Wisconsin–Waukesha. He is the editor of *Homer Simpson Goes to Washington: American Politics through Popular Culture* and *SpongeBob SquarePants and Philosophy*. Foy coedited *Homer Simpson Marches on Washington: Dissent through American Popular Culture* and *Homer Simpson Ponders Politics: Popular Culture as Political Theory* and has written more than two dozen articles and chapters exploring popular culture and politics. His lifelong dream is to let loose with a whizzpopper in front of the Queen.

Jacob M. Held is associate professor of philosophy at the University of Central Arkansas. His primary research interests include political and legal philosophy, applied ethics, and nineteenth-century German philosophy. He is also the editor of *Dr. Seuss and Philosophy: Oh, the Thinks You Can Think!* (2011). Recently he has become interested in philosophy for children and had the opportunity to run a pilot program at a local homeschool co-op run by his amazing wife, Jennifer. When he gets tired of listening to a bunch of squabbling, self-centered, spoiled brats, he leaves academic philosophy and goes to co-op.

Tanya Jeffcoat is associate program coordinator for the Academic Center for Excellence at the University of the Ozarks, where she also teaches in the Humanities Division. Her primary philosophical interests are in classical American pragmatism (especially John Dewey) and ecological sustainability, and she looks for ways to encourage people to become philosophically engaged, no matter their age. In this spirit, she contributed "From There to Here, From Here to There, Diversity is Everywhere" in *Dr. Seuss and Philosophy: Oh, the Thinks You Can Think!* She spends her down time tucked away in the foothills of the Ozark Mountains, where she continually goes out of her way to find new and wonderful things to wonder about.

John V. Karavitis, CPA, MBA, works in the Chicago-land area as a financial analyst. For someone with a lifelong love of learning, writing about Matilda's misadventures in Crunchem Hall Primary School was a matter of course. He began his own educational misadventures in the Chicago public school system. After that, a private college–preparatory high school run by no-nonsense Jesuits, and then a series of private and state colleges. He never stopped learning, as evidenced by his degrees in accounting, business administration, computer science, economics, mathematics, and psychology. Look for his essays in Open Court's upcoming . . . *and Philosophy* books on *Frankenstein*, *Jurassic Park*, the Devil, and *Homeland*. John understands Matilda, and he hopes that one day we will all let go of the fear that children can't and won't learn unless they are forced to.

Chad Kleist is a PhD candidate at Marquette University. He has published in many areas of ethics, including moral psychology and global, theoretical, and applied ethics. His primary interests lie at the intersections of global ethics and feminism. Chad is a bit crodswoggle! He enjoys traveling and cooking, although he tends to avoid giant country. He spends most of his time whizzpopping with other human beans. While gobblefunking in the classroom, he also hopes to pass life lessons from Dahl on to his students for years to come.

Greg Littmann somehow came to be / associate professor in philosophy / at SIU in Edwardsville / (62026, IL). / There he teaches, you will find, / metaphysics, epistemology and philosophy of mind. / He's published on evolutionary epistemology / and the philosophy of logic, and I see / twenty chapters that relate / philosophy to pop culture—Wait! / Do you like books? Like *Game of Thrones*? / Or *Frankenstein*? Or Sherlock Holmes? / Or *Dune* or *Ender's Game*? Or these, / Neil Gaiman's modern fantasies? / Anyhow, Greg wrote on those / and was eaten by a rhinoceros, / which shows that thinking does not pay / and dirty beasts have right of way.

Marc Napolitano is assistant professor of English at the US Military Academy, West Point. His primary areas of interest include Victorian literature, children's literature, and adaptation theory. He has published articles on these subjects in journals such as *Dickens Studies Annual*, *Studies in Children's Literature*, *Neo-Victorian Studies*, and *Journal of Adaptation in Film and Performance*. He would like to thank his mother, Joann, for reading *Charlie and the Chocolate Factory* aloud to him in his childhood and mitigating the harshness of the factory's disciplinary punishments with the sweetness of her narratorial voice.

Miranda Nell received her doctorate in philosophy from the New School for Social Research and teaches at Saginaw Valley State University in Michigan. She is a regular contributor to the Talking Philosophy blog of *The Philosophers' Magazine* and the LSE Book Review website. Her interests include aesthetics, epistemology, and peach-flying.

Ron Novy is director of the University College at the University of Central Arkansas and lecturer in philosophy and the humanities there as well. Most recently, he has contributed chapters for volumes on Dr. Seuss and Spider-Man. Other volumes in which he appears generally involve someone in tights and a cape chasing someone else in more stylish tights and a cape. He loved *James and the Giant Peach* as a kid, which likely influenced his aversion to stomping spiders even when they can't be conveniently shooed away (this annoys some people tremendously).

Janelle Pötzsch is a PhD student in philosophy at Ruhr-Universität Bochum, Germany. Her research interests include business ethics and political philosophy. She has contributed essays to *The Big Bang Theory and Philosophy* (2012), *Frankenstein and Philosophy* (2013), and the forthcoming *Jurassic Park and Philosophy*. Being more of an owl person, she often wonders whether there isn't a marvelous medicine to cure being grumpy in the mornings.

Benjamin A. Rider is (by now) associate professor of philosophy at the University of Central Arkansas. He has written about Plato's views about moral and philosophical education, as well as on other topics in ancient philosophy and applied ethics. He probably spends more time than is healthy examining his life and trying to get others to do the same.